THE EXCLUSIVE LEARNINGEXPRESS® ADVANTAGE

Unlike any other publisher in the critical fields of career development and test preparation, LEARNINGEXPRESS customizes its preparation guides to fit the specialized requirements of the state in which you live. Because each state's tests can vary widely in the questions they ask and the subjects they cover, customization is a key factor in both how thoroughly you come prepared to the specific test you are taking, and how well you do.

Each guide in the series represents the combined efforts of top experts in the field, from leading educators and experts in test preparation and career development to civil service professionals familiar with the test in your field in your state.

LEARNINGEXPRESS is an affiliate of RANDOM HOUSE, one of the most respected names in the world of publishing.

WHAT TEST-TAKERS ARE SAYING ABOUT LEARNINGEXPRESS PREPARATION GUIDES

"The information from the last two study guides I ordered from your company was invaluable. . . .
Better than the $200 6-week study courses being offered. . . . After studying from dozens of books I
would choose yours over any of the other companies."
S. Frosch

"Excellent . . . It was like having the test in advance!"
J. Kennedy

"Without this book, I wouldn't have understood the test."
R. Diaz

"Told me everything that was going to be on the test [and] gave me
a good understanding of the whole process, too."
J. Molinari

"The best test-prep book I've used!"
H. Hernandez

"I felt 100% prepared when I took the Suffolk County exam this past June. I scored a 96
on it. I had taken it previously in 1992 and only scored an 82. Your guide
helped me add 14 points to my score!"
R. Morrell

STATE POLICE
EXAM
MASSACHUSETTS

LearningExpress

NEW YORK

Library of Congress Cataloging-in-Publication Data

State police exam Massachusetts.
      p. cm. — (The LearningExpress law enforcement library)
  ISBN 1-57685-058-7
   1. Police—Massachusetts—Examinations, questions, etc.
2. Police—Vocational guidance—Massachusetts.   3. Employment
tests—Massachusetts.   I. LearningExpress (Organization)   II. Series.
HV8145.M4S73   1997
363.2'076—dc21   97-22840
                                                                                                 CIP

Printed in the United States of America
9 8 7 6 5 4 3 2 1
First Edition

Regarding the Information in this Book
We attempt to verify the information presented in our books prior to publication. It is always a good idea, however, to double-check such important information as minimum requirements, application and testing procedures, and deadlines with your local law enforcement agency, as such information can change from time to time.

For Further Information
For information on LearningExpress, other LearningExpress products, or bulk sales, please call or write to us at:
  LearningExpress®
  900 Broadway
  Suite 604
  New York, NY 10003
  212-995-2566

ISBN 1-57685-058-7

7 85555 85058 3

CONTENTS

LIST OF CONTRIBUTORS

The following individuals contributed to the content of this book.

Elizabeth Chesla is an adult educator and curriculum developer at Polytechnic University in New York who has also taught reading and writing at New York University School of Continuing Education and New York Institute of Technology in New York City.

Jan Gallagher, Ph.D., is a test-development specialist, editor, and teacher living in Jersey City, New Jersey.

Mary Hesalroad, a former police officer for the Austin, Texas, Police Department, now works as a special investigator for the Office of the Attorney General in Texas.

Judith N. Meyers is an instructor in reading and study skills at Wagner College, Staten Island, New York; director of the Two Together Tutorial Program of the Jewish Child Care Assosciation in New York City; and an Adult Basic Education Practitioner at City University New York.

Judith F. Olson, M.A., is chairperson of the language arts department at Valley High School in West Des Moines, Iowa, where she also conducts test preparation workshops.

Judith Robinovitz is an independent educational consultant and director of Score at the Top, a comprehensive test preparation program in Vero Beach, Florida.

Judith Schlesinger, Ph.D., is a writer and psychologist whose background includes years of working with police officers in psychiatric crisis interventions.

Jay Smith is an exercise physiologist and Director of Physical Fitness and Health Maintenance Programs for the Massachusetts Criminal Justice Training Council.

INTRODUCTION

HOW TO USE THIS BOOK

SUMMARY
Read this first!

If you want to be a State Police Officer in Massachusetts, this book will help you reach your goal. It will give you:

- Must-know information about how to become a state police officer in Massachusetts
- Practice exams and instruction to help you score your best on the written exam
- Vital tips on dealing with the other parts of the selection process

As this book went to press, the Massachusetts State Police Personnel Department had not yet finalized the content of its written exam. The Personnel Department was able, however, to give us an outline of the skills it planned to test: memorization, reading comprehension, logic and reasoning, basic math, and writing. The test is expected to be multiple-choice, like the exams presented in this book, although it is possible that your writing skills will be assessed using an actual writing sample rather than by multiple-choice questions.

The practice exams in this book are based on this information supplied by the Personnel Department. While the format of the actual exam may differ somewhat from that of the exams in this book, you should find that the skills tested in these practice exams are the same ones that appear on your exam.

Your first step in using this book is to turn to Chapter 1, "Becoming a State Police Officer in Massachusetts." There you'll find vital information on minimum requirements, how to apply, and the entire selection process.

Next, turn to the "Massachusetts State Police Exam Planner," Chapter 2. This chapter guides you through the exam-related materials in this book, presenting study schedules that will help you prepare based on how much time you have before exam day.

In addition to taking the practice exams and studying the instructional chapters on the various skills tested in those exams, you should also read Chapters 12–15, which cover the other parts of the selection process after the written exam. After all, you're plan-

ning to do well enough on the exam to be invited back for the next steps, and there is much you can do to get ready for the physical ability test, the personal history statement and oral interview, and the psychological assessment.

If you find, after taking the practice exams and working through the instructional chapters on the various skills tested on the exam, that you need more help in the basic skills that will help you succeed on the exam, LearningExpress has more help to offer. The LearningExpress series Skill Builders for Test Takers offers vital guidance for people who need to improve their reading, writing, and math skills. See the order information at the back of this book, or ask your local bookseller for *Practical Math in 20 Minutes a Day, Writing Skills in 20 Minutes a Day, Vocabulary and Spelling in 20 Minutes a Day,* and *Reading Comprehension in 20 Minutes a Day.*

BECOMING A STATE POLICE OFFICER IN MASSACHUSETTS

1

CHAPTER SUMMARY

This chapter describes in detail the selection process for becoming a State Police Officer in Massachusetts. It offers the applicant useful information in such key areas as requirements and procedures, training, salary and benefits, and initial assignment.

assachusetts Department of State Police officials expect thousands of men and women to come looking for something very soon—and that "something" is a spot in law enforcement history as a graduate of the next class of Troopers from the State Police Academy in New Braintree.

Competition is stiff, of course, but there's room for those who are up to exacting standards. Recruit classes aren't all that small, usually ranging in size from 100 to 150 recruits. That may not seem like many until you compare those numbers to the one Constable and 33 men who had state policing chores back in 1865. State policing did get a little easier in 1921 when 50 men patrolled rural Massachusetts as members of the first uniformed branch of troopers.

Recent times have brought the biggest changes for state troopers, though. In 1992 the Massachusetts State Police consolidated with the Metropolitan, Registry, and Capitol Police and is now known as the Department of State Police. In November 1996, the 73rd Recruit Training Troop

IMPORTANT ADDRESSES & PHONE NUMBERS

Massachusetts State Police Academy
340 West Brookfield Road
New Braintree, MA 01531
508-867-1000

Department of State Police
Personnel Office
508-820-2295

graduated, earning its place in history as the first class to graduate under this new system. These graduates work out of seven State Police installations spread throughout the Commonwealth, patrolling their assigned areas, conducting investigations, and restoring order when necessary.

The men and women who slip on the famed Boots and Breeches of the Massachusetts State Police today hit the highways knowing they are amongst the best-equipped, best-trained troopers in the nation. Earning the right to wear French and Electric Blue isn't easy, however, and there are over 2,200 men and women who will testify to this truth.

The Massachusetts State Police statement of values that reflects its mission to the community should look pretty familiar to citizens of this state:

"The end of the institution, maintenance and administration of government . . . is to secure the body politic and to furnish the individuals who compose it with the power of enjoying in safety and tranquillity their natural rights . . ."

These words are quoted from the preamble of the Massachusetts Constitution by Colonel Reed V. Hillman and reflect the goals and attitudes of those who serve with the Massachusetts State Police.

APPLYING TO BECOME A TROOPER IN MASSACHUSETTS

MINIMUM REQUIREMENTS

To apply for the entry-level position of **Trainee** with the Massachusetts State Police, you must meet the following minimum requirements:

- Be between ages 19 and 35
- Be a U.S. citizen
- Be a high school graduate or possess an equivalence certificate issued by the Department of Education (college credits may become a requirement in the near future)
- Possess a valid driver's license
- Be of good reputation and sound moral character
- Be able to swim
- Be able to pass a required physical exam and a fitness exam

SELECTION PROCESS

The selection process begins with a written entrance examination. Exam announcements will be made through radio stations, television, and newspapers throughout Massachusetts. Applications aren't available until *after* these announcements come out, so don't waste

MASSACHUSETTS STATE POLICE: AT A GLANCE	
Full-Time Sworn State Police Officers	2,259
Females	207
Caucasians	2,026
African-Americans	171
Hispanics	51
Asians (including Filipinos)	11
Applicants for Full-Time Sworn Trooper in 1992	16,503

Note: Figures supplied by the Commonwealth of Massachusetts Department of State Police Personnel Office.

your time hunting for one until you get the word—nor do they keep mailing lists of people who request to be notified when applications are available.

The selection process for becoming a Trainee consists of seven steps, each of which assesses a certain area of your abilities and character. You must successfully complete each step, which usually follow in this order:

1. Exam Announcement/ Application Procurement

2. Written Entrance Exam

3. Fitness Assessment

4. Background Investigation

5. Oral Interview Board

6. Psychological Assessment

7. Medical Assessment

Step One: Exam Announcement/ Application Procurement

When the State Department of Police decides to test they will make an exam announcement throughout the Commonwealth via radio, television, and newspapers. Applications are *not* available until the exam announcement is made. Applications can be picked up at any State Police installation at that time.

Step Two: Written Entrance Exam

The written exam tests your general knowledge and basic skills (see sidebar on page 5). According to the Massachusetts State Police Personnel Office, the exam is expected to find out how well you read, how well you understand what you read, your ability to memorize people and/or objects, and how well you use logic and reasoning skills. Your basic math skills will be called into play and you can also expect your writing ability to be tested.

If you pass the written exam, you'll be ranked on an eligibility list, with the person posting the highest score being ranked number one. When officials decide it's time to fill an academy class, they'll begin notifying applicants, starting at the top of the list.

Step Three: Fitness Assessment

The fitness assessment will be the first test you will encounter after you are notified that a class is being filled. This test is currently based on the Cooper Standards for testing and includes:

- 1.5-Mile Run/Walk
- Push-Ups
- Sit-Ups
- Sit and Reach (tests flexibility)
- Body Fat Analysis

You'll be timed on the run/walk, push-ups, and sit-ups and your performance will be assessed based on your gender, age, and test percentile that you fall into. For example, if you are a male, aged 26, you'll be expected to complete the 1.5-mile run/walk within 12 minutes and 51 seconds.

Flexibility is measured in inches according to how far you can reach while in a seated position. These measurements are evaluated by age and percentile. Body fat analysis is based on your percentage of body fat according to your age and gender.

Step Four: Background Investigation

The next step in the process is a thorough check into your past and present. Your criminal record (if any) will be examined, along with in-depth checks with co-workers, present and past employers, and personal references. If your background checks out, you'll be allowed to proceed to the oral interview board.

Step Five: Oral Interview Board

The oral interview board usually consists of a three-member interview team. The length of the interview varies, of course, since no two individuals take the same amount of time to answer questions. You can expect to be asked about the decisions you've made in your life, your past experiences, and your hopes for the future.

Step Six: Psychological Assessment

Once you pass the oral board, you should expect a conditional offer of employment, followed by a psychological assessment. Although you may be required to take only a written test for evaluation purposes, you should also be prepared for an interview with psychological professionals.

Step Seven: Medical Assessment

The last hurdle you'll face in the hiring process is the exam by medical personnel. This exam is performed by a licensed physician and determines that you have no physical problems that may limit your capacity to perform all the duties of the position. Such problems may be a bad back, cardiovascular abnormality, or pelvic bone or tissue abnormality.

When you receive a thumb's up from the doc, you'll be on the list to start the next academy.

TRAINING

Academy training is about 23 weeks long. All recruits train at the 780-acre State Police Academy near New Braintree. If you have prior military experience, then get ready for a feeling of *deja vu*. All trainees live on-site and train Monday through Friday in an intense, paramilitary environment.

A typical day starts with a wakeup call at 5 a.m., followed by:

- Physical Training
- Breakfast
- Cleaning Chores in Quarters
- Drill and Ceremonies Training
- Lunch

. . . and so goes the training day, sometimes ending around 8 or 9 p.m.

You'll spend time in the classroom studying criminal law, motor vehicle law, search and seizure laws, and evidence identification—just to name a few subjects. Not all your time will be spent behind a classroom desk, though. You'll become quite familiar with the inside of the gym where you'll learn defensive tactics, handcuffing techniques, and how to properly use the PR24NX Expandable Baton, as well as other techniques. You'll also learn to role play in practical exercises designed to prepare you for real-life patrol situations.

This academy isn't a cake walk. The discipline-intensive regime is designed to instill self-confidence, order, and self-discipline in each trainee—all tools that you'll need to feel comfortable when you slide behind the wheel of a cruiser on your own.

Initial Assignment

After graduating from the Academy, you'll spend time in a French and Electric Blue patrol cruiser with an experienced field training officer. You'll be assigned to one of the seven Troops located throughout the Commonwealth. After an appropriate length of time in the field you will be eligible to apply for special units such as Narcotics, Airwing, Motorcycles, K-9, or the Violent Fugitive Arrest Squad, just to name a few.

SALARY & BENEFITS

The accompanying chart lists *base* monthly and annual salaries for different ranks within the Department of State Police.

Educational Incentives

The Department of State Police encourages men and women with a good education to apply. It offers

Your Written Exam

What specific skills or areas are tested?

According to the Massachusetts State Police Personnel Office, the written exam is likely to test the following skills:

- Reading Comprehension
- Recall—Your Ability to Memorize Objects and People
- Logic and Reasoning
- Basic Math
- Writing Skills

What is the format of the exam?

The exam is multiple choice. It may include a writing sample to test your writing skills.

What is the passing score?

A minimum of 70% is the passing score.

Which chapters of this book would be helpful to prepare for the exam?

Useful information on combating test anxiety is covered in Chapter 3, "The Secrets of Test Success." For help on preparing for the specific areas you'll be tested on, refer to Chapter 5, "Memory and Observation," Chapter 6, "Reading Comprehension," Chapter 7, "Logic and Reasoning," Chapter 8, "Math," Chapter 9, "Writing," and Chapter 10, "Vocabulary and Spelling." And don't forget the two State Police Officer Practice Exams, Chapters 4 and 11.

Where is the test given?

Entrance exams are usually scheduled on the same day at State Police installations throughout the Commonwealth. You may take the exam at the site located nearest to you.

SALARY: AT A GLANCE		
Position	**Monthly Salary**	**Annual Salary**
Trainee	$1,681.60	$21,860.00
Trooper	$2,395.40	$31,140.20
Sergeant	$3,239.72	$42,116.38
Lieutenant	$4,028.00	$52,364.00
Captain	$4,632.00	$60,216.00

Note: Figures supplied by the Commonwealth of Massachusetts Department of State Police Personnel Office.

a bonus based on a percentage of your base pay and that percentage breakdown is:

- 10% of your base salary for an Associate's Degree (hours must be in criminal justice)
- 15% of your base salary for a Bachelor's Degree
- 25% of your base salary for a Master's Degree

Approximately 75% of the department is educated with a Bachelor's degree or above.

Vacation

After one year you'll get ten days' paid vacation. It gets even better as times goes on:

- 15 days' paid vacation after four and a half years;
- 20 days' paid vacation after nine and a half years; and
- 25 days' paid vacation after nineteen and a half years

Personal Leave

You'll be granted five days' paid personal leave during the year.

Holidays

You'll have 11 paid holidays per year.

Military Leave

Up to 15 days' leave may be granted for you to fulfill reserve or National Guard obligations. If further time off is required, arrangements can be made for leave on unpaid status.

Uniform and Equipment Allowance

Uniforms and equipment are issued by the Commonwealth.

Sick Leave

You'll have 15 days of sick leave per year, and those days can be carried over from one year to the next.

Health Coverage

Your hospital, medical, and surgical insurance is 90% paid by the Commonwealth.

Retirement

Massachusetts State Troopers can retire after 20 years of service. State law currently requires a mandatory retirement at age 55, but this requirement is being challenged in state court. The Department of State Police is currently allowing personnel to keep working past 55 until the issue is settled.

If you retire after 20 years of service you will receive 60% of the salary you were receiving at the time you retired. If you continue to serve, you'll receive an additional 3% for every year over 20. There is a cap on the percentage, however. You cannot receive over 75%.

C·H·A·P·T·E·R 2

MASSACHUSETTS STATE POLICE EXAM PLANNER

CHAPTER SUMMARY

This chapter helps you prepare for Massachusetts' written State Trooper exam by presenting a study plan specially designed for you. After gathering information and conducting a self-evaluation to see how much work you need to do in how much time, you can choose from four customized test-preparation schedules.

The customized schedules in this chapter are designed to give you a reasonable amount of time to study for the kinds of questions that appear on the State Trooper exam in Massachusetts, depending on how much time is left before exam day. Before you begin your preparation, you need to know two things: just what you're preparing *for* and how prepared you already are.

These customized exam planners lead you through practice exams that are based on the real test and chapters that help you sharpen your test-taking skills and knowledge. Whether you have six months to prepare—or just three weeks—here's how to prepare to score your best.

STEP 1: GET INFORMATION

When: Today   **Time to complete: 1½ hours**

The first thing you need is information. If you haven't already done so, read Chapter 1 to learn about the selection process. Then contact the recruiting office at the phone number listed in Chapter 1. Request a position announcement or exam bulletin and ask when the next exam is scheduled. If no exam is scheduled, ask if you can be put on a mailing list for notification.

Both Chapter 1 and the exam bulletin give an outline of what skills will be tested on the written exam. You can use this information to help you construct your plan in Step 3.

If the exam is scheduled:	do the following self-evaluation and then:
six months or more from now	go to Schedule A
three to six months from now	go to Schedule B
one to three months from now	go to Schedule C
three weeks or less from now	go to Schedule D

STEP 2: SELF-EVALUATION

When: This week   **Time to complete: 4-5 hours**

Find out whether you're ready to take the written exam. First, read Chapter 3, "The Secrets of Test Success." Then take the practice exam in Chapter 4. Score your exam using the answer key at the end. Then match your score with the following analysis.

Score	Analysis
under 60	You need concentrated work in the skills tested. Consider taking classes at the local community college in the areas you're weakest in, or use some of the additional resources listed in Chapters 5–10. After you've spent at least four months working on your skills, retake the test in Chapter 4 and check your score.
61–70	You should spend some time working on your skills. Consider the LearningExpress Skill Builders listed at the back of this book or other books from the library or bookstore. Enlist friends or former teachers to give you some extra help.
71–85	You're in the ballpark. While you only need a score of approximately 70 to pass the real exam, you need to score your *best* to have a good chance of being hired. Work through all the exercises in Chapters 5–10 and then take the second practice test in Chapter 11. If your score hasn't improved much, try some of the tactics listed above.
86–100	You're well on the way to a score that will make you look good when you're evaluated for hiring. For those extra few points that can make the difference in whether or not you get the job, work through the exercises in Chapters 5–10, concentrating on the areas where a little practice will do the most good. Then take the second practice exam in Chapter 11.

STEP 3: MAKE A PLAN

When: This week, after Step 2   **Time to complete: 1 hour**

There are four sample schedules below, based on the amount of time you have before the exam. If you're the kind of person who needs deadlines and assignments to motivate you for a project, here they are. If you're the kind of person who doesn't like to follow other people's plans, you can use the suggested schedules here to construct your own.

In constructing your plan, you should take into account how much work you need to do. If your score on the practice test wasn't what you had hoped, consider taking some of the steps from Schedule A and getting them into Schedule D somehow, even if you do have only three weeks before the exam.

Even more important than making a plan is making a commitment. You can't improve your skills in reading, writing, and logical reasoning overnight. You have to set aside some time every day for study and practice. Try for at least 20 minutes a day. Twenty minutes daily will do you much more good than two hours on Saturday.

If you have months before the exam, you're lucky. Don't put off your study until the week before the exam! Start now. Even ten minutes a day, with half an hour or more on weekends, can make a big difference in your score—and in your chances of getting the job!

SCHEDULE A: THE LEISURE PLAN

You've already taken the sample test and know that you have at least six months in which to build on your strengths and improve in areas where you're weak. Make the most of your time.

Time	Preparation
Exam minus 6 months	Study the explanations for the practice exam in Chapter 4 until you know you could answer all the questions right. Start going to the library once every two weeks to read books or magazines about law enforcement.
Exam minus 5 months	Read Chapters 5 and 6 and work through the exercises. Use at least one of the additional resources listed in each chapter. Find other people who are preparing for the test and form a study group.
Exam minus 4 months	Read Chapter 7 and work through the exercises. Use at least one of the additional resources listed there. Start preparing for the rest of the selection process by reading Chapters 12–15.
Exam minus 3 months	Read Chapter 8 and work through the exercises. You're still doing your library reading, aren't you?
Exam minus 2 months	Read Chapters 9 and 10 and work through the exercises. Make flash cards of vocabulary words you come across in your reading.
Exam minus 1 month	Take the practice test in Chapter 11. Use your score to help you decide where to concentrate your efforts this month. Go back to the relevant chapters and use the extra resources listed there, or get the help of a friend or teacher.
Exam minus 1 week	Review both practice tests. See how much you've learned in the past months? Review Chapter 3 and make sure you've taken all the steps to get ready for the exam.
Exam minus 1 day	Relax. Do something unrelated to the exam. Eat a good meal and go to bed at your usual time.

SCHEDULE B: THE JUST-ENOUGH-TIME PLAN

If you have three to six months before the exam, that should be enough time to prepare for the written test, especially if you scored above 60 on the first practice test. This schedule assumes four months; stretch it out or compress it if you have more or less time.

Time	Preparation
Exam minus 4 months	Read Chapters 5 and 6 and work through the exercises. Use at least one of the additional resources listed in each chapter. Find other people who are preparing for the test and form a study group. Start going to the library once every two weeks to read books about law enforcement.
Exam minus 3 months	Read Chapters 7 and 8 and work through the exercises. Use at least one of the additional resources for Chapter 7. Keep up your reading program.
Exam minus 2 months	Read Chapters 9 and 10 and work through the exercises. Make flash cards of vocabulary words you come across in your reading.
Exam minus 1 month	Take the practice test in Chapter 11. Use your score to help you decide where to concentrate your efforts this month. Go back to the relevant chapters and use the extra resources listed there, or get the help of a friend or teacher.
Exam minus 1 week	Review both practice tests. See how much you've learned in the past months? Review Chapter 3 and make sure you've taken all the steps to get ready for the exam.
Exam minus 1 day	Relax. Do something unrelated to the exam. Eat a good meal and go to bed at your usual time.

SCHEDULE C: MORE STUDY IN LESS TIME

If you have one to three months before the exam, you still have enough time for some concentrated study that will help you improve your score. This schedule is built around a two-month timeframe. If you have only one month, spend an extra couple of hours a week to get all these steps in. If you have three months, take some of the steps from Schedule B and fit them in.

Time	Preparation
Exam minus 8 weeks	Evaluate your performance on the practice test in Chapter 4 to find one or two areas you're weakest in. Choose one or two chapter(s) from among Chapters 5–10 to read in these two weeks. Use some of the additional resources listed there. When you get to those chapters in this plan, review them.
Exam minus 7 weeks	Read Chapter 5 and work through the exercises.
Exam minus 6 weeks	Read Chapter 6 and work through the exercises.
Exam minus 5 weeks	Read Chapter 7 and work through the exercises.
Exam minus 4 weeks	Read Chapter 8 and work through the exercises.
Exam minus 3 weeks	Read Chapters 9 and 10 and work through the exercises.
Exam minus 2 weeks	Take the second practice test in Chapter 11. Then score it and read the answer explanations until you're sure you understand them. Review the areas where your score is lowest.
Exam minus 1 week	Review Chapters 5–10, concentrating on the areas where a little work can help the most. Review Chapter 3 to make sure you've taken all the steps to get ready for the exam.
Exam minus 1 day	Relax. Do something unrelated to the exam. Eat a good meal and go to bed at your usual time.

SCHEDULE D: THE CRAM PLAN

If you have three weeks or less before the exam, you really have your work cut out for you. Carve half an hour out of your day, *every day,* for study. This schedule assumes you have the whole three weeks to prepare in; if you have less time, you'll have to compress the schedule accordingly.

Time	Preparation
Exam minus 3 weeks	Read Chapters 5, 6, and 7 and work through the exercises.
Exam minus 2 weeks	Read Chapters 8, 9, and 10 and work through the exercises. Take the practice test in Chapter 11.
Exam minus 1 week	Evaluate your performance on the second practice test. Review the parts of Chapters 5–10 that you had the most trouble with. Get a friend or teacher to help you with the section you had the most difficulty with.
Exam minus 2 days	Review both practice tests. Make sure you understand the answer explanations.
Exam minus 1 day	Relax. Do something unrelated to the exam. Eat a good meal and go to bed at your usual time.

STEP 4: SCORE YOUR BEST

When: On Exam Day

If you've followed the plan presented in this chapter, or invented your own based on these guidelines, you *will* score your best—because you're prepared.

C·H·A·P·T·E·R 3

THE SECRETS OF TEST SUCCESS

CHAPTER SUMMARY

This chapter contains valuable advice for those planning to take a written law enforcement exam: how to prepare, how to beat test anxiety, how to pace yourself as you move through the test, and when to guess. Read this chapter before you take the first sample written exam in this book.

 little preparation goes a long way when it comes to taking a test. If you know about the test beforehand and come prepared physically and mentally, you're already a step ahead. Test preparation reduces your test anxiety, allows you to pace yourself properly on the test, and helps you to do as well as you possibly can. It's a good feeling to walk into a test knowing you've done your best to prepare for it.

FINDING OUT ABOUT THE TEST

The first step is to learn as much as possible about the test you'll be taking. The information you need to know is summarized in the list that follows on the next page.

Must-Know Information

- When and where will the test be given?
- Do I have more than one opportunity to take the test?
- How long will the test take?
- Do most people who take the test finish on time?
- What do I need to bring to the test?

Make sure you know the answers to these questions before you take the test.

Structure and Format of the Test

Find out as much as you can about how the test is organized. Every test is different, but chances are the test you take will be timed and contain mostly multiple-choice questions. Learn as much as you can ahead of time.

- What skills are tested?
- How many sections does the test have?
- How many questions does each section have?
- Are the questions ordered from easy to hard, or is the sequence random?
- How much time is allotted for each section? Are there breaks between sections?
- What is the passing score? How many questions do I have to get right to get that score?
- Will a higher score give me any advantages, like a higher salary or a better rank on the eligibility list? If so, what score would be ideal, yet within reason for me?
- How is the test scored? Is there a penalty for wrong answers? If so, what is it?
- If I finish a section early, can I return to a previous section or move ahead to the next section?
- Can I write in the test booklet, or will I be given scrap paper for my work?

- What should I bring to the test with me? Pencils? Calculator? Ticket of admission? Photo identification? Proof of citizenship?

Some standardized tests are scored in such a way that you are penalized for wrong answers. You *need* this information before you take the test because it will affect how you approach the test. More on that later.

If you complete the *Test Information Sheet* on the next page, you'll be sure to have all the information you need.

COMBATING TEST ANXIETY

Knowing what to expect and being prepared for it is the best defense against test anxiety—that worrisome feeling that keeps you from doing your best. Practice and preparation keep you from succumbing to that feeling.

Nevertheless, even the brightest, most well-prepared test-takers may suffer from occasional bouts of test anxiety. But don't worry—you can overcome it.

Take the Test One Question at a Time

Focus all of your attention on the one question you're answering. Block out any thoughts about questions you've already read or concerns about what's coming next. Concentrate your thinking where it will do the most good—on the question you're answering.

Develop a Positive Attitude

Keep reminding yourself that you're prepared. The fact that you're reading this book means that you're better prepared than most of the others who are taking the test. Remember, it's only a test, and you're going to do your BEST. That's all anyone can ask of you. If that nagging drill sergeant voice inside your head starts send-

TEST INFORMATION SHEET

Must-Know Data

When is the test?_____

Where will it be given?_____

Do you know how to get to the testing site?
❏ Yes   Make a trial run to see how long it takes to get there at the time of day you'll be making the real trip.
❏ No   Find out how to get to the testing site and make your trial run.

How long does it take to get to the testing site? _____

What time do you need to leave to get there on time? _____

How long is the test? _____

List the items you need to bring to the test:

_____

_____

Structure and Format of the test

Format: ❏ Multiple-choice   ❏ Fill-in-the-blanks
          ❏ True/false   ❏ Essay
          ❏ Other

Total # questions: _____

Total # sections: _____

	# Questions	Skills Tested
Section 1		
Section 2		
Section 3		
Section 4		

Passing score:_____   Ideal score:_____

Knowing this information helps you prepare mentally for the test. You'll be able to walk into the test relaxed and confident, knowing you'll do your best.

---

ing negative messages, combat them with positive ones of your own.

- "I'm doing just fine."
- "I've prepared for this test."
- "I know exactly what to do."
- "I know I can get the score I'm aiming for."

You get the idea. Remember to drown out negative messages with positive ones of your own.

If You Lose Your Concentration

Don't worry about it! It's normal. During a long test it happens to everyone. When your mind is stressed or overexerted, it takes a break whether you want it to or not. It's easy to get your concentration back if you simply acknowledge the fact that you've lost it and take a quick break. You brain needs very little time (seconds really) to rest.

Put your pencil down and close your eyes. Take a few deep breaths and listen to the sound of your breathing. Picture yourself doing something you really enjoy, like playing sports or listening to music. The ten seconds or so that this takes is really all the time your brain needs to relax and get ready to focus again.

Try this technique several times in the days before the test when you feel stressed. The more you practice, the better it will work for you on test day.

If You Freeze

Don't worry about a question that stumps you even though you're sure you know the answer. Mark it and go on to the next question. You can come back to the "stumper" later. Try to put it out of your mind completely until you come back to it. Just let your subconscious mind chew on the question while your conscious mind focuses on the other questions (one at a time, of course). Chances are, the memory block will be gone by the time you return to the question.

If you freeze before you ever begin the test, here's what to do:

1. Take a little time to look over the test.
2. Read a few of the questions.
3. Decide which ones are the easiest and start there.

Before long, you'll be "in the groove."

DURING THE TEST

As you are taking your test, you want to use your time wisely and avoid making errors. Here are a few suggestions for making the most of your time.

TIME MANAGEMENT STRATEGIES
Pace Yourself

The most important time management strategy is pacing yourself. Pacing yourself doesn't just mean how quickly or slowly you can progress through the test. It means knowing how the test is organized, the number of questions you have to get right, and making sure you have enough time to do them. Before you begin a section, take just a few seconds to survey it, noting the number of questions, their organization, and the type of questions that look easier than the rest. Rough out a time schedule based on the time allotted for the section. Mark the halfway point in the section and make a note beside that mark of what time it will be when the testing period is half over.

Keep Moving

Once you begin the test, keep moving! Don't stop to ponder a difficult question. Skip it and move on. Mark the question so you can quickly find it later, if you have time to come back to it. If all questions count the same, then a question that takes you five seconds to answer counts as much as one that takes you several minutes, so pick up the easy points first. Besides, answering the easier questions first helps to build your confidence and gets you in the testing groove. Who knows? As you go through the test, you may even stumble across some relevant information to help you answer those tough questions.

Don't Rush

Keep moving, but don't rush. Think of your mind as a teeter-totter. On one side is your emotional energy. On the other side is your intellectual energy. When your emotional energy is high, your intellectual capacity is low. Remember how difficult it is to reason with someone when you're angry? On the other hand, when your intellectual energy is high, your emotional energy is low.

Rushing raises your emotional energy. Remember the last time you were late for work? All that rushing around causes you to forget important things—like your lunch. Move quickly to keep your mind from wandering, but don't rush and get yourself flustered.

Check Yourself

Check yourself at the halfway mark. If you're a little ahead, you know you're on track and may even have time left to go back and check your work. If you're behind, you have several choices. You can pick up the pace a little, but do this only if you can do it comfortably. Remember—DON'T RUSH! You can also skip around in the remaining portion of the test to pick up as many easy points as possible. This strategy has one drawback, however. If you are marking a score sheet with circles (or "bubbles") and you put the right answers in the wrong bubbles—they're wrong. So pay close attention to the question numbers if you decide to do this.

Set a Target Score

Earlier, you were asked to find out what constituted a passing score and if there was any advantage in earning a higher score. Here's how to use this information to your advantage.

First, let's assume that your only objective is to pass the test because there is no advantage to be gained from a higher score. Figure out how many questions you must answer correctly to pass. *That's how long your test is.* For example, if the test has 100 questions and you need only 70 right to pass, once you're quite sure you've answered 70 questions correctly, you can just breeze through the rest of the test. You'll probably do even better than you did before you hit the passing mark.

Now, let's assume that you need to pass the test, but scoring higher than others who take the test gives you some advantage, a higher placement for example.

In this case, you still want to calculate a passing score. Then set a goal, an ideal score you'd like to earn. Try to make your target score realistic, yet challenging. As you take the test, work first to pass it, then concentrate on earning your target score. This strategy focuses you on the questions you answered correctly, rather than the ones you think are wrong. That way you can build confidence as you go and keep emotional energy to a minimum.

Caution: Don't waste too much time scoring as you go. Just make rough estimates along the way.

AVOIDING ERRORS

When you take the test, you want to make as few errors as possible in the questions you answer. Here are a few tactics to keep in mind.

Control Yourself

Remember the comparison between your mind and a teeter-totter that you read about a few paragraphs ago? Keeping your emotional energy low and your intellectual energy high is the best way to avoid mistakes. If you feel stressed or worried, stop for a few seconds. Acknowledge the feeling (Hmmm! I'm feeling a little pressure here!), take two or three deep breaths, and send yourself a few positive messages. This relieves your emotional anxiety and boosts your intellectual capacity.

Directions

In most testing situations, a proctor reads the instructions aloud before the test begins. Make certain you understand what is expected. If you don't, *ask!* Listen carefully for instructions about how to answer the questions and whether there's a penalty for wrong answers. Make certain you know how much time you have. You may even want to write the amount of time on your test. If you miss this vital information, *ask for it.* You need it to do well on your test.

Answers

This may seem like a silly warning, but it is important. Place your answers in the right blanks or the corresponding bubbles. Right answers in the wrong place earn no points. It's a good idea to check every 5-10 questions, and every time you skip a question, to make sure you're in the right spot. That way you won't need much time to correct your answer sheet if you have made an error.

Choosing the Right Answer by Process of Elimination

As you read a question, you may find it helpful to underline important information or make some notes about what you're reading. When you get to the heart of the question, circle it and make sure you understand what it is asking. If you're not sure of what's being asked, you'll never know whether you've chosen the right answer. What you do next depends on the type of question you're answering.

- If it's math, take a quick look at the answer choices for some clues. Sometimes this helps to put the question in a new perspective and makes it easier to answer. Then make a plan of attack to solve the problem.
- Otherwise, follow this simple *process of elimination* plan to manage your testing time as efficiently as possible: Read each answer choice and make a *quick* decision about what to do with it, marking your test book accordingly:

  The answer seems reasonable; keep it. Put a ✔ next to the answer.

  The answer is awful. Get rid of it. Put an **X** next to the answer.

  You can't make up your mind about the answer, or you don't understand it. Keep it for now. Put a **?** next to it.

Whatever you do, don't waste time dilly-dallying over each answer choice. If you can't figure out what an answer choice means, don't worry about it. If it's the right answer, you'll probably be able to eliminate all the others, and, if it's the wrong answer, another answer will probably strike you more obviously as the right answer.

If you haven't eliminated any answers at all, skip the question temporarily, but don't forget to mark the question so you can come back to it later if you have time. If the test has no penalty for wrong answers, and you're certain that you could never answer this question in a million years, pick an answer and move on!

If you've eliminated all but one answer, just reread the circled part of the question to make sure you're answering exactly what's asked. Mark your answer sheet and move on to the next question.

Here's what to do when you've eliminated some, but not all of the answer choices. Compare the remaining answers looking for similarities and differences, reasoning your way through these choices. Try to eliminate those choices that don't seem as strong to you. But DON'T eliminate an answer just because you don't understand it. You may even be able to use relevant information from other parts of the test. If you've narrowed it down to a single answer, check it against the circled question to be sure you've answered it. Then mark your answer sheet and move on. If you're down to only two or three answer choices, you've improved your odds of getting the question right. Make an *educated* guess and move on. However, if you think you can do better with more time, mark the question as one to return to later.

If You're Penalized for Wrong Answers

You *must know* whether you'll be penalized for wrong answers before you begin the test. If you don't, ask the proctor before the test begins. Whether you make a guess or not depends upon the penalty. Some standardized tests are scored in such a way that every wrong answer reduces your score by a fraction of a point, and these can really add up against you! Whatever the penalty, if you can eliminate enough choices to make the odds of answering the question better than the penalty for getting it wrong, make a guess. This is called *educated guessing*.

Let's imagine you are taking a test in which each answer has five choices and you are penalized ¼ of a point for each wrong answer. If you cannot eliminate any of the answer choices, you're better off leaving the answer blank because the odds of guessing correctly are one in five. However, if you can eliminate two of the choices as definitely wrong, the odds are now in your favor. You have a one in three chance of answering the question correctly. Fortunately, few tests are scored using such elaborate means, but if your test is one of them, know the penalties and calculate your odds before you take a guess on a question.

If You Finish Early

Use any time you have left to do the following:

- Go back to questions you marked to return to and try them again.
- Check your work on all the other questions. If you have a good reason for thinking a response is wrong, change it.
- Review your answer sheet. Make sure that you've put the answers in the right places and that you've marked only one answer for each question. (Most tests are scored in such a way that questions with more than one answer are marked wrong.)
- If you've erased an answer, make sure you've done a good job of it.
- Check for stray marks on your answer sheet that could distort your score.

Whatever you do, don't just take a nap when you've finished a test section. Make every second count by checking your work over and over again until time is called.

THE DAYS BEFORE THE TEST

Physical Activity

Get some exercise in the days preceding the test. You'll send some extra oxygen to your brain and allow your thinking performance to peak on test day. Moderation is the key here. Don't exercise so much that you feel exhausted, but a little physical activity will invigorate your body and brain.

Balanced Diet

Like your body, your brain needs the proper nutrients to function well. Eat plenty of fruits and vegetables in the days before the test. Foods that are high in lecithin, such as fish and beans, are especially good choices. Lecithin is a mineral your brain needs for peak performance. You may even consider a visit to your local pharmacy to buy a bottle of lecithin tablets several weeks before your test.

Rest

Get plenty of sleep the nights before you take the test. Don't overdo it, though, or you'll make yourself as groggy as if you were overtired. Go to bed at a reasonable time, early enough to get the number of hours you need to function effectively. You'll feel relaxed and rested if you've gotten plenty of sleep in the days before you take the test.

Trial Run

At some point before you take the test, make a trial run to the testing center to see how long it takes to get there. Rushing raises your emotional energy and lowers your intellectual capacity, so you want to allow plenty of time on test day to get to the testing center. Arriving 10–15 minutes early gives you time to relax and get situated.

The Night Before

Get ready all those things you need to bring with you to the test, such as pencils, identification, admission ticket, etc. Make sure you have at least three pencils, including one with a dull point for faster gridding of a bubble answer sheet. You don't want to waste time the morning of the test hunting around for these things.

TEST DAY

It's finally here, the day of the big test. Set your alarm early enough to allow plenty of time. Eat a good breakfast. Avoid anything that's really high in sugar, such as donuts. A sugar high turns into a sugar low after an hour or so. Cereal and toast or anything with complex carbohydrates is a good choice. Eat only moderate amounts. You don't want to take a test feeling stuffed!

Dress in layers. You can never tell what the conditions will be like in the testing room. Your proctor just might be a member of the polar bear club.

Pack a high energy snack to take with you. You might get a break sometime during the test when you can grab a quick snack. Bananas are great. They have a moderate amount of sugar and plenty of brain nutri-

ents, such as potassium. Most proctors won't allow you to eat a snack while you're testing, but a peppermint shouldn't pose a problem. Peppermints are like smelling salts for your brain. If you lose your concentration or suffer from a momentary mental block, a peppermint can get you back on track.

Leave early enough so you have plenty of time to get to the test center. Allow a few minutes for unexpected traffic. When you arrive, locate the restroom and use it. Few things interfere with concentration as much as a full bladder. Then check in, find your seat, and make sure it's comfortable. If it isn't, tell the proctor and ask to change to a location you find more suitable.

Now relax and think positively! Before you know it the test will be over, and you'll walk away knowing you've done the best you can.

AFTER THE TEST

Two things:

1. Plan a little celebration.
2. Go to it.

If you have something to look forward to after the test is over, you may find it easier to prepare well for the test and to keep moving during the test.

GOOD LUCK!

MASSACHUSETTS STATE POLICE PRACTICE EXAM 1

4

CHAPTER SUMMARY

This is the first practice exam in this book based on the areas most likely to be tested on the Massachusetts State Police written exam. Use this test to see how you would do if you had to take the exam today.

The skills tested on the exam that follows are those the State of Massachusetts plans to assess on its State Police Exam. While the actual exam may look somewhat different from this one, or test skills in a somewhat different way, this exam will provide vital practice that will help you get ready. The practice exam consists of 100 multiple-choice questions in the following areas: memorization, reading comprehension, logic and reasoning, basic mathematics, and writing skills.

The test begins with the memory portion. You will have ten minutes to study five Wanted posters and the text that accompanies them. After those ten minutes, the exam begins with questions about those Wanted posters. You should not refer back to the Wanted posters to answer the questions on them in this practice exam. In the real exam, the material you have to memorize will have been taken away from you before the test booklets are passed out.

Normally you would have about two and a half hours for a test like this, but for now, don't worry about timing—except for the ten minutes for memorization. For the rest of the exam, just take the test in as relaxed a manner as you can. The answer sheet you should use for answering the questions is on the following page. Then comes the exam itself, and after that is the answer key, with each correct answer explained. The answer key is followed by a section on how to score your exam.

1.	ⓐ	ⓑ	ⓒ	ⓓ	36.	ⓐ	ⓑ	ⓒ	ⓓ	71.	ⓐ	ⓑ	ⓒ	ⓓ
2.	ⓐ	ⓑ	ⓒ	ⓓ	37.	ⓐ	ⓑ	ⓒ	ⓓ	72.	ⓐ	ⓑ	ⓒ	ⓓ
3.	ⓐ	ⓑ	ⓒ	ⓓ	38.	ⓐ	ⓑ	ⓒ	ⓓ	73.	ⓐ	ⓑ	ⓒ	ⓓ
4.	ⓐ	ⓑ	ⓒ	ⓓ	39.	ⓐ	ⓑ	ⓒ	ⓓ	74.	ⓐ	ⓑ	ⓒ	ⓓ
5.	ⓐ	ⓑ	ⓒ	ⓓ	40.	ⓐ	ⓑ	ⓒ	ⓓ	75.	ⓐ	ⓑ	ⓒ	ⓓ
6.	ⓐ	ⓑ	ⓒ	ⓓ	41.	ⓐ	ⓑ	ⓒ	ⓓ	76.	ⓐ	ⓑ	ⓒ	ⓓ
7.	ⓐ	ⓑ	ⓒ	ⓓ	42.	ⓐ	ⓑ	ⓒ	ⓓ	77.	ⓐ	ⓑ	ⓒ	ⓓ
8.	ⓐ	ⓑ	ⓒ	ⓓ	43.	ⓐ	ⓑ	ⓒ	ⓓ	78.	ⓐ	ⓑ	ⓒ	ⓓ
9.	ⓐ	ⓑ	ⓒ	ⓓ	44.	ⓐ	ⓑ	ⓒ	ⓓ	79.	ⓐ	ⓑ	ⓒ	ⓓ
10.	ⓐ	ⓑ	ⓒ	ⓓ	45.	ⓐ	ⓑ	ⓒ	ⓓ	80.	ⓐ	ⓑ	ⓒ	ⓓ
11.	ⓐ	ⓑ	ⓒ	ⓓ	46.	ⓐ	ⓑ	ⓒ	ⓓ	81.	ⓐ	ⓑ	ⓒ	ⓓ
12.	ⓐ	ⓑ	ⓒ	ⓓ	47.	ⓐ	ⓑ	ⓒ	ⓓ	82.	ⓐ	ⓑ	ⓒ	ⓓ
13.	ⓐ	ⓑ	ⓒ	ⓓ	48.	ⓐ	ⓑ	ⓒ	ⓓ	83.	ⓐ	ⓑ	ⓒ	ⓓ
14.	ⓐ	ⓑ	ⓒ	ⓓ	49.	ⓐ	ⓑ	ⓒ	ⓓ	84.	ⓐ	ⓑ	ⓒ	ⓓ
15.	ⓐ	ⓑ	ⓒ	ⓓ	50.	ⓐ	ⓑ	ⓒ	ⓓ	85.	ⓐ	ⓑ	ⓒ	ⓓ
16.	ⓐ	ⓑ	ⓒ	ⓓ	51.	ⓐ	ⓑ	ⓒ	ⓓ	86.	ⓐ	ⓑ	ⓒ	ⓓ
17.	ⓐ	ⓑ	ⓒ	ⓓ	52.	ⓐ	ⓑ	ⓒ	ⓓ	87.	ⓐ	ⓑ	ⓒ	ⓓ
18.	ⓐ	ⓑ	ⓒ	ⓓ	53.	ⓐ	ⓑ	ⓒ	ⓓ	88.	ⓐ	ⓑ	ⓒ	ⓓ
19.	ⓐ	ⓑ	ⓒ	ⓓ	54.	ⓐ	ⓑ	ⓒ	ⓓ	89.	ⓐ	ⓑ	ⓒ	ⓓ
20.	ⓐ	ⓑ	ⓒ	ⓓ	55.	ⓐ	ⓑ	ⓒ	ⓓ	90.	ⓐ	ⓑ	ⓒ	ⓓ
21.	ⓐ	ⓑ	ⓒ	ⓓ	56.	ⓐ	ⓑ	ⓒ	ⓓ	91.	ⓐ	ⓑ	ⓒ	ⓓ
22.	ⓐ	ⓑ	ⓒ	ⓓ	57.	ⓐ	ⓑ	ⓒ	ⓓ	92.	ⓐ	ⓑ	ⓒ	ⓓ
23.	ⓐ	ⓑ	ⓒ	ⓓ	58.	ⓐ	ⓑ	ⓒ	ⓓ	93.	ⓐ	ⓑ	ⓒ	ⓓ
24.	ⓐ	ⓑ	ⓒ	ⓓ	59.	ⓐ	ⓑ	ⓒ	ⓓ	94.	ⓐ	ⓑ	ⓒ	ⓓ
25.	ⓐ	ⓑ	ⓒ	ⓓ	60.	ⓐ	ⓑ	ⓒ	ⓓ	95.	ⓐ	ⓑ	ⓒ	ⓓ
26.	ⓐ	ⓑ	ⓒ	ⓓ	61.	ⓐ	ⓑ	ⓒ	ⓓ	96.	ⓐ	ⓑ	ⓒ	ⓓ
27.	ⓐ	ⓑ	ⓒ	ⓓ	62.	ⓐ	ⓑ	ⓒ	ⓓ	97.	ⓐ	ⓑ	ⓒ	ⓓ
28.	ⓐ	ⓑ	ⓒ	ⓓ	63.	ⓐ	ⓑ	ⓒ	ⓓ	98.	ⓐ	ⓑ	ⓒ	ⓓ
29.	ⓐ	ⓑ	ⓒ	ⓓ	64.	ⓐ	ⓑ	ⓒ	ⓓ	99.	ⓐ	ⓑ	ⓒ	ⓓ
30.	ⓐ	ⓑ	ⓒ	ⓓ	65.	ⓐ	ⓑ	ⓒ	ⓓ	100.	ⓐ	ⓑ	ⓒ	ⓓ
31.	ⓐ	ⓑ	ⓒ	ⓓ	66.	ⓐ	ⓑ	ⓒ	ⓓ					
32.	ⓐ	ⓑ	ⓒ	ⓓ	67.	ⓐ	ⓑ	ⓒ	ⓓ					
33.	ⓐ	ⓑ	ⓒ	ⓓ	68.	ⓐ	ⓑ	ⓒ	ⓓ					
34.	ⓐ	ⓑ	ⓒ	ⓓ	69.	ⓐ	ⓑ	ⓒ	ⓓ					
35.	ⓐ	ⓑ	ⓒ	ⓓ	70.	ⓐ	ⓑ	ⓒ	ⓓ					

MASSACHUSETTS STATE POLICE EXAM 1

You have 10 minutes to study the following Wanted Posters. When the 10 minutes are up, turn the page and proceed with taking the exam.

MISSING
Valencia Camacho

DESCRIPTION:

    Age: 10

    Race: Hispanic

    Height: 4'10"

    Weight: 80 lb.

    Hair: Black, straight, shoulder-length

    Eyes: Brown

    Skin: Dark brown

REMARKS: Last seen alone at Dixon's Ice Cream Shoppe in Highpoint Mall in Daytona at noon on Saturday, April 1. Wearing red shorts, white t-shirt, with her hair in a pony tail. Front right tooth missing.

IF LOCATED: Call Daytona Sheriff's Department, Juvenile Unit, at 344-555-1220.

WANTED
James Wilson Baker

ALIASES: Willie James

WANTED BY: Chicago Police Department

CHARGES: Burglary

DESCRIPTION:

> Age: 18
> Race: White
> Height: 5'11"
> Weight: 195 lb.
> Hair: Red
> Eyes: Green

IDENTIFYING SCARS OR MARKS: Tattoo on inner right forearm of black Nazi swastika.

REMARKS: Rides a black Kawasaki 750 with cracked headlight. Last seen in Chicago and believed to be headed for Cambridge, Massachusetts.

WANTED
Jean Chan

ALIASES: Jean Cho

WANTED BY: New Mexico State Police

CHARGES: Auto Theft

DESCRIPTION:

> Age: 30
> Race: Asian
> Height: 5'2"
> Weight: 110 lb.
> Hair: Black
> Eyes: Brown

IDENTIFYING SCARS OR MARKS: Scar above right eye.

REMARKS: Last seen at Edward's Texaco Gasmart in Albuquerque, New Mexico. Chan may be headed for Oakland, California, driving a stolen white Trans Am.

WANTED
Louis Robert Hart

ALIASES: Hart-Break; Robert Louis
WANTED BY: FBI
CHARGES: Conspiracy
DESCRIPTION:

    Age: 45
    Race: Black
    Height: 6'3"
    Weight: 255 lb.
    Hair: Black
    Eyes: Brown

REMARKS: Hart is addicted to gambling and frequents the Blue Streak Greyhound Raceway in Jacksonville, Mississippi. Is thought to still be in the area.
CAUTION: Hart is known to carry a diving knife strapped to his right leg.

WANTED
Larry Edward Cloud

ALIASES: Eddie One-Eye
WANTED BY: Florida State Police
CHARGES: DUI
DESCRIPTION:

    Age: 62
    Race: White
    Height: 5'8½"
    Weight: 180 lb.
    Hair: Gray
    Eyes: Blue

IDENTIFYING SCARS OR MARKS: Wears black patch over missing right eye.
REMARKS: Last seen in Pensacola. Is known to frequent the Dew Drop Inn downtown and drives a sky-blue Ford Escort. Sources say he is moving to Race Point, Massachusetts.

PART ONE: MEMORIZATION

Questions 1–20 are based on the Wanted Posters you have just studied. **Do not turn back to the Wanted posters to answer these questions.** When you finish Part One, continue with the rest of the exam.

1. James Wilson Baker is wanted for
   a. theft
   b. fraud
   c. conspiracy
   d. burglary

2. James Wilson Baker wears a tattoo on his right arm depicting a
   a. motorcycle
   b. ring
   c. swastika
   d. greyhound

3. How old is Valencia Camacho?
   a. 18
   b. 10
   c. 30
   d. 17

4. Larry Edward Cloud also goes by which of the following names?
   a. Eddie One-Eye
   b. Robert Louis
   c. Edward Cloud
   d. Willie James

5. When last seen, Valencia Camacho wore her hair in
   a. tight curls
   b. braids
   c. a pony tail
   d. a spike cut

6. Identifying scars or marks on Larry Edward Cloud include which of the following?
   a. missing right eye
   b. tattoo of a swastika
   c. a scar above the right eye
   d. tattoo of an eye on the inner right forearm

7. Jean Chan weighs approximately
   a. 180 lbs.
   b. 110 lbs.
   c. 120 lbs.
   d. 80 lbs.

8. Jean Chan was last seen driving a
   a. Ford Escort
   b. Ford F-150
   c. Trans Am
   d. Kawasaki 750

9. Louis Robert Hart is wanted by the
   a. FBI
   b. Jacksonville Police
   c. New Mexico State Police
   d. Florida State Police

10. Jean Chan is wanted for
    a. carrying a concealed weapon
    b. conspiracy
    c. reckless driving
    d. auto theft

11. Louis Robert Hart is believed to be in which state?
    a. New Mexico
    b. Mississippi
    c. California
    d. Florida

12. Which of the following best describes Louis Robert Hart's facial hair?
   a. He is clean-shaven.
   b. He wears a full beard and mustache.
   c. He wears a goatee.
   d. He wears a thin mustache.

13. Which of these females is listed as missing?
   a. Camacho
   b. Chan
   c. Cho
   d. both Chan and Camacho

14. Which of the suspects is wanted for conspiracy?
   a. Chan
   b. Hart
   c. Cloud
   d. Baker

15. Which suspect frequents the Dew Drop Inn in Pensacola?
   a. Hart
   b. Camacho
   c. Baker
   d. Cloud

16. Which suspect may be moving to Race Point, Massachusetts?
   a. Cloud
   b. Baker
   c. Chan
   d. Hart

17. Which suspect is known to strap a diving knife to his or her leg?
   a. Chan
   b. Hart
   c. Cloud
   d. both Chan and Hart

18. Which suspect has gray hair?
   a. Hart
   b. Chan
   c. Baker
   d. Cloud

19. Based on the wanted posters, which of the following statements is TRUE?
   a. Both Hart and Cloud have tattoos.
   b. Both Hart and Cloud are under 40.
   c. Hart is younger than Cloud.
   d. Cloud is taller than Hart.

20. Based on the wanted posters, which of the following statements is FALSE?
   a. Baker has red hair.
   b. Hart is black.
   c. Baker and Hart both have mustaches.
   d. Baker and Hart are not close in age.

PART TWO: READING COMPREHENSION

Following are several reading passages. Answer the questions that come after each, based solely on the information in the passage.

   Law enforcement officers often do not like taking time from their regular duties to testify in court, but testimony is an important part of an officer's job. To be good witnesses, officers should keep complete notes detailing any potentially criminal or actionable incidents. When on the witness stand, officers may refer to those notes to refresh their memory about particular events. It is also very important for officers to listen carefully to the questions asked by the lawyers and to provide only the information requested. Officers should never volunteer opinions or any extra information that is beyond the scope of a question.

21. According to the passage, an officer who is testifying in court
   a. will be questioned by the judge
   b. may refer to his or her notes while on the witness stand
   c. must testify without pay
   d. appreciates taking a break from routine assignments

22. This passage is probably taken from a
   a. memo entitled "Proper Arrest Procedure"
   b. newspaper article about crime prevention
   c. recruitment pamphlet for law enforcement officers
   d. officers' training manual

23. According to the passage, testifying in court is
   a. difficult, because lawyers try to trick witnesses
   b. an important part of a law enforcement officer's job
   c. less stressful for law enforcement officers than for other witnesses
   d. a waste of time, because judges usually let criminals off

Detectives who routinely investigate violent crimes can't help but become somewhat jaded. Paradoxically, the victims and witnesses with whom they work closely are often in a highly vulnerable and emotional state. The emotional fallout from a sexual assault, for example, can be complex and long-lasting. Detectives must be trained to handle people in emotional distress and must be sensitive to the fact that for the victim the crime is not routine. At the same time, detectives must recognize the limits of their role and resist the temptation to act as therapists or social workers, instead referring victims to the proper agencies,

24. What is the main idea of the passage?
   a. Detectives who investigate violent crime must never become emotionally hardened by the experience.
   b. Victims of violent crime should be referred to therapists and social workers.
   c. Detectives should be sensitive to the emotional state of victims of violent crime.
   d. Detectives should be particularly careful in dealing with victims of sexual assault.

25. According to the passage, what is "paradoxical" about the detective's relationship to the victim?
   a. Detectives know less about the experience of violent crime than do victims.
   b. What for the detective is routine is a unique and profound experience for the victim.
   c. Detectives must be sensitive to victims' needs but can't be social workers or psychologists.
   d. Not only must detectives solve crimes, but they must also handle the victims with care.

26. Which of the following is NOT advocated by the passage for detectives who investigate violent crimes?
   a. They should refer victims to appropriate support services.
   b. They should be aware of the psychological consequences of being victimized.
   c. They should not become too personally involved with victims' problems.
   d. They should never become jaded.

On occasion, corrections officers may be involved in receiving a confession from an inmate under their care. Sometimes, one inmate may confess to another inmate, who may be motivated to pass the information on to corrections officers. Often, however, these confessions are obtained by placing an undercover agent, posing as an inmate, in a cell with the prisoner. On the surface, this may appear to violate the principles of the constitutional Fifth Amendment privilege against self-incrimination. However, the courts have found that the Fifth Amendment is intended to protect suspects from coercive interrogation, which is present when a person is in custody and is subject to official questioning. In the case of an undercover officer posing as an inmate, the questioning does not appear to be official; therefore, confessions obtained in this manner are not considered coercive.

27. According to the passage, corrections officers
   a. are allowed to question inmates about crimes they have committed
   b. sometimes receive confessions from inmates
   c. should try to become friendly with inmates in order to gather information
   d. should always read inmates their rights before talking to them

28. According to the passage, prison inmates
   a. sometimes make confessions to fellow inmates
   b. lose their privilege against self-incrimination
   c. do not know they can refuse to answer corrections officers' questions
   d. may be coerced into confessing

29. The privilege against self-incrimination can be found in
   a. a Supreme Court opinion
   b. prison rules and regulations
   c. state law governing prisons
   d. the U.S. Constitution

30. The privilege against self-incrimination does not apply to inmates who
   a. were read their rights when they were arrested

   b. have already been convicted
   c. believe they are talking to a fellow inmate
   d. have received life sentences

Adolescents are at high risk for violent crime. Although they make up only 14 percent of the population age 12 and over, 30 percent of all violent crimes—1.9 million—were committed against them. Because crimes against adolescents are likely to be committed by offenders of the same age (as well as same sex and race), preventing violence among and against adolescents is a twofold challenge. Adolescents are at risk for becoming both victims and perpetrators of violence. New violence-prevention programs in urban middle schools help reduce the crime rate by teaching both victims and perpetrators of such violence the skills of conflict resolution and how to apply reason to disputes, as well as by changing attitudes towards achieving respect through violence and towards the need to retaliate. These programs provide a safe place for students to discuss their conflicts and therefore prove appealing to students at risk.

31. What is the main idea of the passage?
   a. Adolescents are more likely to commit crimes than older people and must therefore be taught nonviolence in order to protect society.
   b. Middle school students appreciate the conflict resolution skills they acquire in violence-prevention programs.
   c. Middle school violence-prevention programs are designed to help to lower the rate of crimes against adolescents.
   d. Violence against adolescents is increasing.

32. Which of the following is NOT mentioned in the passage as a skill taught by middle school violence-prevention programs?
   a. settling disputes without violence
   b. avoiding the need for vengeance
   c. being reasonable in emotional situations
   d. keeping one's temper

33. According to the passage, which of the following statements about adolescents is true?
   a. Adolescents are disproportionately likely to be victims of violent crime.
   b. Adolescents are more likely to commit violent crimes than other segments of the population.
   c. Adolescents are the victims of 14% of the nation's violent crimes.
   d. Adolescents are reluctant to attend violence-prevention programs.

34. According to the passage, why is preventing violence against adolescents a "twofold challenge"?
   a. because adolescents are twice as likely to be victims of violent crime as members of other age groups
   b. because adolescents must be prevented from both perpetrating and being victimized by violent crime
   c. because adolescents must change both their violent behavior and their attitudes towards violence
   d. because adolescents are vulnerable yet reluctant to listen to adult advice

In many law enforcement departments, law enforcement officers who want to be promoted further must first spend an extended period of time working in the internal affairs division. Not only do these offi-cers become thoroughly versed in detecting law enforcement officer misconduct, they also become familiar with the circumstances and attitudes out of which such conduct might arise. Placement in internal affairs reduces the possibility that a commanding officer might be too lenient in investigating or disciplining a colleague. The transfer to internal affairs also separates a detective from his or her precinct, reducing the prospect of cronyism, and it familiarizes the detective with serving in a supervisory capacity.

35. According to the passage, law enforcement officers are transferred to internal affairs in order to
   a. enable them to identify situations that might lead to officer misconduct
   b. familiarize them with the laws regarding officer misconduct
   c. ensure that they are closely supervised
   d. increase the staff of the internal affairs division

36. Who, according to the passage, must spend an extended period working for the internal affairs department?
   a. law enforcement officers interested in officer misconduct
   b. all law enforcement officers
   c. law enforcement officers interested in advancement
   d. law enforcement officers who want to become internal affairs investigators

37. The internal affairs requirement is apparently intended to
   a. teach law enforcement officers how to conduct their own work properly
   b. demonstrate to the community that the law enforcement agency takes law enforcement officer misconduct seriously
   c. strengthen the internal affairs division
   d. make supervisors more effective in preventing officer misconduct

Law enforcement officers should be aware of the cultural beliefs and habits of the subcultures they are likely to serve in an urban environment. In one case, an African American man was arrested for the murder of a woman who had been strangled with a pair of stockings missing their tops; he was arrested because he had stocking tops in his drawer. The white officers were not aware that stocking tops were used in a hair styling process common in African American communities at that time. Neither was the all-white jury. This shows why it is important not only that officers be culturally aware, but also that both law enforcement agencies and juries reflect the diversity of their communities.

38. According to the passage, law enforcement officers need to be aware of the subcultures they serve because
   a. they are likely to be prejudiced
   b. there could be hostility between the officers and cultural minorities
   c. their ignorance could lead to injustice
   d. improved community relations will lead to more effective law enforcement

39. The African American man mentioned in the passage was suspected of murder because
   a. he was African American
   b. the officers believed only the murderer would be likely to possess stocking tops
   c. the officers looked down on his culture
   d. witnesses had identified him

40. The passage suggests that juries should reflect the diversity of the communities they serve in order to
   a. ensure that juries will be able to place the suspect in the context of the community
   b. make juries more sympathetic to members of cultural minorities
   c. reduce the possibility of bias in their verdicts
   d. improve relations between the community and the criminal justice system

In order for our society to make decisions about the kinds of punishments we will impose on convicted criminals, we must understand why we punish criminals. Some people argue that retribution is the purpose of punishment and that, therefore, the punishment must in some direct way fit the crime. This view is based on the belief that a person who commits a crime deserves to be punished. Because the punishment must fit the specific crime, the theory of retribution allows a sentencing judge to consider the circumstances of a each crime, criminal and victim in imposing a sentence.

Another view, the deterrence theory, promotes punishment in order to discourage commission of future crimes. In this view, punishment need not relate directly to the crime committed, because the point is to deter both a specific criminal and the general public from committing crimes in the future. However, punishment must necessarily be uniform and consistently applied, in order for the members of the public to understand how they would be punished if they committed a crime. Laws setting sentencing guidelines are based on the deterrence theory and do not allow a judge to consider the specifics of a particular crime in sentencing a convicted criminal.

41. According to the passage, punishment
   a. is rarely an effective deterrent to future crimes
   b. must fit the crime in question
   c. may be imposed for differing reasons
   d. is imposed solely at the discretion of a judge

42. The retribution theory of punishment
   a. is no longer considered valid
   b. holds that punishment must fit the crime committed
   c. applies only to violent crimes
   d. allows a jury to recommend the sentence that should be imposed

43. The passage suggests that a person who believes that the death penalty results in fewer murders most likely also believes in
   a. the deterrence theory
   b. the retribution theory
   c. giving judges considerable discretion in imposing sentences
   d. the integrity of the criminal justice system

44. A good title for this passage would be
   a. Sentencing Reform: A Modest Proposal
   b. More Criminals Are Doing Time
   c. Punishment: Deterrent or Retribution?
   d. Why I Favor Uniform Sentencing Guidelines

45. A person who believes in the deterrence theory would probably also support
   a. non-unanimous jury verdicts

   b. early release of prisoners because of prison overcrowding
   c. a broad definition of the insanity defense
   d. allowing television broadcasts of court proceedings

PART THREE: LOGIC AND REASONING

Answer question 46 on the basis of the following definition.

Perjury consists of making a false statement while under oath or swearing to a false statement previously made.

46. Which situation below is the best example of perjury?
   a. Under oath, Jason states that he was not in town on the night of the burglary; however, the prosecutor shows a videotape of Jason, taken on that night, entering a bar near the house that was burglarized.
   b. Just before he takes the witness stand, Tim tells the defense attorney that he's not at all nervous about testifying because he intends to tell the truth; however, his hands are shaking and his voice is quivering.
   c. Under oath, Edna tells the prosecutor that she does not understand his question and asks him to repeat it; after he does so, she says she still doesn't understand the question and doesn't want to testify anymore.
   d. During an arrest, a state trooper asks Hector where he was on the night of the bank robbery and Hector says he can't remember, but the trooper knows Hector to be a confirmed liar and is almost certain he is lying now.

47. Trooper Rannick is off-duty and is meeting his girlfriend at the mall to see a movie. He is running late and is afraid she may have given up on him and left the theater. As he enters the mall, he sees a man grab a woman's purse, push her down, and take off running through the crowded mall. What should Trooper Rannick do?

   a. shout at the man, "Halt or I'll shoot!"

   b. have a store manager call mall security, then hurry on his way

   c. go find mall security himself to handle the situation

   d. chase the suspect and try to apprehend him

48. Officer Kemp has worked more night shifts in a row than Officer Rogers, who has worked five. Officer Miller has worked fifteen night shifts in a row, more than Officers Kemp and Rogers combined. Officer Calvin has worked eight night shifts in a row, less than Officer Kemp. How many night shifts in a row has Officer Kemp worked?

   a. eight

   b. nine

   c. ten

   d. eleven

49. Trooper Bettis has arrived at the scene of a family disturbance in a rural area. Two other troopers are in the front yard attempting to arrest family members who are attacking the troopers. Trooper Bettis pulls his departmentally approved expandable baton and runs up to help the troopers. A woman steps up and swings a broken beer bottle at Trooper Bettis' head. What should he do next?

   a. use his baton in the approved manner on this woman

   b. attempt to grab the broken bottle out of her hand

   c. go back to the cruiser and call for more backup

   d. dodge her blows and continue running to help the other troopers

50. Four eyewitnesses saw a vehicle being stolen and noted the license plate number. Each wrote down a different number, which appear below. Which one is probably right?

   a. KLV 017

   b. XIW 007

   c. XIW 017

   d. XIV 017

51. The owner of the Sun Times Chevrolet dealership mentions to Trooper Chervenack that late at night someone has been stealing parts off of the vans he has parked in the back lot. Trooper Chervenack drives past this location every night while on patrol and tells the car dealer she will keep an eye out for trouble. Which of the following situations should she investigate?

   a. after midnight an Hispanic male in his early twenties is walking up and down the well-lit rows of new cars parked near the front of the lot

   b. after midnight two young men in baggy pants and T-shirts are rollerblading in the aisles between the cars in the lot

   c. after midnight a station wagon drives into the lot and stops near the main showroom; a man gets out and walks toward the door carrying a ladder

   d. after midnight a panel truck pulls out of the vacant lot next to the rear of the car lot where the vans are parked

52. Randy Wade comes home and surprises a burglar in his house. The burglar runs past Randy out the door. Which one of the following parts of Randy's description of the burglar will be most helpful to police in identifying him?
   a. He walked with a limp.
   b. He carried a VCR.
   c. He wore a ski mask.
   d. He smelled like fish.

53. Trooper Mattox is issuing a speeding ticket to Claude Sims, an angry citizen. Mr. Sims is furious because he feels he doesn't deserves the ticket. At what point should Trooper Mattox consider taking Mr. Sims into physical custody?
   a. when Mr. Sims gets out of his car and shouts, "Why aren't you out catching real crooks instead of bothering honest citizens?"
   b. when Mr. Sims gets out of his car and paces back and forth, gesturing angrily while the ticket is being written
   c. when Mr. Sims points his pen at Trooper Mattox and says, "You better watch your step, buddy."
   d. when Mr. Sims pokes his finger hard in Trooper Mattox's chest and says, "You're gonna get yours now, buster!"

54. The police are staking out a suspected crack house. Officer Michaels is in front of the house. Officer Roth is in the alley behind the house. Officer Jensen is covering the windows on the north side, Officer Sheen on the south. If Officer Michaels switches places with Officer Jensen, and Jensen then switches places with Officer Sheen, where is Officer Sheen?
   a. in the alley behind the house
   b. on the north side of the house

   c. in front of the house
   d. on the south side of the house

55. State troopers often have to decide when it is appropriate to use force when confronting hostile situations. In which of the situations below is it appropriate for a trooper to use force to subdue an individual?
   a. a woman brushes past a trooper on the sidewalk, gesturing wildly and muttering angrily to herself
   b. a man stopped for speeding leaps out of his car and starts yelling at the trooper about how he is a taxpayer
   c. a fight has broken out at a rural tavern; when the trooper arrives, one of the fighters walks toward the trooper with his arm cocked and his fist doubled up
   d. a trooper arrives at a rural bar to handle a fight in the parking lot between two men and sees one of the men walking away from the other gesturing angrily

56. In a four day period—Monday through Thursday—each of the following officers worked only one day, each a different day. Trooper Johnson was scheduled to work on Monday, but she traded with Trooper Carter, who was originally scheduled to work on Wednesday. Trooper Falk traded with Trooper Kirk, who was originally scheduled to work on Thursday. After all the switching was done, who worked on Tuesday?
   a. Carter
   b. Falk
   c. Johnson
   d. Kirk

Use the following information to answer question 57.

State troopers follow certain procedures when placing a person under arrest and transporting that person in a cruiser. Troopers are expected to:

1. Handcuff the prisoner securely.

2. Search the prisoner carefully for possible weapons and contraband.

3. Before seating the prisoner, check the area where the prisoner will be seated in the cruiser for possible weapons and contraband from a previous arrest.

4. Place the prisoner in the cruiser and place a seatbelt on the prisoner.

5. Drive the prisoner directly to jail.

6. After arrival at the jail, check the cruiser's seat and floorboard area where the prisoner was sitting for possible contraband or weapons tossed down by the prisoner during the ride.

57. Trooper DeVero arrests Joe Smith after discovering a vial of cocaine in the man's car during a traffic stop. She places handcuffs on Smith, searches him for weapons and contraband, and then places him in the back seat of her cruiser after checking the seat and floorboard area. She places the seatbelt around Smith and drives toward the jail. On the way, she sees a driver roll through a stop sign. She stops the car and issues the driver a citation and then drives on to the jail where she helps Smith out of the back seat and then checks the area where he was sitting for weapons or contraband. Under these circumstances and according to the procedure outlined, the actions taken by Trooper DeVero were

a. improper, because she did not call for backup after discovering the cocaine

b. proper, because she followed right procedure in arresting and transporting Smith to jail

c. improper, because she should have driven Smith directly to jail without stopping

d. proper, because she was able to efficiently handle two situations: Smith's arrest and the woman's traffic violation

58. The state police department needs to appoint a new captain, which will be based on seniority. Sergeant West has less seniority than Sergeant Temple, but more than Sergeant Brody. Sergeant Rhodes has more seniority than Sergeant West, but less than Sergeant Temple. Sergeant Temple doesn't want the job. Who will be the new captain?

a. Rhodes

b. Temple

c. West

d. Brody

Answer question 59 on the basis of the following definition.

The crime of **Filing a False Police Report** occurs when a person gives a false statement to a peace officer who is conducting a criminal investigation, and that person knows his or her statement is a key part of the investigation.

59. Which situation below is the best example of Filing a False Police Report?

  a. The resident of a nearby mental hospital calls Trooper Edmundson to report seeing space aliens stealing dogs from the park.

  b. A man reports to Trooper Ericson that his car has been stolen, but Trooper Ericson finds out that the man paid friends to steal the car.

  c. A woman who is a witness to a homicide tells Trooper Becker that she thinks the suspect who ran from the scene was wearing a dark green shirt; later investigators find out that the shirt was navy blue.

  d. A man reports to Trooper Blacke that his television has been stolen, and then calls the next day to say that a friend came over and borrowed the set without telling him.

60. Four people witnessed a mugging. Each gave a different description of the mugger. Which description is probably right?

  a. He was average height, thin, and middle aged.

  b. He was tall, thin, and middle-aged.

  c. He was tall, thin, and young.

  d. He was tall, average weight, and middle-aged.

61. Due to jail over-crowding, one prisoner must be moved from the city jail to the county jail. The officers have been instructed to move the prisoner who is charged with committing the most severe offense and who has the longest record. Robb has been arrested this time for a misdemeanor and has been arrested seven times before. James has been arrested for a felony and has been arrested fewer times than Robb. Bush has been arrested for a more serious crime than James and has been arrested more times than Robb. Michaels has been arrested for a misdemeanor and it is his third offense. Who will be moved to the county jail?

  a. Robb

  b. Bush

  c. Michaels

  d. James

Answer question 62 on the basis of the following definition.

Assault by Means of a Dangerous Weapon occurs when a person uses a dangerous weapon to cause serious bodily injury to another person or threatens to use a dangerous weapon during the assault.

62. Which situation below is the best example of Assault by Means of a Dangerous Weapon?

  a. Elliot and Tom get into an argument, and Tom yells that he should go home, get his gun, and shoot Elliot.

  b. Hank breaks Joe's leg by hitting him with a baseball bat during an argument after the game.

  c. Harriet shoves Brad, who falls off the bed and breaks both wrists.

  d. Martin pokes Larry in the chest and tells him to stay away from his girlfriend; Larry loses his balance, falls down the stairs, and breaks his back.

63. Four police officers are chasing a suspect on foot. Officer Calvin is directly behind the suspect. Partners Jenkins and Burton are side by side behind Calvin. Officer Zeller is behind Jenkins and Burton. Burton trips and falls and Calvin turns back to help him. An officer tackles the suspect. Which officer caught the suspect?

a. Burton
b. Zeller
c. Jenkins
d. Calvin

Use the following information to answer questions 64 and 65.

When a state trooper suspects that a person may be guilty of driving a motor vehicle while under the influence of alcohol or drugs, the trooper should:

1. Stop the suspect vehicle and have the driver get out.

2. Tell the driver that he or she will be asked to perform field sobriety tests.

3. Demonstrate each portion of the sobriety tests before the driver attempts it.

4. Place the driver under arrest if he or she fails the test.

5. Arrange for the driver's vehicle to be towed from the scene.

64. Trooper Marcos is on patrol when he sees a white Ford Thunderbird run a red light. The vehicle is weaving back and forth over the double yellow line in the center of the roadway. Trooper Marcos pulls the driver over and the driver gets out of his car at Trooper Marcos' request. When Trooper Marcos smells a strong odor of alcohol on the driver's breath, he tells the driver he must perform field sobriety tests. The driver tries to stand on one leg but falls down. Trooper Marcos places him under arrest for driving under the influence and calls for a tow truck to come pick up the Thunderbird.

Under these circumstances the actions taken by Trooper Marcos were

a. proper, because he remembered all steps, up through arranging for the vehicle to be towed

b. improper, because he failed to demonstrate the sobriety tests for the driver

c. proper, because he could smell alcohol on the driver's breath and knew he'd been drinking

d. improper, because he did not first ask the driver whether he had been drinking

65. Trooper Richeson is patrolling late one evening a few miles outside of Peabody when the car about 50 yards ahead of him suddenly swerves and careens off the roadway onto the shoulder and stops. Trooper Richeson pulls in behind the car and approaches the driver. He smells alcohol on the driver's breath and asks her to step out of the vehicle. He tells the driver he will be asking her to perform a few sobriety tests and demonstrates each test before allowing her to attempt them. The driver fails the tests and Trooper Richeson tells her she is under arrest, places her in his cruiser, and drives away. Under these circumstances the actions taken by Trooper Richeson were

a. improper, because he did not have the driver's vehicle towed from the scene

b. proper, because he demonstrated each sobriety test for the driver

c. improper, because the driver stopped her car voluntarily

d. proper, because he determined that the driver failed the sobriety tests

PART FOUR: BASIC MATHEMATICS

Choose the correct solution to problems 66–80.

66. If a state police cruiser travels at the speed of 62 mph for 15 minutes, how far will it travel? (Distance = Rate × Time)
a. 15.5 miles
b. 9.3 miles
c. 16 miles
d. 24.8 miles

67. The cost of a list of supplies for a police station is as follows: $19.98, $52.20, $12.64, and $7.79. What is the total cost?
a. $91.30
b. $92.61
c. $93.60
d. $93.61

68. In a given area of the United States, in one year, there were 215 highway accidents associated with drinking alcohol. Of these, 113 were caused by excessive speed. About what percent of the accidents were speed-related?
a. 47%
b. 49%
c. 51%
d. 53%

69. A law enforcement agency receives a report of a drunk driver on the roadway on August 3 at 10:42 p.m. and another similar report on August 4 at 1:19 a.m. How much time has elapsed between reports?
a. 1 hour 37 minutes
b. 2 hours 23 minutes
c. 2 hours 37 minutes
d. 3 hours 23 minutes

70. How many feet of tape will a law enforcement officer need to tie off a crime scene area that is 34 feet long and 20 feet wide?
a. 54
b. 88
c. 680
d. 108

71. A locked ammunition box is about $2\frac{1}{2}$ centimeters thick. About how thick is this box in inches? (1 cm = 0.39 inches)
a. 1 inch
b. $\frac{1}{4}$ inch
c. 2 inches
d. 5 inches

72. What is the approximate total weight of four boxes of confiscated firearms weighing 152 pounds, 168 pounds, 182 pounds, and 201 pounds?
a. 690 pounds
b. 700 pounds
c. 710 pounds
d. 750 pounds

73. State Trooper Tate earns $26,000 a year. If she receives a 4.5% salary increase, how much will she earn?
a. $27,170
b. $26,450
c. $27,260
c. $29,200

74. Which of the following rooms has the greatest perimeter?
a. a square room 10 feet by 10 feet
b. a square room 11 feet by 11 feet
c. a rectangular room 12 feet by 8 feet
d. a rectangular room 14 feet by 7 feet

75. If it takes four law enforcement officers 1 hour and 45 minutes to perform a particular job, how long would it take one officer working at the same rate to perform the same task alone?

a. 4.5 hours

b. 5 hours

c. 7 hours

d. 7.5 hours

76. Which of the following diameters is the smallest?

a. $\frac{17}{20}$ inches

b. $\frac{3}{4}$ inches

c. $\frac{5}{6}$ inches

d. $\frac{7}{10}$ inches

77. When a burglar alarm system is installed in a home that is under construction, the system costs about 1.5% of the total building cost. The cost of the same system installed after the home is built is about 4% of the total building cost. How much would a homeowner save by installing an alarm system in a $150,000 home while the home is still under construction?

a. $600

b. $2,250

c. $3,750

d. $6,000

78. Which of the following rope lengths is longest? (1 cm = 0.39 inches)

a. 1 meter

b. 1 yard

c. 32 inches

d. 85 centimeters

79. A safety box has three layers of metal, each with a different width. If one layer is $\frac{1}{8}$ inch thick, a second layer is $\frac{1}{6}$ inch thick, and the total thickness is $\frac{3}{4}$ inch thick, what is the width of the third layer?

a. $\frac{5}{12}$

b. $\frac{11}{24}$

c. $\frac{7}{18}$

d. $\frac{1}{2}$

80. A person can be scalded by hot water at a temperature of about 122°F. At about what temperature Centigrade could a person be scalded? $C = \frac{5}{9}(F - 32)$

a. 35.5°C

b. 55°C

c. 216°C

d. 50°C

PART FIVE: WRITING SKILLS

Choose the best answer for questions 81–85 based on the information given in the question.

81. The following information was obtained by Officer Gunter at the scene of an altercation over a parking space in a supermarket parking lot.

Date of altercation:	June 17, 1997
Time of altercation:	5:45 p.m.
Place of altercation:	Eagle Supermarket parking lot
Persons involved:	Dr. Sam Boswell and Ms. Lorene Webb
Action taken:	No arrests; both parties advised to go home

Officer Gunter is writing a report of the incident. Which of the following expresses the above information *most clearly and accurately*?

a. On June 17, 1997, at 5:45 p.m. in the Eagle Supermarket parking lot, Dr. Sam. Boswell and Ms. Lorene Webb were involved in an altercation over a parking space. There were no arrests. Both parties were advised to go home.

b. Dr. Sam Boswell and Ms. Lorene Webb were not arrested at Eagle Supermarket parking lot. They were involved in an altercation at 5:45 p.m. on June 17,1997, over a parking space and were advised to go home.

c. In Eagle Supermarket parking lot, an altercation occurred involving Dr. Sam Boswell and Ms. Lorene Webb over a parking space. On June 17, 1997, at 5:45 p.m. no arrests were made, and both parties advised to go home.

d. Dr. Sam Boswell and Ms. Lorene Webb were involved in an altercation over a parking space on June 17, 1997. No arrests were made at 5:45 p.m. in the Eagle Supermarket parking lot, and they were advised to go home.

82. State Troopers Aljanaidi and Benson receive a radio dispatch to respond to a 911 report of a child having been abducted from a farm on Sand Road. They obtain the following information.

Date of occurrence: September 20, 1997
Time of occurrence: Between 3:30 and 4:00 p.m.
Place of occurrence: 90120 Sand Road
Victim: Maya Jackson, age 6
Crime: Abduction
Suspect: Unknown

State Trooper Aljanaidi is writing a memo book entry regarding the incident. Which of the following expresses the above information *most clearly and accurately?*

a. At age 6, Maya Jackson was abducted on September 20, 1997, by an unknown person from 90120 Sand Road, between 3:30 and 4:00 p.m.

b. Maya Jackson was abducted by an unknown person from 90120 Sand Road on September 20, 1997, between 3:30 and 4:00 p.m., she was age 6.

c. On September 20, 1997 Maya Jackson, between 3:30 and 4:00 p.m., was abducted by an unknown person at age 6 from 90120 Sand Road.

d. On September 20, 1997, between 3:30 and 4:00 p.m., Maya Jackson, age 6, was abducted from 90120 Sand Road by an unknown person.

83. The following information was obtained by Officer Moy at the scene of a warehouse fire.

Place of incident: Icarus Publishing Co. warehouse, 1132 Battery St.
Date of incident: February 27,1997
Time of onset of fire: Between 2:00 a.m. and 3:30 a.m.
Crime: Suspected arson

Officer Moy is writing a crime report on the above incident. Which of the following expresses the above information *most clearly and accurately?*

a. Icarus Publishing Co., a warehouse at 1132 Battery, was on fire by suspected arson, between 2:00 a.m. and 3:30 a.m. at 1132 Battery St., February 27, 1997.

b. On February 27, 1997, between 2:00 a.m. and 3:30 a.m., a fire occurred at the Icarus Publishing Co. warehouse, 1132 Battery St. Arson is suspected.

c. A suspected arson fire on February 27, 1997 at Icarus Publishing Co., 1132 Battery St., a warehouse, happened between 2:00 a.m. and 3:30 a.m.

d. A warehouse at Icarus Publishing Co., 1132 Battery St., is on fire between 2:00 a.m. and 3:00 a.m. by suspected arson. It was on February 27, 1997.

84. Trooper Billings has completed an investigation of an incident involving destruction of property. Billings has obtained the following information.

Date of incident:	November 4, 1996
Time of incident:	Between 11:00 and midnight
Place of incident:	Waynesville High School
Crime:	Vandalism
Suspects:	Gary Talerino and Jennifer O'Brien, students
Action taken:	Suspects arrested

Trooper Billings is writing up a report of the crime. Which of the following expresses the above information *most clearly and accurately?*

a. Vandalism occurred at Waynesville High School, suspecting Gary Talerino and Jennifer O'Brien. They were arrested between 11:00 p.m. and midnight, November 4, 1996.

b. On November 4, 1996, between 11:00 p.m. and midnight, Gary Talerino and Jennifer O'Brien were suspected of vandalism. They were arrested at Waynesville High School.

c. On November 4, 1996, between 11:00 p.m. and midnight, vandalism occurred at Waynesville High School. Suspects Gary Talerino and Jennifer O'Brien were arrested.

d. Arrested at Waynesville High School on November 4, 1996, between 11:00 p.m. and midnight, Gary Talerino and Jennifer O'Brien were suspected of vandalism.

85. State Troopers Liang and Freeman arrest a motorist for driving while intoxicated. The officers obtain the following information.

Time of occurrence:	2:20 a.m.
Place of occurrence:	Route 17 near Orlando Drive
Offense:	Driving while intoxicated
Driver:	Chad Washburn, age 23
Disposition:	Driver arrested and taken to county jail

Trooper Liang is making a memo book entry of the incident. Which of the following expresses the above information *most clearly and accurately?*

a. Arrested for driving while intoxicated, officers took driver Chad Washburn, age 23, to the county jail at 2:20 a.m. at Route 17 near Orlando Drive.

b. Driving while intoxicated, Chad Washburn, age 23, was arrested at Route 17 near Orlando Drive and taken by officers to the county jail at 2:20 a.m.

c. At 2:20 a.m. at Route 17 near Orlando Drive, Chad Washburn, age 23, was arrested for driving while intoxicated. He was taken by officers to the county jail.

d. Chad Washburn, age 23, driving while intoxicated at Route 17 near Orlando Drive at 2:20 a.m., was taken to the county jail and arrested by officers.

Answer questions 86–88 by choosing the sentence that best combines the underlined sentences into one.

86. He did not return from the stakeout until 6:00 a.m.
We were all concerned.
a. He did not return from the stakeout until 6:00 a.m.; however, we were all concerned.
b. While we were all concerned, he did not return from the stakeout until 6:00 a.m.
c. He did not return from the stakeout until 6:00 a.m., whether we were all concerned.
d. Because he did not return from the stakeout until 6:00 a.m., we were all concerned.

87. Everyone believed the suspect's story.
Trooper Rinehart thought he was lying.
a. Everyone believed the suspect's story, and Trooper Rinehart thought he was lying.
b. Everyone believed the suspect's story, whereas Trooper Rinehart thought he was lying.
c. Everyone believed the suspect's story, when Trooper Rinehart thought he was lying.
d. Everyone believed the suspect's story, or Trooper Rinehart thought he was lying.

88. Trooper Garcia is an intelligent woman.
Trooper Garcia tends to be reckless.
a. Trooper Garcia tends to be reckless while she is an intelligent woman.
b. Trooper Garcia tends to be reckless and is an intelligent woman.
c. Although Trooper Garcia tends to be reckless, she is an intelligent woman.
d. Tending to be reckless, Trooper Garcia is an intelligent woman.

Answer questions 89–90 by choosing the sentence that uses verbs correctly from among the four choices.

89. a. All the officers got out their weapons and cleaned them.
b. All the officers have gotten out their weapons and cleaning them.
c. All the officers got out their weapons and have cleaned them.
d. All the officers gotten out their weapons and cleaned them.

90. a. At first I was liking the long hours of surveillance, but later they got on my nerves.
b. At first I liked the long hours of surveillance, but later they have gotten on my nerves.
c. At first I like the long hours of surveillance, but later they got on my nerves.
d. At first I liked the long hours of surveillance, but later they got on my nerves.

Answer questions 91–95 by choosing the word or phrase that means the same or nearly the same as the underlined word.

91. Officer Michaels was an indispensable member of the department.
a. determined
b. experienced
c. creative
d. essential

92. The attorney wanted to expedite the process.
a. accelerate
b. evaluate
c. reverse
d. justify

93. Trooper Riggs gave a <u>plausible</u> explanation for being late for work.
a. unbelievable
b. insufficient
c. apologetic
d. credible

94. Although the neighborhood was said to be safe, they heard <u>intermittent</u> gunfire all night long.
a. protracted
b. periodic
c. disquieting
d. vehement

95. As soon as the Department of Corrections' recommendations for prison reform was released, the department was <u>inundated</u> with calls from people who said they approved.
a. provided
b. bothered
c. rewarded
d. flooded

Answer questions 96–100 by choosing the word that is spelled correctly and best completes the sentence.

96. It is my _____ that the state police in this area do a fine job.
a. beleif
b. bilief
c. belief
d. bilieff

97. She seems to have no _____ into her shoplifting problem.
a. insite
b. incite
c. ensight
d. insight

98. Trooper Richards is too _____ for his own good.
a. sinsitive
b. sensitive
c. sensative
d. sinsative

99. My sister is going to be on the cover of *Soldier of Fortune* _____.
a. magizine
b. magazene
c. magezine
d. magazine

100. The suspect, Mysterious Marvin, performs in _____ shows all around the country.
a. magic
b. magick
c. magek
d. maggic

ANSWERS

PART ONE: MEMORIZATION

1. **d.** Refer to the Charges section about James Wilson Baker.
2. **c.** Refer to Baker's Identifying Scars or Marks section.
3. **b.** Refer to the Description section where Camacho's age is listed.
4. **a.** Refer to the Aliases section.
5. **c.** Refer to the drawing of Camacho and to the Remarks section.
6. **a.** Refer to the Identifying Scars or Marks section. Remembering the alias Eddie One-Eye would also give you the answer to this question.
7. **b.** Refer to Chan's Description section.
8. **c.** Refer to the Remarks section on Chan.
9. **a.** Refer to the Wanted By section on Hart.
10. **d.** Refer to the Charges section on Chan.
11. **b.** Refer to the Remarks section on Hart.
12. **d.** Refer to the drawing of Hart.
13. **a.** Camacho is listed as "missing" while Chan is listed as "wanted."
14. **b.** Refer to the Charges section on Hart.
15. **d.** Refer to the Remarks section on Cloud.
16. **a.** Refer to the Remarks section on Cloud.
17. **b.** Refer to the Caution section on Hart.
18. **d.** Refer to the Description of Cloud.
19. **c.** Refer to Description sections of both Hart and Cloud. None of the other choices are true.
20. **c.** Baker does not have a mustache so this choice is false. (Don't miss the part of this question that asks you which statement is *false*.)

PART TWO: READING COMPREHENSION

21. **b.** The third sentence of the passage states that officers may refer to their notes.
22. **d.** The passage provides information for law enforcement officers and choice **d** is therefore the most logical choice. Choice **a** refers to a memo directed to law enforcement officers, but the subject matter is incorrect. In choice **b** the subject matter is also incorrect. The wording and tone of the passage do not seem to be attempting recruitment, as in choice **c**.
23. **b.** The first sentence states the importance of officer testimony.
24. **c.** Choice **a** is incorrect because the first sentence suggests that becoming hardened is unavoidable. Choices **b** and **d** are mentioned in the passage but neither is the main idea.
25. **b.** See the first two sentences of the passage.
26. **d.** The passage claims that becoming jaded is inevitable.
27. **b.** See the first sentence of the passage.
28. **a.** See the second sentence of the passage.
29. **d.** The fourth sentence of the passage refers to the *constitutional Fifth Amendment privilege against self-incrimination*.
30. **c.** The distinction between coercive questioning by an officer and obtaining information from an inmate who believes he or she is talking to another inmate is the point of the passage as a whole.
31. **c.** The other choices, though mentioned in the passage, are not the main idea.
32. **d.** While keeping one's temper probably an aspect of the program, it is not explicitly mentioned in the passage.

33. **a.** See the second sentence of the passage.

34. **b.** This idea is explicitly stated in the fourth sentence.

35. **a.** See the second sentence of the passage.

36. **c.** See the first sentence.

37. **d.** This reason is implied throughout the passage.

38. **c.** The suspect mentioned in the passage was arrested because the officers were ignorant of a cultural practice in the black community. The passage doesn't discuss racial prejudice.

39. **b.** This is implied in the second and third sentences of the passage.

40. **a.** Both the jury and the law enforcement officers in the case mentioned in the passage were unaware of the black community's hair-styling practice.

41. **c.** The passage presents two reasons for punishment. The second sentence notes a view that *some people* hold. The first line of the second paragraph indicates *another view*.

42. **b.** This is the main idea of the first paragraph.

43. **a.** This is an application of the main idea of the second paragraph to a specific crime.

44. **c.** The first sentence indicates that the passage is about punishment. The first paragraph is about retribution; the second is about deterrence.

45. **d.** The second sentence notes that one reason behind the deterrence theory is the effect of deterring not only criminals but also the public.

PART THREE: LOGIC AND REASONING

46. **a.** Of the four options you have to choose from, choice **a** is the only option that involves lying while under oath or swearing to a false statement previously made.

47. **d.** Even though he is not on the clock, the trooper cannot ignore the situation and at the same time honor his oath to protect and serve. He should try his best to catch the suspect. To shout that he is going to shoot in a crowded mall might cause a panic. To try to get mall security would take too much time, and the perpetrator would almost certainly get away.

48. **b.** Officer Kemp has worked more shifts in a row than Officer Calvin; therefore Kemp has worked more than eight shifts. The number of Kemp's shifts plus the number of Rogers' shifts (five) cannot equal fifteen or more, the number of Miller's shifts. Therefore, Kemp has worked nine shifts in a row $(5 + 9 = 14)$.

49. **a.** Trooper Bettis should defend himself immediately and handle this woman with his baton in a professional, approved manner. Grabbing broken glass barehanded isn't using common sense, and dodging her blows or running back to the cruiser does not take care of the threat to his safety and the safety of the other troopers involved.

50. **c.** The elements of the license plate number that most often repeat in the eyewitnesses descriptions are XIW and 017. Therefore, the correct license number is most likely XIW 017.

51. **d.** Seeing a panel truck pulling away from the back of the lot where the vans are parked should cause Trooper Chervenack to be very suspicious. It's not as likely that the individuals in the other situations could be stealing parts from the vans even if they are at the right place at the right time.

52. a. "He walked with a limp" is the only element of the description likely to remain constant over time and will therefore be most helpful to the police.

53. d. The situation has escalated to the point where Mr. Sims not only appears to be threatening violence, but has already committed an assault by poking the trooper in the chest. The time to pull out the handcuffs is now! The other situations described only require a bit of patience and tolerance on the part of the trooper.

54. c. After all the switches were made, Officer Sheen is in front of the house. Officer Roth is in the alley behind the house, Officer Michaels on the north side, and Officer Jensen on the south.

55. c. This man appears ready to attack the trooper. Under the circumstances outlined in choices **a**, **b**, and **d**, neither the trooper nor the public is in any danger.

56. d. After all the switches were made, Trooper Kirk worked on Tuesday. Carter worked on Monday, Johnson on Wednesday, and Falk on Thursday.

57. c. According to step 5 in the procedure for arresting and transporting a suspect, the trooper should have driven the prisoner directly to jail. Her actions were improper since she decided to conduct a traffic stop on the way.

58. a. Sergeant Temple has the most seniority, but does not want the job. Next in line is Sergeant Rhodes, who has more seniority than West or Brody.

59. b. In the other options given, everyone else is giving statements to authorities in good faith. In this situation the man intentionally misleads Trooper Ericson.

60. b. Tall, thin, and middle aged are the elements of the description repeated most often and are therefore most likely accurate.

61. b. Bush committed the most serious offense and has served the most time.

62. b. Choice **b** is the only situation where an assault occurs with a deadly weapon. In choice **a** there is a threat of assault by means of a deadly weapon, but no assault takes place. In choices **c** and **d**, serious injury takes place but no weapon is involved.

63. c. After all the switching was done, Officer Jenkins was directly behind the suspect. Officer Burton had fallen and Officer Calvin turned back to help him. Officer Zeller remained in the rear.

64. b. Trooper Marcos did not follow the procedure outlined for this kind of arrest. He skipped step 3, demonstrating the sobriety tests.

65. a. Trooper Richeson followed the procedure right down the list except that he failed to perform step 6, calling for a tow truck.

PART FOUR: BASIC MATHEMATICS

66. a. Solving this problem requires converting 15 minutes to 0.25 hour, which is the time, then using the formula: 62 mph times 0.25 hour is 15.5 miles.

67. b. You simply add all the numbers together to solve this problem.

68. d. Division is used to arrive at a decimal, which can then be rounded to the nearest hundredth and converted to a percentage: 113 divided by 215 is 0.5255. 0.5255 rounded to the nearest hundredth is 0.53, or 53%.

69. c. Subtraction and addition will solve this problem. From 10:42 to 12:42, two hours have elapsed. From 12:42 to 1:00, another 18 minutes have elapsed (60 minus 42 is 18). Then from 1:00 to 1:19, there is another 19 minutes.

70. d. There are two sides 34 feet long and two sides 20 feet long. Using the formula P = 2L + 2W will solve this problem. Therefore, you should multiply 34 times 2 and 20 times 2, and then add the results: 68 plus 40 is 108.

71. **a.** The problem is solved by first converting a fraction to a decimal, then multiplying: 2.5 times 0.39 is 0.975, which is rounded to 1.

72. **b.** Add all four weights for a total of 703. 703 rounded to the nearest ten is 700.

73. **a.** There are three steps involved in solving this problem. First, convert 4.5% to a decimal: 0.045. Multiply that by $26,000 to find out how much the salary increases. Finally, add the result ($1,170) to the original salary of $26,000 to find out the new salary, $27,170.

74. **b.** First you have to determine the perimeters of all four rooms. This is done by using the formula for a square (P = 4S), or for a rectangle (P = 2L + 2W), as follows: 4 × 10 = 40 for choice **a**; 4 × 11 = 44 for the correct choice, **b**; (2 × 12) + (2 × 8) = 40 for choice **c**; and (2 × 14) + (2 × 7) = 42 for choice **d**.

75. **c.** To solve the problem you have to first convert the total time to minutes (105 minutes), then multiply by 4 (420 minutes), and then convert the answer back to hours by dividing by 60 minutes to arrive at the final answer (7 hours). Or you can multiply $1\frac{3}{4}$ hours by 4 to arrive at the same answer.

76. **d.** To solve the problem, one must first find the common denominator, in this instance 60. Then the fractions must be converted: $\frac{17}{20}$ is equal to $\frac{51}{60}$ (for choice **a**); $\frac{3}{4}$ is equal to $\frac{45}{60}$ (for choice **b**); $\frac{5}{6}$ is equal to $\frac{50}{60}$ (for choice **c**); and $\frac{7}{10}$ is equal to $\frac{42}{60}$ (for the correct choice, **d**).

77. **c.** First you must subtract the percentage of the installation cost during construction (1.5%) from the percentage of the installation cost after construction (4%). To do this, begin by converting the

percentages into decimals: 4% equals 0.04; 1.5% equals 0.015. Now subtract: 0.04 minus 0.015 equals 0.025. This is the percentage of the total cost which the homeowner will save. Multiply this by the total cost of the home to find the dollar amount: 0.025 times $150,000 is $3,750.

78. **a.** First it is necessary to convert centimeters to inches. To do this for choice **a**, multiply 100 cm (1 meter) by 0.39 inches, yielding 39 inches. For choice **b**, 1 yard is 36 inches. For choice **d**, multiply 85 cm by 0.39 inches, yielding 33.15 inches. Choice **a**, 39 inches, is the longest.

79. **b.** To solve the problem, you must first find the common denominator, in this instance, 24. Then the fractions must be converted: $\frac{1}{8}$ equals $\frac{3}{24}$; $\frac{1}{6}$ equals $\frac{4}{24}$; $\frac{3}{4}$ equals $\frac{18}{24}$. Add the values for first and second layers together: $\frac{3}{24} + \frac{4}{24} = \frac{7}{24}$, then subtract the sum from the total thickness ($\frac{18}{24}$): $\frac{18}{24} - \frac{7}{24} = \frac{11}{24}$.

80. **d.** First convert Fahrenheit to Centigrade using the formula given: $C = \frac{5}{9}(122 - 32)$; that is, C is equal to $\frac{5}{9} \times 90$; so C = 50.

PART FIVE: WRITING SKILLS

81. **a.** This choice represents the most logical order of time and place. Unlike the other choices, it makes clear that the parties were advised to go home immediately after the altercation occurred.

82. **d.** This choice represents the most logical order of time and place. Unlike the other choices, it makes clear that it is Maya Jackson who is age 6 and that the abduction—not the abductor—was *from 90120 Sand Road*.

83. **b.** This choice represents the most logical order of time and place. Unlike the other choices, it does not imply that Icarus Publishing Co. is simply a

warehouse and makes clear where the warehouse is located; it does not imply that the warehouse is currently on fire.

84. c. This choice represents the most logical order of time and place. It makes clear when the vandalism occurred but does not give information about when the suspects were arrested. (This information cannot be known from the facts presented.)

85. c. This choice represents the most logical order of time and place and makes clear who was driving while intoxicated. It does not imply that the arrest took place while the driver was still actually driving.

86. d. This choice establishes the causal relationship between the two sentences.

87. b. The transitional word *whereas* correctly establishes a contrast.

88. c. The transitional word *although* correctly establishes a contrast.

89. a. The verbs *got* and *cleaned* agree in tense.

90. d. The verbs *liked* and *got* agree in tense.

91. d. To be *indispensable* is to be necessary or *essential*.

92. a. To *expedite* a process is to speed it up or *accelerate* it.

93. d. A *plausible* explanation is one that is believable or *credible*.

94. b. Something that is *intermittent* happens now and then or is *periodic*.

95. d. To be *inundated* is to be overwhelmed or *flooded*.

96. c. *Belief* is the correct spelling.

97. d. *Insight* is the correct spelling.

98. b. *Sensitive* is the correct spelling.

99. d. *Magazine* is the correct spelling.

100. a. *Magic* is the correct spelling.

SCORING

You will need to get 70 percent of the questions right (that is, 70 questions right) in order to pass the exam. However, your rank on the eligibility list depends on your score on the written exam. The higher your score, the more likely you are to be called to go through the rest of the selection process. In fact, a score in the 90s has been necessary in the past to get candidates to the next steps in the process. So your goal is to score as high as you possibly can.

What's much more important than your total score, for now, is how you did on each of the kinds of question on the exam. You need to diagnose your strengths and weaknesses so that you can concentrate your efforts as you prepare for the exam. The exam is divided into five parts, so you must look at each part to find out which kinds of questions you did well in and which kinds gave you more trouble. Then you can plan to spend more of your preparation time on the chapters of this book that correspond to the questions you found hardest and less time on the chapters in areas in which you did well.

To see where your trouble spots are, break down your scores according to the five parts:

Part One: _____ questions right out of 20

Part Two: _____ questions right out of 25

Part Three: _____ questions right out of 20

Part Four: _____ questions right out of 15

Part Five: _____ questions right out of 20

Next, use the table on this page to see which part of the exam corresponds to which chapter in this book. You'll want to spend the most time on the chapters that cover the parts that gave you the most trouble.

Exam Part	Chapter
One	5
Two	6
Three	7
Four	8
Five	9 and 10

Even if you got a perfect score on a particular kind of question, you'll probably want to at least glance through the relevant chapter. On the other hand, you should spend a lot of time with the chapters on the question types that gave you the most difficulty. After you work through those chapters, take the second practice exam in Chapter 11 to see how much you've improved.

C·H·A·P·T·E·R 5

MEMORY AND OBSERVATION

CHAPTER SUMMARY

This chapter contains hints and tips to help you answer questions that test your memory skills. Memory questions can be based on pictures or on written materials; you may get the materials ahead of time or on test day. However the memory questions are structured, this chapter will help you deal with them.

It's amazing what your mind will file away in that cabinet we call *memory.* You remember every snippet of dialogue uttered by Clint Eastwood in his first Dirty Harry movie from years ago, but you can't remember which bus route you used yesterday to get to the dentist. Some people remember names well, but can't put them with the right faces. Others forget names quickly, but know exactly when, where, and why they met the person whose name they've forgotten. There are a few lucky individuals with what is commonly referred to as a photographic memory or total recall. And then there are those of us who wake up every morning to a radio alarm so we can find out what day of the week it is. Fortunately for most of us, a good memory is actually a skill that can be developed—with the right incentive.

A high score on the civil service exam is plenty of incentive.

Civil service exams may test your short-term memory or longer-term memory skills. In tests of short-term memory, you're often required to look at a sketch of a street scene; drawings of men and women with differing facial features, weapons and other property; or photographs. Usually, you'll be given a set amount of time (5 minutes is common) to look at the scene, and then you'll be asked to answer test questions about what you saw. Your goal is to memorize as much of that drawing or photograph as you can in the allotted time.

Some departments are more interested in longer-term memory skills. They may send you a study booklet a few weeks in advance of the test and ask you to memorize several items in the booklet. In that case, you'll answer questions based on what you've been memorizing from the study booklet.

This chapter covers both kinds of memory questions, so you'll be prepared for either one.

SHORT-TERM MEMORY QUESTIONS

QUESTIONS BASED ON WRITTEN PASSAGES

A common method of testing short-term memory is to have you read a lengthy, detailed block of text and then answer several multiple-choice questions based on that material. Here is an example:

Answer questions 1, 2, and 3 based on the following passage.

Police dispatchers sent Officer Becky Mann to 2400 Ulit Avenue. Officer Mann received the call at 10:49 p.m. and arrived on the scene at 10:55 p.m. She met Lisa Garret, who told her that she had just moved into the garage apartment behind 2400 Ulit Avenue, which carries the address of 2400½ Ulit Avenue, three days ago on Monday, November 26. Larry Goddard, who lives at 2400 Ulit Avenue, let Garret use

his phone to call 911. Her other neighbor, Karen Ellen, was not at home. Officer Mann asked Garret to tell her what happened. Garret said she got home late tonight from an overtime assignment at her job at the tropical fish food plant. She said she pulled into the driveway at around 10:45 p.m., got out of her Jeep, and walked up the wooden stairs to the landing next to her front door. While she was digging in her purse for the keys to the front door, a man stepped from the shadows of the landing and grabbed her from behind. He held a knife to her throat and told her to give him her purse or he would slit her throat. She said she handed him the purse which had two twenty-dollar bills inside, along with one credit card and her driver's license. He pushed her down on the floor and told her to stay down, hide her face, and count out loud to 100, or he'd kill her. She said she hid her face in both of her hands and started counting aloud. She heard him run down the stairs. Garret said she counted to 20 before she sat up, ran down the stairs to 2400 Ulit Avenue, and begged her neighbor, Larry Goddard, to let her inside to call police.

1. What is the victim's address?
   a. 2400 Ulit Avenue
   b. 2400.5 Ulit Avenue
   c. 240 Ulit Avenue
   d. 2400½ Ulit Avenue

2. Who called 911?
   a. the victim's landlord
   b. Larry Goddard
   c. Lisa Garret
   d. Karen Ellen

3. When did the victim move into this garage apartment?
   a. two days ago
   b. three days ago
   c. three months ago
   d. the day of the robbery

What To Do

Short-term memory questions based on what you have read are fairly straightforward. Your best approach to these questions is to:

1. Read the instructions to find out what questions you will have to answer based on the passage you are about to read.
2. Read the questions before the passage so that your mind will be primed for the kind of information that should catch your eye as you read the passage.
3. After reading the passage, read the answers and try to eliminate the wrong ones first.
4. When you have the right answer, glance back at the passage to check your accuracy.

Using the example above, let's try these techniques. The instructions in the example tell you to answer questions 1 through 3 after reading the passage. That's simple enough. Let your eyes drop down to the first question: "What is the victim's address?" As you read the passage, your eyes will be on the lookout for the victim's address. The next question asks, "Who called 911?" Once again, your brain is primed to wave red flags when you read the passage. The final question is, "When did the victim move into this garage apartment?" Since you are primed with the questions, you are ready to read the passage. You'll find that the answers are **1. d., 2. c.,** and **3. b.**

What Not To Do

- Do not read through the passage looking for only the right answers. Read the entire story before you make your decisions. A lazy reader who skims this passage and stops reading as each question is apparently answered might get an unpleasant surprise when the "obvious" answer is wrong. For example, it's not exactly clear at first that the victim lives at 2400½ Ulit Avenue. The first address you see is 2400 Ulit Avenue. If you didn't read past that point, you could choose the wrong answer for question 2.
- **Do not** make this task harder than it is by trying to draw conclusions. Your memory skills are being tested here, not your crime-solving abilities or your knowledge of the law. Don't add elements to the story that aren't really there.

QUESTIONS BASED ON PICTURES

Looking at a picture for a set length of time—usually 5 minutes—and then answering a series of questions about details in the scene is a very common way for civil service exams to test your short-term memory. This is a simple test of your ability to recall details. You aren't being asked to solve crimes, use judgment skills, or draw conclusions about what you see.

The picture will usually be a scene of a busy city street with plenty of details for you to pick up on: store names, buses, taxis, people, clothing, action scenes (a mugging or maybe someone changing a flat tire on a car), and street signs. You'll be asked to study this drawing or photograph until a specific time limit is up, then you will turn to a set of questions in the test booklet. Let's assume that the picture you studied for five minutes showed a man holding a knife in his left hand while stealing a woman's purse. You might see a test question like this:

4. What is the man who is stealing the woman's purse holding in his left hand?
    a. a gun
    b. a stick
    c. a bottle
    d. a knife

The questions are simple and the answers are simple. If you don't remember what the robber had in his hand or didn't notice the scene in the picture, then you will have to give this question your best guess.

At the end of this chapter you'll find a street scene and several questions about it that you can use to practice.

What To Do

Use a methodical approach to studying what you see. When you read sentences on a page, you read from left to right. This skill is as unconscious as breathing for most English-language readers. Approach memorizing a picture the same way you read, taking in the information from left to right. Instead of staring at the street scene with the whole picture in focus, make yourself start at the left and work your way across the page until you get to the right.

What Not To Do

■ **Do not** go into brain-lock when you first see the busy street scene. Take a deep breath and decide to be methodical.

■ **Do not** try to start memorizing with a shotgun approach, letting your eyes roam all over the page without really taking in the details.

QUESTIONS BASED ON A VIDEOTAPE

Some departments will show you a video and then have you answer questions about what you have observed. This test is not widely used because it's difficult to have large numbers of people watch a video, but this is a method you may encounter. Your best bet is to relax, study the situation on the screen carefully and with *confidence* that you will remember what you see, and then tackle the questions.

LONG-TERM MEMORY QUESTIONS

For questions that test long-term memory, you will be sent a study booklet a few weeks in advance of the test. The booklet contains detailed instructions on what you will be expected to know for the test. The expectation is that you will have plenty of time to memorize the information and that you will be able to answer questions based on what you have memorized.

For example, you may see several pictures of items stolen in a burglary—maybe a wristwatch or a crown inlaid with six rubies. On test day, you may see a question like this:

5. In the study booklet provided to you, there are several drawings of items taken in a burglary. One of the items was a crown. How many jewels did you see on the crown?
    a. three
    b. four
    c. none
    d. six

The questions are simple. No tricks here. You just have to be able to recall details.

What To Do

If you get material to study in advance, study it *in advance*. Don't start the day before the test. Spend a little time on your study booklet every day from the day you get it until the day before the test.

What Not To Do

- **Do not** read the questions too quickly. If you're having trouble remembering the details, going with what initially feels like the correct answer is usually a good idea—but *you must make sure you're answering the right question.* If you were reading quickly and didn't look at the last sentence in the example above, you might anticipate that the question asks you how many crowns you saw in the drawing, not how many jewels were on the crown. Haste can produce easily avoidable errors.

MEMORIZATION TIPS

Memorization is much easier if you approach the task with the expectation that you *will* remember what you see. Call it positive thinking, self-hypnosis, or concentration—it doesn't really matter as long as you get results. When you run through the practice questions in this book, prepare your mind before you start. Tell yourself over and over that you will remember what you see as you study the images. Your performance level will rise to meet your expectations.

Yes, it's easy for your brain to seize up when you see a drawing filled with details, a test section full of questions, and a test proctor standing above you with a stopwatch in one hand intoning, "You have five minutes to study this drawing. You may begin." But if you've programmed yourself to stay calm, stay alert, and execute your plan, you'll remember the details when you need them.

Plan? Yes, you need a plan. If you have a method for memorizing, say, a busy urban street scene—like the left-to-right scheme outlined above—then you will be more likely to relax and allow yourself to retain what you've seen long enough to answer the test questions. Keep in mind that you aren't trying to memorize the scene to learn it for life, you are doing it to retain the information long enough to answer the test questions. What will it matter if you remember the scene three months from now? Your goal is to retain the information long enough to get through this test.

OBSERVATION TIPS

It's almost impossible to talk about memorization without bringing up observation. Some people are naturally observant. Some drift off into never-never land frequently and have no awareness of the world around them. Whatever category you think you are in, it's never too late to sharpen, or acquire, strong observation skills. How? Practice, of course.

Newspaper photos make great practice tools. News photos are action-oriented and usually have more than one person in the scenes. Sit down in a quiet place, clear your mind, remind yourself for several minutes that you will retain all the details you need when you study the picture, and then turn to a picture and study it for about five minutes. At the end of the time, turn the picture over, get a piece of paper and a pencil, then write down all the details you can think of in the picture. Make yourself do this as often as possible before the test.

You can tone up your observation skills on the way to work or school, too. Instead of sitting in your car waiting for the light to change with a blank stare on your face, look around you and say out loud what you see. "I'm at the corner of 12th and Walnut. I see a man in a black,

full-length raincoat standing on the northeast corner looking in the display window of Hank's Motorcycle Shop. There's a black Subaru station wagon parked at a meter near the motorcycle shop. The license plate is. . ." (If you ride to work on a bus or train, you can say these things silently to yourself.) Not only are you practicing a basic skill you will need to become an excellent police officer, you are training your mind to succeed at whatever memory questions the test maker throws your way.

MEMORY AND OBSERVATION PRACTICE

On the previous page is a street scene like those found on some police exams. Below are several questions asking about details of the scene. Use this scene to practice your memory skills. Take five minutes (no more!) to study the picture and then answer the questions that follow, without looking back at the picture.

Then check your answers by looking back at the scene. If you get all the questions right, you know you're well prepared for memory questions. If you miss a few, you know you need to spend more time practicing, using the tips outlined above. Remember, you *can* improve your memory with practice.

6. What does the woman wearing sunglasses have in her hand?
   a. money
   b. a bag
   c. a wallet
   d. an envelope

7. The man carrying flowers is wearing
   a. a beard
   b. a mustache
   c. wire-rimmed glasses
   d. a goatee

8. The bus stop in this scene is labeled
   a. M1
   b. M16
   c. M3
   d. M14

9. What is printed on the sleeve of the jacket worn by the young man who is holding out his hand to the woman in the sunglasses?
   a. the letter J
   b. the letter L
   c. the letter T
   d. the letter O

10. What name is printed on the side of the panel van driving down the street?
   a. Jake's Flowers
   b. Jim's Mercantile
   c. Joe's Market
   d. John's Delivery

11. What is the man with a skull and the word "Kill" on his t-shirt doing?
   a. snatching a woman's purse
   b. distributing leaflets
   c. sprinting to catch the bus
   d. walking down the street

12. What phone number is written on the Acme Moving truck?
   a. 553-9444
   b. 555-9994
   c. 555-9444
   d. 553-4944

Tips for Memory and Observation Questions

- Use a methodical approach to memorization.
- For questions based on passages, read the questions first so you'll know what to look for.
- For questions based on pictures, "read" the picture from left to right.
- For questions based on materials you receive in advance, study the materials for a few minutes every day before the test.
- Read the questions carefully; make sure you're answering the question that's being asked.
- Practice your memory and observation skills in your daily routine.

C·H·A·P·T·E·R 6
READING COMPREHENSION

CHAPTER SUMMARY

Reading is a vital skill for any potential law enforcement officer, so most civil service tests include reading comprehension questions. The tips and exercises in this chapter will help you improve your reading comprehension so that you can increase your score in this area.

ost civil service tests attempt to measure how well applicants understand what they read. Understanding written materials is part of almost any job, including law enforcement. The tests are usually in a multiple-choice format and have questions based on brief passages, much like the standardized tests that are offered in schools. For that matter, almost all standardized test questions test your reading skill. After all, you can't answer the question if you can't read it! Similarly, you can't study your course material at the academy or learn new procedures once you're on the job if you can't read well. So reading comprehension is vital not only on the test but also for the rest of your career.

TYPES OF READING COMPREHENSION QUESTIONS

You have probably encountered reading comprehension questions before, where you are given a passage to read and then have to answer multiple-choice questions about it. The advantages of these questions for you, the test taker, are that you don't have to know anything about the topic in the passage and that the answers are usually right there—if you just know where to find them. This leads to one of the disadvantages: you have to search quickly for answers in an unfamiliar text. It's easy to fall for one of the wrong answer choices, which may be designed to mislead you.

The best way to do well on this passage/question format is to be very familiar with the kinds of questions that are typically asked on the test. Questions most frequently ask you to:

1. identify a specific **fact or detail** in the passage
2. note the **main idea** of the passage
3. define a **vocabulary** word from the passage
4. make an **inference** based on the passage

PRACTICE PASSAGE 1:
USING THE FOUR QUESTION TYPES

The following is a sample test passage, followed by four questions. Read the passage, and then answer the questions, based on your reading of the text, by circling your choice. Then note under your answer the letter of the type of question you believe each to be based on the list above. Correct answers appear immediately after the questions.

In the last decade, community policing has been frequently touted as the best way to reform urban law enforcement. The idea of putting more officers on foot patrol in high crime areas, where relations with police have frequently been strained, was initiated in Houston in 1983 under the leadership of then-Commissioner Lee Brown. He believed that officers should be accessible to the community at the street level. If officers were assigned to the same area over a period of time, those officers would eventually build a network of trust with neighborhood residents. That trust would mean that merchants and residents in the community would let officers know about criminal activities in the area and would support police intervention. Since then, many large cities have experimented with Community-Oriented Policing (COP) with mixed results. Some have found that police and citizens are grateful for the opportunity to work together. Others have found that unrealistic expectations by citizens and resistance from officers have combined to hinder the effectiveness of COP. It seems possible, therefore, that a good idea may need improvement before it can truly be considered a reform.

1. Community policing has been used in law enforcement since
    a. the late 1970s
    b. the early 1980s
    c. the Carter administration
    d. Lee Brown was New York City Police Commissioner

    Question type_____

2. The phrase "a network of trust" in this passage suggests that
   a. police officers can rely only on each other for support
   b. community members rely on the police to protect them
   c. police and community members rely on each other
   d. community members trust only each other

   Question type_____

3. The best title for this passage would be
   a. Community Policing: The Solution to the Drug Problem
   b. Houston Sets the Pace in Community Policing
   c. Communities and Cops: Partners for Peace
   d. Community Policing: An Uncertain Future?

   Question type_____

4. The word "touted" in the first sentence of the passage most nearly means
   a. praised
   b. denied
   c. exposed
   d. criticized

   Question type_____

ANSWERS AND EXPLANATIONS FOR PRACTICE PASSAGE 1

Don't just look at the right answers and move on. The explanations are the most important part. Use these explanations to help you understand how to tackle each kind of question the next time you come across it.

1. b. Question type: 1, fact or detail. The passage says that community policing began "in the last decade." A decade is a period of ten years. In addition, the passage identifies 1983 as the first large-scale use of community policing in Houston. Don't be misled by trying to figure out when Carter was president. Also, if you happen to know that Lee Brown was New York City's police commissioner, don't let that information lead you away from the information contained in the passage alone. Brown was commissioner in Houston when he initiated community policing.

2. c. Question type: 4, inference. The "network of trust" referred to in this passage is between the community and the police, as you can see from the sentence where the phrase appears. The key phrase in the question is *in this passage.* You may think that police can rely only on each other, or one of the other answer choices may appear equally plausible to you. But your choice of answers must be limited to the one suggested *in this passage.* Another tip for questions like this: Beware of absolutes! Be suspicious of any answer containing words like *only, always,* or *never.*

3. d. Question type: 2, main idea. The title always expresses the main idea. In this passage, the main idea comes at the end. The sum of all the details in the passage suggests that community policing is not without its critics and that therefore its future is uncertain. Another key phrase is *mixed* *results,* which means that some communities haven't had full success with community policing.

4. **a.** Question type: 3, vocabulary. The word *touted* is linked in this passage with the phrase *the best way to reform.* Most people would think that a good way to reform something is praiseworthy. In addition, the next few sentences in the passage describe the benefits of community policing. Criticism or a negative response to the subject doesn't come until later in the passage.

DETAIL AND MAIN IDEA QUESTIONS

Main idea questions and fact or detail questions are both asking you for information that's right there in the passage. All you have to do is find it.

DETAIL OR FACT QUESTIONS

In detail or fact questions, you have to identify a specific item of information from the test. This is usually the simplest kind of question. You just have to be able to separate important information from less important information. However, the choices may often be very similar, so you must be careful not to get confused.

MAIN IDEA QUESTIONS

The main idea of a passage, like that of a paragraph or a book, is what it is *mostly* about. The main idea is the summary of all the details. Sometimes the main idea is stated, often in the first or last sentence. Sometimes it is implied in the overall text. The key word in the definition is *mostly.* There may be much information in the passage. The trick is to understand what all that information adds up to—the gist of what the author wants us to know. Often some of the wrong answers on main idea questions are specific facts or details from the passage.

PRACTICE PASSAGE 2:
DETAIL AND MAIN IDEA QUESTIONS

Practice answering main idea and detail questions by working on the questions that follow this passage. Circle the answers to the questions, and then check your answers against the key that appears immediately after the questions.

There is some evidence that crime rates are linked to social trends such as demographic and socio-economic changes. Crime statistics showed a decline in the post-World War II era of the 1940s and 50s. Following the Vietnam War in the 1970s, however, reported crimes were on the rise again, only to be followed by lower numbers of such reports in the 1980s. One of the reasons for these fluctuations appears to be age. When the population is younger, as in the 1960s when the baby boomers came of age, there was a greater incidence of crime nationwide. A second cause for the rise and fall of crime rates appears to be economic. Rising crime rates appear to follow falling economies. A third cause cited for the cyclical nature of crime statistics appears to be the ebb and flow of public policy decisions, which sometimes protect personal freedoms at the expense of government control. A youthful, economically disadvantaged population that is not secured by social controls of family and community or by government authority is likely to see an upswing in reported crimes.

1. Crime statistics seem to rise when populations are
   a. younger
   b. older
   c. veteran
   d. richer

Question type_____

2. The main idea of the passage is that

    a. times of prosperity show lower crime statistics

    b. when the economy slows, crime statistics rise

    c. incidence of reported crime is related to several social and economic variables

    d. secure families are less likely to be involved in crime

Question type_____

3. The best title for this passage would be

    a. Wars and Crime Statistics

    b. Why Crime Statistics Rise and Fall

    c. Youth and Crime Statistics

    d. Poverty and Crime Statistics

Question type_____

4. Crime statistics show that crime is

    a. random

    b. cyclical

    c. demographic

    d. social

Question type_____

ANSWERS AND EXPLANATIONS FOR PRACTICE PASSAGE 2

1. a. Question type: 1, detail. This is a fairly clear example of how you can look quickly through a passage and locate a clearly stated detail. The word *young* appears in relation to the baby boomers; the idea is also suggested in the last sentence by the word *youthful*.

2. c. Question type: 2, main idea. The other answer choices are details—they're all in the passage, but they're not what the passage is *mostly* about. Answer **c** is the only one that combines several details into a statement that reflects the first sentence, which is also the topic sentence, of the paragraph.

3. b. Question type: 2, main idea. Each of the other choices expresses a detail, one of the reasons listed in the passage for fluctuation in crime rates. Answer **b** is the only one that expresses the sum of those details.

4. b. Question type: 1, detail. The passage mentions "the cyclical nature of crime statistics." Other phrases that suggest this answer include *fluctuations, rise and fall,* and *ebb and flow.*

VOCABULARY AND INFERENCE QUESTIONS

Questions that ask you about the meaning of vocabulary words in the passage and those that ask what the passage *suggests* or *implies* (inference questions) are different from detail or main idea questions. In vocabulary and inference questions, you usually have to pull ideas from the passage, sometimes from more than one place in the passage.

VOCABULARY QUESTIONS

Questions designed to test vocabulary are really trying to measure how well you can figure out the meaning of an unfamiliar word simply by making a good association based on context. Theoretically you should be able to substitute a nonsense word for the one being sought, and you would still make the right choice because you could determine meaning strictly from the sense of the sentence. Try to determine the meaning of this nonsense word from the rest of the sentence:

The chief noted that it gave him great *terivinix* to announce the award for Officer of the Year.

In this sentence, *terivinix* most likely means

a. pain
b. sympathy
c. pleasure
d. anxiety

Clearly, the context of an award makes c, *pleasure*, the best choice. Awards don't usually bring pain, sympathy, or anxiety. When confronted with an unfamiliar word, try substituting a nonsense word and see if the context gives you the clue.

INFERENCE QUESTIONS

Inference questions can be the most difficult to answer because they require you to take meaning from the text even when that meaning is not directly stated. Inferences are hints that we take based on the clues the writer has given us. You have to read between the lines in order to make a judgment about what an author was implying in the passage.

PRACTICE PASSAGE 3: VOCABULARY AND INFERENCE QUESTIONS

The questions that follow this passage are strictly vocabulary and inference questions. Circle the answers to the questions, and then check your answers against the key that appears immediately after the questions.

In recent years, issues of public and personal safety have become a major concern to many Americans. Violent incidents in fast-food restaurants, libraries, hospitals, schools, and offices have led many to seek greater security inside and outside of their homes. Sales of burglar alarms and high-tech security devices such as motion detectors and video monitors have skyrocketed in the last decade. Convenience stores and post offices have joined banks and jewelry stores in barricading staff behind iron bars and safety glass enclosures. Communities employ private security forces and encourage homeowners to keep trained attack dogs on their premises. While some people have sympathy for the impetus behind these efforts, there is also some concern that these measures will create a "siege mentality" leading to general distrust among people that could foster a dangerous isolationism within neighborhoods and among neighbors.

1. The passage suggests which of the following about community security?
   a. Communities are more dangerous today than they were ten years ago.
   b. Too much concern for security can destroy trust among neighbors.
   c. Poor security has led to an increase in public violence.
   d. Isolated neighborhoods are safe neighborhoods.

Question type_____

2. The word "foster" in the last sentence of the passage most nearly means
   a. adopt
   b. encourage
   c. prevent
   d. secure

Question type_____

3. The author believes that
   a. more security is needed to make neighborhoods safer
   b. people should spend more on home security
   c. people should not ignore the problems created by excessive safety concerns
   d. attack dogs and high-tech devices are the best protection against violent crime

Question type_____

4. In the last sentence, the phrase "siege mentality" means
   a. hostility
   b. defensiveness
   c. fear
   d. corruption

Question type_____

ANSWERS AND EXPLANATIONS FOR PRACTICE PASSAGE 3

1. b. Question type; 4, inference. The key word here is *distrust,* which implies that neighbors become suspicious of each other if they are worried about safety.

2. b. Question type: 3, vocabulary. The first answer choice is meant to confuse you if you associate the word *foster* with foster care and, by extension, with adoption. *Foster* means *nurture* or *help to grow.* Look again at the sentence. What could *a general distrust*—the thing that fosters—do to *a dangerous isolationism*—the thing being fostered? A general distrust could *encourage* a dangerous isolationism.

3. c. Question type: 4, inference. By using phrases like *dangerous isolationism,* the author suggests that he or she doesn't approve of the move toward more use of security devices. The other answer choices all indicate the author's approval of the trend being discussed.

4. b. Question type: 3, vocabulary. The key word here is *siege.* People who perceive themselves to be under attack tend to stick together in the face of a common enemy. They become quick to defend themselves against that enemy.

If English Isn't Your First Language

One of the difficulties of taking reading tests for non-native English speakers is the lack of a frame of reference that allows for quick comprehension of the text. People who have not lived in or been educated in the U.S. often don't have the background information that comes from reading American newspapers, magazines, and textbooks.

A second problem for non-native English speakers is the difficulty in recognizing vocabulary and idioms that assist comprehension. In order to read with good understanding, the test taker must have an immediate grasp of as many words as possible in the text.

The Long View

Read newspapers, magazines, and other periodicals that deal with current events and matters of local, state, and national importance. Pay special attention to articles related to law enforcement issues.

Be alert to new or unfamiliar vocabulary or terms that occur frequently in the popular press. Get a highlighter pen and use it to pick out new or unfamiliar words as you read. Keep a list of those words and their definitions. Review them for 15 minutes each day.

During the Test

When you are taking the test, make a picture in your mind of the situation being described in the passage. Ask yourself, "What did the writer mostly want me to think about this subject?"

Locate and underline the topic sentence which carries the main idea of the passage. Remember that the topic sentence may not always be the first sentence.

REVIEW: PUTTING IT ALL TOGETHER

A good way to solidify what you've learned about reading comprehension questions is for *you* to write the questions. Here's a passage, followed by space for you to write your own questions. Write one question of each of the four types: fact or detail, main idea, vocabulary, and inference.

In recent years law enforcement officers have welcomed the advent of a number of new technologies which have aided them greatly in their work. These include long-range eavesdropping devices and computer scanners that allow police to identify possible suspects by merely typing a license number into a computer in the patrol car. The scanner allows instant access to motor vehicle and criminal records and gives officers the opportunity to snare wrongdoers, even when they are not involved in criminal activity at the time. Police departments have praised the use of the computers, which they say help them get criminals off the streets and out of the way of honest citizens. Not all of those citizens agree with this attitude, however; some believe that arrests made solely on the basis of scanner identification constitute an invasion of privacy. They regard the accessing of records as illegal search and seizure. In New Jersey, Florida, and Arizona, lawsuits have been filed by citizens who believe that their constitutional rights have been violated. They believe that much computer-generated information is inaccurate and vulnerable to computer hackers who invade computer data bases. Some believe that such information from scanners could be used to charge innocent citizens with crimes or to target particular neighborhoods for harassment.

1. Detail question:_____
   a.
   b.
   c.
   d.

2. Main idea question:_____
   a.
   b.
   c.
   d.

3. Inference question_____
   a.
   b.
   c.
   d.

4. Vocabulary question_____
   a.
   b.
   c.
   d.

Possible Questions

Here is one question of each type based on the passage above. Your questions may be very different, but these will give you an idea of the kinds of questions that could be asked.

1. Main idea question: Which of the following best expresses the main idea of the passage?
   a. New technologies are available to police officers.
   b. Police are skeptical of new policing technologies.
   c. New technologies raise questions of privacy.
   d. New technologies may be discriminatory.

2. Detail question: Computer scanners allow police to
   a. identify suspects
   b. access computer databases
   c. locate wrongdoers
   d. all of the above

3. Vocabulary question: In this passage the word "snare" means
   a. question
   b. interrupt
   c. capture
   d. free

4. Inference question: The writer implies, but does not directly state, that
   a. computer technologies must be used with care
   b. high-tech policing is the wave of the future
   c. most citizens believe that high-tech policing is beneficial
   d. most police officers prefer using the new technologies

HOW TO ANSWER FILL-IN-THE-BLANK READING QUESTIONS

Some exams test your reading skills by having you fill in the missing words in a reading passage. If you're lucky, such questions come in standard multiple-choice format, and you'll be given choices of words to fill in the blank. Some tests, however, require you to fill in only the first letter of the missing word. To do well, you need both good reading skills and good test-taking skills. Below are some tips to help you sharpen your test-taking techniques, particularly for those tests that have you determine the first letter of the missing word.

FINDING THE MISSING WORD

You will be given reading passages with words omitted. Each missing word is indicated by a series of dashes. There is one dash for each letter in the missing word. You will have to determine the missing words and mark them correctly on your answer sheet. Here's how:

- Read the paragraph through quickly to get the general idea of it.
- Now go back to fill in the blanks by putting one letter on each line. Do the easy words first, then work on the harder ones. Choose only one word for each blank space. Make sure that word has exactly as many letters as there are dashes *and* makes sense in the sentence.
- Try to fill in every blank. Guess if you have to.
- Don't be alarmed if you're not sure of some of your answers. You can miss several words and still do well.

Look at the following sample sentence:

Fortunately, no one was hurt when the _ _ _ _ _ was derailed.

There are five dashes so the word you need must have five letters. The correct answer is **train** because it makes sense and has five letters. The word *engine* makes sense in the sentence, but it is incorrect because it is not a five-letter word. *Plane* is a five-letter word but is incorrect because planes cannot be derailed. Write the word *train* in the blank space.

MARKING THE ANSWER SHEET

Once you have completed the passage, you will have to mark your answers on the answer sheet. On the answer sheet, you will find numbered columns. Each column contains the letters A–Z, and the number at the top of the column corresponds to the number of a missing word in the passage. To mark your answer on the answer sheet, print the **first letter** of the word you wrote in the blank space in the passage in the box directly under the appropriate item number. Then, completely blacken the circle in that column containing the letter you wrote in the box.

· ·

IMPORTANT:

The words you wrote in the blank spaces in the passage will not be scored. Neither will the letters you write at the top of the columns on the answer sheet. Only the darkened circles of the letters you have chosen will be scored. Make sure you mark your answers correctly.

· ·

As you mark your answer sheet, check to make sure that:

1. the item number on the answer sheet is the same as the item number in the passage
2. you have written the correct first letter in the box
3. you have completely blackened the correct circle below the box

For example, if you chose *train* as the first missing word in a passage, you would find column 1, print T in the box, and blacken the circle with T in it.

PRACTICE FILL-IN-THE-BLANK PASSAGE

Now read the following sample paragraph.

> Fortunately, no one was hurt when the 1)_ _ _ _ _ was derailed. The derailment occurred 2)_ _ _ _ _ _ _ lumber and other debris were piled on the tracks. Investigators believe a 3)_ _ _ _ _ _ of people were involved. They are looking into the possibility 4)_ _ _ _ a local gang caused the accident for 5)_ _ _. It would not be the first 6)_ _ _ _ that members of this 7)_ _ _ _ caused serious damage.

First write the answers in the blank spaces (one letter per line), then mark them on the answer sheet below. Work as quickly as you can without sacrificing accuracy. Double check often to be sure you are marking your answers correctly. See the end of the chapter for answers.

WRITE 1ST LETTER OF WORD HERE

CODE LETTERS HERE

1	2	3	4	5	6	7	8	9	10
A	A	A	A	A	A	A	A	A	A
B	B	B	B	B	B	B	B	B	B
C	C	C	C	C	C	C	C	C	C
D	D	D	D	D	D	D	D	D	D
E	E	E	E	E	E	E	E	E	E
F	F	F	F	F	F	F	F	F	F
G	G	G	G	G	G	G	G	G	G
H	H	H	H	H	H	H	H	H	H
I	I	I	I	I	I	I	I	I	I
J	J	J	J	J	J	J	J	J	J
K	K	K	K	K	K	K	K	K	K
L	L	L	L	L	L	L	L	L	L
M	M	M	M	M	M	M	M	M	M
N	N	N	N	N	N	N	N	N	N
O	O	O	O	O	O	O	O	O	O
P	P	P	P	P	P	P	P	P	P
Q	Q	Q	Q	Q	Q	Q	Q	Q	Q
R	R	R	R	R	R	R	R	R	R
S	S	S	S	S	S	S	S	S	S
T	T	T	T	T	T	T	T	T	T
U	U	U	U	U	U	U	U	U	U
V	V	V	V	V	V	V	V	V	V
W	W	W	W	W	W	W	W	W	W
X	X	X	X	X	X	X	X	X	X
Y	Y	Y	Y	Y	Y	Y	Y	Y	Y
Z	Z	Z	Z	Z	Z	Z	Z	Z	Z

ADDITIONAL RESOURCES

Here are some other ways you can build the vocabulary and knowledge that will help you do well on reading comprehension questions.

- Practice asking the four sample question types about passages you read for information or pleasure.
- If you belong to a computer network such as America Online or Compuserve, search out articles related to law enforcement. Exchange views with others on the Internet. All of these exchanges will contribute to the knowledge needed to relate to the passage material on the tests.
- Use your library. Many public libraries have sections, sometimes called "Lifelong Learning Centers," that contain materials for adult learners. In these sections you can find books with exercises in reading and study skills. It's also a good idea to enlarge your base of information about the criminal justice field by reading books and articles on subjects related to criminology. Many libraries have computer systems that allow you to access information quickly and easily. Library personnel will show you how to use the computers and microfilm and microfiche machines.
- Begin now to build a broad knowledge of the law enforcement profession. Get in the habit of reading articles in newspapers and magazines on law enforcement issues. Keep a clipping file of those articles. This will help keep you informed of trends in the profession and aware of pertinent vocabulary related to policing issues.
- Consider reading or subscribing to professional journals. The journals listed below are written for

a general readership among law-enforcement personnel and are available for a reasonable annual fee. They may also be available in your public library.

Corrections Today
American Correctional Association
4380 Forbes Boulevard
Lanham, MD 20706

FBI Law Enforcement Bulletin
Madison Building, Rm. 209
FBI Academy
Quantico, VA 22135

Law and Order
Hendon, Inc.
1000 Skokie Boulevard
Willamette, IL 60091

Police Chief
International Association of Chiefs of Police, Inc.
515 North Washington Street
Alexandria, VA 22314

Police: The Law Officer's Magazine
Hare Publications
P.O. Box 847
Carlsbad, CA 92018

If you need more help building your reading skills and taking reading comprehension tests, consider *Reading Comprehension in 20 Minutes a Day* by Elizabeth Chelsa, published by LearningExpress. Order information is in the back of this book.

ANSWERS TO FILL-IN-THE-BLANK
READING QUESTIONS

1. train
2. because
3. number
4. that
5. fun
6. time
7. gang

C·H·A·P·T·E·R 7
LOGIC AND REASONING

CHAPTER SUMMARY
This chapter shows you how to deal with exam questions that test your judgment and common sense. Reading carefully and learning to think like a trooper are the keys to doing well on these types of questions.

The State Police Department can train you and give you everything you will need to become one of the best. Before they invest in you, however, they want to know if you already have something they cannot hand out and cannot teach—common sense and good judgment. While it might seem obvious that a state trooper needs logic, common sense, and good judgment, not everyone has these traits, and some people who *do* have them need to be reminded to use them. Law enforcement agencies have to have some way of determining who has these traits and who is clueless. Multiple-choice exams are the quickest, most cost-effective method of finding out.

Judgment questions are designed to see if you can make a sound decision—pick the right multiple-choice answer—based on the information given to you. To come to the right conclusion, you will need your common sense, good judgment, and good reading skills. (A little good luck never hurts either, so feel free to stick that four-leaf clover in your pocket.)

Judgment questions fall into three categories: situational judgment, application of rules and procedures, and judgment based on eyewitness accounts. This chapter will look at each category, take apart an example of each type of judgment question, and then identify the best approach to answering the question. There are also tips on what is most likely to trip up the unwary test-taker.

SITUATIONAL JUDGMENT QUESTIONS

Situational judgment questions ask you to climb inside the mind of a state trooper and make decisions from this viewpoint. It isn't necessary for you to know the laws of any state or the policies and procedures of any law enforcement agency. The test itself will give you the information you need to answer the question.

Some exams load you right into the hot seat with language such as "You are on patrol in a high-crime area. . ." while other exams use a more subtle approach: "Trooper Jones is on patrol when she sees a man breaking into a car." Although the approach is different, both test makers are asking you to look at their questions from the same viewpoint—a trooper's view.

The structure of the questions is pretty simple. You'll be given a situation, and then you'll be asked to choose how you would handle the situation if you were the trooper handling this call. The nice part is that you don't have to come up with your own plan. You get to choose the best answer from four multiple-choice options listed below the question. Eye-bulging panic, of course, will make all of the options appear to be the right one, but keep in mind that there is only *one* best answer.

Here's an example:

1. Trooper Cloud is driving through Newbury just after the end of a high school football game. A small car a few vehicles ahead of him stalls in the lane, block-ing the one lane of traffic leading out of the stadium area. This stretch of road is flat and there is a shoulder. What should Trooper Cloud do?

a. Call for a tow truck to move the vehicle.

b. Push the car onto the shoulder of the road so that the other traffic may proceed.

c. Tell the driver to keep trying to start the engine in hope that the car will start after a brief wait.

d. Direct traffic around the stalled vehicle by having the cars drive on the shoulder of the road.

In this situation, all of the options could conceivably happen, but only one answer is the best answer. The best way to approach this type of question is to start by eliminating the options that you know aren't going to work. Option **a** is not as appealing as some of the other options because traffic would be snarled until the tow truck arrived to clear the lane. Option **c** is not much of an option for the same reason. The idea here is to keep traffic moving safely. Now we've narrowed the choices down to two, which makes the odds of getting this question right much better. If you compare the two, option **d** is not as good as option **b** because it is not as practical or as safe as simply pushing the small car several feet until it is on the shoulder of the road. The shoulder of the road is intended for this sort of emergency. Also, this option should appeal to your good judgment and common sense: you want to remove the problem (the stalled vehicle) in the safest, most effective manner.

The temptation with situational judgment questions is to project your thoughts and feelings into the scenario. You may catch yourself chewing on your pencil thinking, "Well, I'd have the driver behind the stalled vehicle get out and help the other driver push the car to the side of the road. That's what I would do." That may be how this situation would play out in real life if the other driver were amenable, but that's not one of your options, so this kind of thinking merely complicates the question.

Another temptation is to read more into the situation than is there. You may think, "Maybe the car is too heavy to push, or it won't roll right, or maybe this department doesn't allow its troopers to push cars . . . ." The list goes on. Use the information you *see on the page*, not the information that *could* be there, to make your decision.

You will be required to exercise your good judgment and common sense. And it certainly helps to know what it means to "think like a trooper."

THROUGH THEIR EYES

It's easy to say "think like a trooper" if you know how troopers think. The ideal way to learn is to ride with troopers in your area and ask tons of questions. See what they handle in real, day-to-day settings, find out how they feel about the calls they make, and *ask* them—in calmer moments, of course—what they were looking for when they handled specific calls. Do what you can to look at the world through their eyes.

If ride-alongs are not an option, then arm yourself with the next few paragraphs.

Safety First

If you got tired of hearing your momma say, "Safety first!" when you were growing up, get ready for an exhausting experience. In every action a trooper takes, the safety and well-being of everyone involved is Priority Number One. Even the bad guy's safety is an issue. Protecting life is a trooper's first responsibility.

When you look at a test question, remember that troopers have the importance of safety drilled into them from day one at the academy. Is it safer to let the man stand in the street while he tells you how the accident happened, or is it better to have him move onto the sidewalk? Is it safer for the accident victims if the cruiser is blocking this lane of traffic or that lane of traffic? Is it safer for you to stand in front of a car or to the side of a car when making a stop?

The safety issue may not surface in every question, but when it does, be aware that safety is a state trooper's highest priority.

Use of Force

The smallest amount possible is the right amount of force. You don't need to go through six months in a state police academy to recognize that it's a monumental waste of effort to swat a fly with a ten-pound sledgehammer when a one-ounce plastic flyswatter will get the same result. Common sense comes into play heavily in this area. Expect to see test questions asking you what the proper amount of force is for a trooper to use when physical control is necessary, and what kind of force is appropriate out of the choices you see. When answering judgment questions, keep in mind that test makers know that the best officers will use the least force possible in all situations.

The Choices: Lecture, Cite, or Arrest

Do you write a ticket, or are the law and the public better served with a warning and a brief lecture on good driving? Is every breach of the peace a signal to break out the handcuffs? Situational judgment questions will demand that you know the answers. For example, you might see a question like this:

2. You are driving past a convenience store parking lot when you see one man punch another man in the stomach. You separate the two men and find out that it was a minor disturbance. The two men are embarrassed that you witnessed the altercation because they are

good friends. They assure you that no one is hurt. The victim laughs and says "no" when you ask if he wants to file criminal charges. What should you do about this obvious breach of the peace that has occurred in your presence?

a. Arrest the suspect anyway because the assault occurred in front of you.

b. Arrest the suspect because the victim may change his mind later.

c. Let the suspect go free because the victim does not want to file charges.

d. Arrest the suspect because bystanders are watching to see what kind of action you will take.

Once again, the process of elimination will come in handy to answer this question. After reading all of the options, you should reason immediately that option **d** is not a good choice. Law enforcement is rarely conducted in total privacy. The opinions of bystanders should not affect how you enforce the law. Option **a** is not the best choice either. It is not in the best interest of the public or the overcrowded justice system to physically take a person into custody each and every time a violation of the law occurs in your presence. Option **b** is a bad choice for the same reason. The victim obviously knows the suspect. In the unlikely event that he changes his mind later and wants to file charges, he knows the identity of his attacker and can contact the department with that information. A warrant can always be issued for the suspect.

That leaves us with option **c**, the best choice. Maybe you've heard the expression "no victim, no crime." If the man who was assaulted did not consider himself a victim of a crime then you have no need to arrest the "suspect" for assault. Arresting the suspect for any other violation in this situation would not be in the

best interest of the law, the public, or the police department. Common sense should tell you that arrest is not warranted because the two men resolved the situation themselves, no one was hurt, no damage to property occurred, and no one else was affected by the altercation. And by not arresting this man you remain available for more serious calls.

Tips for Answering Situational Judgment Questions

- Read carefully, but don't read anything into the situation that isn't there.
- Think like a trooper:
  Safety first.
  Use the least possible force.
- Use your common sense.

APPLICATION OF LAWS AND PROCEDURES

Another kind of test question asks you to read rules, laws, policies, or procedures and then apply those guidelines to a hypothetical situation. You may still be able to use your good judgment and common sense in these questions, but even more important is your ability to read carefully and accurately.

These kinds of questions ask you to do something troopers do every day: take their knowledge of the laws of their state or of their department's procedures and use that knowledge to decide what to do in a given situation. The questions don't expect you to know the laws or procedures; they're right there as part of the test question. And that's why your reading skills really come into play.

Questions that ask you to apply rules and laws are a little different from ones that ask you to apply procedures, so each kind of question is treated separately in this chapter.

APPLICATION OF LAWS

Some questions will give you a definition of a crime and then ask you to apply that definition to hypothetical situations to see which situation matches the definition. Here's an example:

Shoplifting is a theft of goods from a store, shop, or place of business during business hours where the suspect takes the good(s) past the last point of opportunity to pay for the merchandise without attempting to offer payment.

3. Which situation below is the best example of shoplifting?
   a. Terry walks into the Bag and Save grocery store and gets a piece of candy. He takes it to the counter and discovers he has no money. The clerk tells him to go ahead and keep the candy this time. Terry leaves the store eating the candy.
   b. Gloria walks into an electronics store to get a pack of triple-A batteries. She sticks the small package in her coat pocket while she looks at the computer display. After a few minutes, she turns to walk out. Before she reaches the door, she remembers the batteries and turns back to the counter to pay for them.
   c. Gail enters Philo's Pharmacy on 12th Street to pick up a prescription. After paying for the medicine, she walks over to the perfume counter where she finds a small bottle of cologne she likes. She puts the cologne in her purse and walks out of the front door of the pharmacy.
   d. Pete and his mother, Abby, are grocery shopping. Pete picks up a candy bar, peels off the wrapper, and hands Abby the wrapper. When they reach the checkout counter, Pete walks out of the store while Abby puts the groceries, along with the candy wrapper, on the stand for checkout. The clerk rings up the price of the candy along with the groceries.

The best approach to application of definition questions is to read each option carefully and decide whether or not it fits the definition. You have to rely on your good judgment, your careful reading skills, and your ability to put two and two together to reach a conclusion. The questions do not assume that you have any knowledge of the law or of police procedures; you are given all the information you need to reason out the best possible answer.

Let's look at the options in our example. Option **a** is not an example of shoplifting because the clerk told Terry he did not have to pay for the candy. Terry did not hide the candy or try to leave the business without an attempt to pay. The clerk had the option of having Terry put back the candy, but he instead chose to give it away.

Option **b** is not an example of shoplifting because Gloria did not pass the last point of opportunity to pay before leaving the store without making an attempt to pay for the batteries. In businesses where the checkout stands are located in the middle or toward the rear of the store, the benefit of the doubt goes to the shopper until he or she walks out the door.

Option **c** *is* an example of shoplifting because Gail made no attempt to pay for the cologne before leaving the business.

Option **d** is not an example of shoplifting because Abby paid for her son's candy, even though he ate the candy in the store and eventually walked out of the store.

Again, careful reading is the key to getting the application of definition questions correct. You have to read exactly what is there while not reading anything more into the situation than is actually written on the page. For example, if while reading option **b** you focus on Gloria putting the batteries in her pocket instead of whether or not she attempted to pay for the item, you may end up with an incorrect answer. Reread the definition and note that *where* someone carries goods while they are shopping has no bearing on the crime as defined. Do not complicate the situation.

APPLICATION OF PROCEDURES

Application of procedures questions are a lot like the previous type. You'll be given information about law enforcement procedures and then asked to apply these procedures to a hypothetical situation. You might have to decide which step in a set of procedures is the next step to be taken in the situation, or you might have to decide whether a hypothetical trooper followed the procedures properly in the situation given. In either case, you're being tested on your ability to follow directions, including your reading comprehension skills.

The question is usually preceded by a brief passage telling you about the procedure; for example:

When a trooper handles "found" property—property that has been discovered by someone, but is not necessarily evidence from a crime scene—the officer should follow these procedures:

1. Write a report detailing who found the property, what the property is, where it was found, and where it is now located, and turn in the report before the end of his or her shift.
2. Attach a tag to the property.
3. Write the report number on the tag, along with the officer's name, badge number, and the date and time the property was turned in.
4. Turn the property into the Property Room before the end of his or her shift.

4. Trooper Smith is on patrol when he is flagged down by a motorist on Route 1. The motorist has found an expensive jack lying on the side of the road and tells Trooper Smith he thinks someone forgot it after changing their flat. He gives the jack to the trooper and provides his name and other information for the report. Trooper Smith writes a found property report using all of the details provided by the motorist, places a tag on the jack and writes the report number, his name, his badge number, and the date and time the jack came into his possession. He then puts the jack in the trunk of his cruiser. He turns in his report an hour after writing it, and at the beginning of his next shift he takes the jack to the property room. In this situation, Trooper Smith acted
   a. improperly, because he should have let the motorist keep the jack until someone reported it as missing
   b. properly, because he turned in his report before the end of his shift
   c. improperly, because he failed to take the property to the property room before the end of his shift
   d. properly, because he wrote all the pertinent information in his report

What the test maker wants you to do is study how Trooper Smith handled the found property case and see if he followed his department's rules on handling found property.

Each option actually has two parts that require you to make two decisions. You have to decide if the officer acted properly or improperly, and then you have to decide if the reason stated in the option is correct or incorrect. In this case, option **c** is correct on both counts because the officer did not act properly, according to the procedures for turning in found property. He should have turned the jack in before the end of his shift (Step 4).

One way to approach picking the right option is to see if you can assign a step to the information in the option. For example, option **a** states that Trooper Smith should have let the motorist who found the jack keep it until someone reported it stolen. If you look at the steps in the list of procedures, you will not see that action in any of the steps.

These questions can be tricky if you read too fast or read only part of the answer choices. Take your time and make sure both parts of the answer are correct. For example, in option **b**, the second part of the answer is correct. That action, turning in the report in a timely manner, is what Trooper Smith is supposed to do according to Step 1. However, if you look at the first part of the answer it says Smith acted correctly in this situation because he turned in his report on time. This is not the *best* answer because Smith did *not* act properly since he failed to turn in the found property before the end of his shift. Remember, there's only one *best* answer.

Tips for Answering Application Questions

- Read what's there, not what might have been there.
- Read through all the options before you choose an answer.
- Find the spot in the law or procedure that supports your answer.

JUDGMENT QUESTIONS BASED ON EYEWITNESS ACCOUNTS

You'll need a careful eye for detail for the kinds of judgment questions that ask you to choose among eyewitness accounts. The test maker is looking to see if you can pick out the common elements in the list of answers you have to choose from in order to arrive at the right answer. The question usually will contain a description of suspects, vehicles, or license plates. Here's an example:

5. You are called to the scene of a gasoline theft at a rural gas station. The station manager tells you that a woman in a green Chevy Cavalier pumped $20 of unleaded gasoline into her car and took off northbound on Route 1. He and three other witnesses tell you they saw the license plate on the vehicle. Which of the plates listed below is most likely to be the correct plate?
    a. PG-2889
    b. PG-2089
    c. PG-2880
    d. PC-2889

In eyewitness account questions, the actual situation in the question has little bearing on what the test maker wants you to do. You are being asked to pick out which license plate is most likely to be the license plate for the suspect vehicle. The answer to this question lies in the answers themselves. The end result isn't focusing on the crime that took place so much as on your ability to take information, average it all up, and arrive at a conclusion.

Your best approach to this question is to start comparing the similarities in each answer. You'll notice that all of the answers start with the letter "P." The second letter is the letter "G" in all of the answers except for option **d**. The first number is the number 2 for all of the answers. Then you see that all of the answers except for **b** agree that the number 8 is the second number on the license plate. The third number of the plate is 8 in all of the answers. The final number of the plate is 9 in all of the answers except for **d**. You should have picked option **a** as the right answer because the license plate that has the most common elements is PG-2889.

You'll be asked to use the same kind of reasoning when you see a test question asking you to pick out a suspect description. Once again, the scenario described in the question is not going to carry as much weight as the answers themselves. Your task will be to find the common threads in each answer until you come up with the most likely description of the suspect.

Tips for Answering Eyewitness Account Questions

- Stay calm and work methodically.
- Compare each element of each answer choice until you find the ones that have the common elements.

IMPROVING YOUR JUDGMENT SKILLS

You have more options than you may realize when it comes to honing your judgment skills—not only for the entrance exam, but also for your career as a state trooper. There are some surprisingly simple exercises you can do in your everyday life that will get you ready.

WHAT IF...

There's a game most law enforcement officers play in their minds called "What if." You play too, but you may not be aware of it. "What if I won the lottery tomorrow? If I did, I'd empty my desk drawers on top of my supervisor's desk and run screaming out of the building." Sound familiar?

Some professional baseball players watch slow-motion videos of a batter with perfect form in the hope that by memorizing and studying his moves, they will be able to improve their own performance. And research shows that this works: In times of stress, people are more likely to carry out a task if they've practiced it—mentally or physically.

"What if" uses the same logic. If you've thought about a situation and you've arrived at a conclusion about what you would do under the given circumstances, then you've given your brain a plan for the situation if it actually comes up. Maybe you've heard someone say, "I didn't have any idea what to do. I just froze." That brain didn't have a plan to follow. Playing "What if" can give it a plan.

Train yourself to play "What if." Do it in the grocery store. You're standing in line behind a man in a heavy coat. Ask yourself "If I were a trooper, *what* would I do *if* I saw this man slip a package of batteries into his coat pocket and go through the checkout line and then out of the store without paying for them?" This could turn out to be one of the situational judgment questions you find on the entrance exam. Practice. At the very least it might add a new dimension to your grocery shopping.

SELF-CONFIDENCE CHECKS

Practice your self-confidence. Odd advice? Not really. Self-confidence is what makes most troopers able to make decisions with a minimum of confusion and self-doubt. Although you aren't a trooper yet, you need the same self-confidence so that you will make the right decisions as a test taker. If you aren't confident about your judgment skills and your ability to decide what to do in a situation, then you are likely to torture yourself with every judgment question.

Believe it or not, it is possible to practice self-confidence. Many people practice the opposite of self-confidence by thinking and saying things like "I don't know if I can do that" or "What if I can't do that?"

Start listening to yourself to see if you talk like that. And then turn it around. Tell yourself and others, "The state police entrance exam is coming up and I intend to ace it." And "I know I will make a good trooper. I know that when I read the test questions I can rely on my own good judgment to help me. My common sense will point me in the right direction."

This isn't bragging. It's how you set yourself up for success. You'll start thinking of what you need to do to ace the test. You're practicing self-confidence right now by reading this book. You are getting the tools you need to do the job. Your self-confidence has no option but to shoot straight up—and your score along with it.

READ, READ, READ

Reading is as vital on judgment questions as it is on questions that call themselves reading questions. This isn't the kind of reading you do when you are skimming a novel or skipping through articles in a newspaper. It's the kind where you not only have to pay attention to what the writer is telling you, but you must make decisions based on the information you've received. There's a whole chapter in this book on reading. Check out the suggestions there, under Additional Resources, on ways to improve your reading skills.

C·H·A·P·T·E·R

MATH 8

CHAPTER SUMMARY

This chapter gives you some important tips for dealing with math questions on a civil service exam and reviews some of the most commonly tested concepts. If you've forgotten most of your high school math or have math anxiety, this chapter is for you.

ot all civil service exams test your math knowledge, but many do. Knowledge of basic arithmetic, as well as the more complex kinds of reasoning necessary for algebra and geometry problems, are important qualifications for almost any profession. You have to be able to add up dollar figures, evaluate budgets, compute percentages, and other such tasks, both in your job and in your personal life. Even if your exam doesn't include math, you'll find that the material in this chapter will be useful on the job.

The math portion of the test covers the subjects you probably studied in grade school and high school. While every test is different, most emphasize arithmetic skills and word problems.

MATH STRATEGIES

- **Don't work in your head! Use your test book or scratch paper to take notes, draw pictures, and calculate.** Although you might think that you can solve math questions more quickly in your head, that's a good way to make mistakes. Write out each step.

- **Read a math question in *chunks* rather than straight through from beginning to end.** As you read each *chunk,* stop to think about what it means and make notes or draw a picture to represent that *chunk.*

- **When you get to the actual question, circle it.** This will keep you more focused as you solve the problem.

- **Glance at the answer choices for clues.** If they're fractions, you probably should do your work in fractions; if they're decimals, you should probably work in decimals; etc.

- **Make a plan of attack** to help you solve the problem.

- **If a question stumps you, try one of the *backdoor* approaches** explained in the next section. These are particularly useful for solving word problems.

- **When you get your answer, reread the circled question to make sure you've answered it.** This helps avoid the careless mistake of answering the wrong question.

- **Check your work after you get an answer.** Test-takers get a false sense of security when they get an answer that matches one of the multiple-choice answers. Here are some good ways to check your work *if you have time*:
  - Ask yourself if your answer is reasonable, if it makes sense.
  - Plug your answer back into the problem to make sure the problem holds together.
  - Do the question a second time, but use a different method.

- **Approximate when appropriate.** For example:
  - $5.98 + $8.97 is a little less than $15. (Add: $6 + $9)
  - .9876 × 5.0342 is close to 5. (Multiply: 1 × 5)

- **Skip hard questions and come back to them later.** Mark them in your test book so you can find them quickly.

BACKDOOR APPROACHES FOR ANSWERING QUESTIONS THAT PUZZLE YOU

Remember those word problems you dreaded in high school? Many of them are actually easier to solve by backdoor approaches. The two techniques that follow are terrific ways to solve multiple-choice word problems that you don't know how to solve with a straightforward approach. The first technique, *nice numbers*, is useful when there are unknowns (like *x*) in the text of the word problem, making the problem too abstract for you. The second technique, *working backwards*, presents a quick way to substitute numeric answer choices back into the problem to see which one works.

Nice Numbers

1. When a question contains unknowns, like *x*, plug nice numbers in for the unknowns. A nice number is easy to calculate with and makes sense in the problem.

2. Read the question with the nice numbers in place. Then solve it.

3. If the answer choices are all numbers, the choice that matches your answer is the right one.

4. If the answer choices contain unknowns, substitute the same nice numbers into **all** the answer choices. The choice that matches your answer is the right one. If more than one answer matches, do the problem again with different nice numbers. You'll only have to check the answer choices that have already matched.

> **Example:** Judi went shopping with p dollars in her pocket. If the price of shirts was s shirts for d dollars, what is the maximum number of shirts Judi could buy with the money in her pocket?

> **a.** psd **b.** $\frac{ps}{d}$ **c.** $\frac{pd}{s}$ **d.** $\frac{ds}{p}$

To solve this problem, let's try these nice numbers: $p = \$100$, $s = 2$; $d = \$25$. Now reread it with the numbers in place:

> Judi went shopping with *$100* in her pocket. If the price of shirts was *2* shirts for *$25*, what is the maximum number of shirts Judi could buy with the money in her pocket?

Since 2 shirts cost $25, that means that 4 shirts cost $50, and 8 shirts cost $100. So our answer is *8*. Let's substitute the nice numbers into all 4 answers:

> **a.** $100 \times 2 \times 25 = 5000$ **b.** $\frac{100 \times 2}{25} = 8$ **c.** $\frac{100 \times 25}{2} = 1250$ **d.** $\frac{25 \times 2}{100} = \frac{1}{2}$

The answer is **b** because it is the only one that matches our answer of **8**.

Working Backwards

You can frequently solve a word problem by plugging the answer choices back into the text of the problem to see which one fits all the facts stated in the problem. The process is faster than you think because you'll probably only have to substitute one or two answers to find the right one.

This approach works only when:

- All of the answer choices are numbers.
- You're asked to find a simple number, not a sum, product, difference, or ratio.

Here's what to do:

1. Look at all the answer choices and begin with the one in the middle of the range. For example, if the answers are 14, 8, 2, 20, and 25, begin by plugging 14 into the problem.

2. If your choice doesn't work, eliminate it. Determine if you need a bigger or smaller answer.

3. Plug in one of the remaining choices.

4. If none of the answers work, you may have made a careless error. Begin again or look for your mistake.

> **Example:** Juan ate $\frac{1}{3}$ of the jellybeans. Maria then ate $\frac{3}{4}$ of the remaining jellybeans, which left 10 jellybeans. How many jellybeans were there to begin with?

> **a.** 60 **b.** 80 **c.** 90 **d.** 120 **e.** 140

Starting with the middle answer, let's assume there were **90** jellybeans to begin with:

Since Juan ate $\frac{1}{3}$ of them, that means he ate 30 ($\frac{1}{3} \times 90 = 30$), leaving 60 of them ($90 - 30 = 60$). Maria then ate $\frac{3}{4}$ of the 60 jellybeans, or 45 of them ($\frac{3}{4} \times 60 = 45$). That leaves 15 jellybeans ($60 - 45 = 15$).

The problem states that there were **10** jellybeans left, and we wound up with **15** of them. That indicates that we started with too big a number. Thus, 90, 120, and 140 are all wrong! With only two choices left, let's use common sense to decide which one to try. The next lower answer is only a little smaller than 90 and may not be small enough. So, let's try **60**:

Since Juan ate $\frac{1}{3}$ of them, that means he ate 20 ($\frac{1}{3} \times 60 = 20$), leaving 40 of them ($60 - 20 = 40$). Maria then ate $\frac{3}{4}$ of the 40 jellybeans, or 30 of them ($\frac{3}{4} \times 40 = 30$). That leaves 10 jellybeans ($40 - 30 = 10$).

Because this result of **10** jellybeans left agrees with the problem, the right answer is **a.**

WORD PROBLEMS

Many of the math problems on tests are word problems. A word problem can include any kind of math, including simple arithmetic, fractions, decimals, percentages, even algebra and geometry.

The hardest part of any word problem is translating English into math. When you read a problem, you can frequently translate it *word for word* from English statements into mathematical statements. At other times, however, a key word in the word problem hints at the mathematical operation to be performed. Here are the translation rules:

EQUALS key words: is, are, has

English	Math
Bob **is** 18 years old.	$B = 18$
There **are** 7 hats.	$H = 7$
Judi **has** 5 books.	$J = 5$

ADDITION key words: sum; more, greater, or older than; total; altogether

English	Math
The **sum** of two numbers is 10.	$X + Y = 10$
Karen has $5 **more than** Sam.	$K = 5 + S$
The base is 3″ **greater than** the height.	$B = 3 + H$
Judi is 2 years **older than** Tony.	$J = 2 + T$
The **total** of three numbers is 25.	$A + B + C = 25$
How much do Joan and Tom have **altogether**?	$J + T = ?$

SUBTRACTION key words: difference, less or younger than, remain, left over

English	Math
The **difference** between two numbers is 17.	$X + Y = 17$
Mike has 5 **less** cats **than** twice the number Jan has.	$M = 2J - 5$
Jay is 2 years **younger than** Brett.	$J = B - 2$
After Carol ate 3 apples, R apples **remained**.	$R = A - 3$

MULTIPLICATION   key words: of, product, times

English	Math
20% **of** Matthew's baseball caps	$.20 \times M$
Half **of** the boys	$\frac{1}{2} \times B$
The **product** of two numbers is 12	$A \times B = 12$

DIVISION   key word: per

English	Math
15 drops **per** teaspoon	$\frac{15 \text{ drops}}{\text{teaspoon}}$
22 miles **per** gallon	$\frac{22 \text{ miles}}{\text{gallon}}$

DISTANCE FORMULA: DISTANCE = RATE × TIME

The key words are movement words like: plane, train, boat, car, walk, run, climb, swim

- How far did the **plane** travel in 4 hours if it averaged 300 miles per hour?

  $D = 300 \times 4$

  $D = 1200$ miles

- Ben **walked** 20 miles in 4 hours. What was his average speed?

  $20 = r \times 4$

  5 miles per hour $= r$

SOLVING A WORD PROBLEM USING THE TRANSLATION TABLE

Remember the problem at the beginning of this chapter about the jellybeans?

Juan ate $\frac{1}{3}$ of the jellybeans. Maria then ate $\frac{3}{4}$ of the remaining jellybeans, which left 10 jellybeans. How many jellybeans were there to begin with?

      a. 60   **b.** 80   **c.** 90   **d.** 120   **e.** 140

We solved it by *working backwards.* Now let's solve it using our translation rules.

Assume Juan started with J jellybeans. Eating $\frac{1}{3}$ of them means eating $\frac{1}{3} \times J$ jellybeans. Maria ate a fraction of the **remaining** jellybeans, which means we must **subtract** to find out how many are left: $J - \frac{1}{3} \times J = \frac{2}{3} \times J$. Maria then ate $\frac{3}{4}$, leaving $\frac{1}{4}$ of the $\frac{2}{3} \times J$ jellybeans, or $\frac{1}{4} \times \frac{2}{3} \times J$ *jellybeans. Multiplying out* $\frac{1}{4} \times \frac{2}{3} \times J$ gives $\frac{1}{6} J$ as the number of jellybeans left. The problem states that there were **10 jellybeans left**, meaning that we set $\frac{1}{6} \times J$ **equal to** 10:

$$\frac{1}{6} \times J = 10$$

Solving this equation for J gives $J = 60$. Thus, the right answer is **a** (the same answer we got when we *worked backwards).* As you can see, both methods—working backwards and translating from English to math—work. You should use whichever method is more comfortable for you.

PRACTICE WORD PROBLEMS

You will find word problems using fractions, decimals, and percentages in those sections of this chapter. For now, practice using the translation table on problems that just require you to work with basic arithmetic. Answers are at the end of the chapter.

_____ **1.** Joan went shopping with $100 and returned home with only $18.42. How much money did she spend?

    a. $81.58   **b.** $72.68   **c.** $72.58   **d.** $71.68   **e.** $71.58

_____ **2.** Mark invited ten friends to a party. Each friend brought 3 guests. How many people came to the party, excluding Mark?

    a. 3   **b.** 10   **c.** 30   **d.** 40   **e.** 41

_____ **3.** The office secretary can type 80 words per minute on his word processor. How many minutes will it take him to type a report containing 760 words?

    a. 8   **b.** $8\frac{1}{2}$ **c.** 9   **d.** $9\frac{1}{2}$ **e.** 10

_____ **4.** Mr. Wallace is writing a budget request to upgrade his personal computer system. He wants to purchase 4 mb of RAM, which will cost $100, two new software programs at $350 each, a tape backup system for $249, and an additional tape for $25. What is the total amount Mr. Wallace should write on his budget request?

    a. $724   **b.** $974   **c.** $1049   **d.** $1064   **e.** $1074

FRACTION REVIEW

Problems involving fractions may be straightforward calculation questions, or they may be word problems. Typically, they ask you to add, subtract, multiply, divide, or compare fractions.

WORKING WITH FRACTIONS

A fraction is a part of something.

Example: Let's say that a pizza was cut into 8 equal slices and you ate 3 of them. The fraction $\frac{3}{8}$ tells you what part of the pizza you ate. The pizza below shows this: 3 of the 8 pieces (the ones you ate) are shaded.

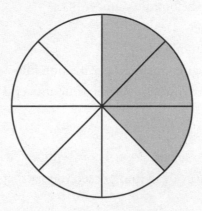

Three Kinds of Fractions

Proper fraction: The top number is less than the bottom number:

$\frac{1}{2}$; $\frac{2}{3}$; $\frac{4}{9}$; $\frac{8}{13}$

The value of a proper fraction is less than 1.

Improper fraction: The top number is greater than or equal to the bottom number:

$\frac{3}{2}$; $\frac{5}{3}$; $\frac{14}{9}$; $\frac{12}{12}$

The value of an improper fraction is 1 or more.

Mixed number: A fraction written to the right of a whole number:

$3\frac{1}{2}$; $4\frac{2}{3}$; $12\frac{3}{4}$; $24\frac{3}{4}$

The value of a mixed number is more than 1: it is the sum of the whole number plus the fraction.

Changing Improper Fractions into Mixed or Whole Numbers

It's easier to add and subtract fractions that are mixed numbers rather than improper fractions. To change an improper fraction, say $\frac{13}{2}$, into a mixed number, follow these steps:

1. Divide the bottom number (2) into the top number (13) to get the whole number portion (6) of the mixed number:

$$\begin{array}{r} 6 \\ 2\overline{)13} \\ \underline{12} \\ 1 \end{array}$$

2. Write the remainder of the division (1) over the old bottom number (2): $6\frac{1}{2}$

3. Check: Change the mixed number back into an improper fraction (see steps below).

Changing Mixed Numbers into Improper Fractions

It's easier multiply and divide fractions when you're working with improper fractions rather than mixed numbers. To change a mixed number, say $2\frac{3}{4}$, into an improper fraction, follow these steps:

1. Multiply the whole number (2) by the bottom number (4). $2 \times 4 = 8$
2. Add the result (8) to the top number (3). $8 + 3 = 11$
3. Put the total (11) over the bottom number (4). $\frac{11}{4}$
4. Check: Reverse the process by changing the improper fraction into a mixed number. If you get back the number you started with, your answer is right.

Reducing Fractions

Reducing a fraction means writing it in *lowest terms*, that is, with smaller numbers. For instance, 50¢ is $\frac{50}{100}$ of a dollar, or $\frac{1}{2}$ of a dollar. In fact, if you have 50¢ in your pocket, you say that you have half a dollar. Reducing a fraction does not change its value.

Follow these steps to reduce a fraction:

1. Find a whole number that divides *evenly* into both numbers that make up the fraction.
2. Divide that number into the top of the fraction, and replace the top of the fraction with the quotient (the answer you got when you divided).
3. Do the same thing to the bottom number.
4. Repeat the first 3 steps until you can't find a number that divides evenly into both numbers of the fraction.

For example, let's reduce $\frac{8}{24}$. We could do it in 2 steps: $\frac{8 \div 4}{24 \div 4} = \frac{2}{6}$; then $\frac{2 \div 2}{6 \div 2} = \frac{1}{3}$. Or we could do it in a single step: $\frac{8 \div 8}{24 \div 8} = \frac{1}{3}$.

Shortcut: When the top and bottom numbers both end in zeroes, cross out the same number of zeroes in both numbers to begin the reducing process. For example, $\frac{300}{4000}$ reduces to $\frac{3}{40}$ when you cross out 2 zeroes in both numbers.

Whenever you do arithmetic with fractions, reduce your answer. On a multiple-choice test, don't panic if your answer isn't listed. Try to reduce it and then compare it to the choices.

Reduce these fractions to lowest terms:

_____ **5.** $\frac{3}{12}$

_____ **6.** $\frac{14}{35}$

_____ **7.** $\frac{27}{72}$

Raising Fractions to Higher Terms

Before you can add and subtract fractions, you have to know how to raise a fraction to higher terms. This is actually the opposite of reducing a fraction.

Follow these steps to raise $\frac{2}{3}$ to 24ths:

1. Divide the old bottom number (3) into the new one (24): $3\overline{)24} = 8$
2. Multiply the answer (8) by the old top number (2): $2 \times 8 = 16$
3. Put the answer (16) over the new bottom number (24): $\frac{16}{24}$
4. Check: Reduce the new fraction to see if you get back the original one: $\frac{16 \div 8}{24 \div 8} = \frac{2}{3}$

Raise these fractions to higher terms:

_____ 8. $\frac{5}{12} = \frac{}{24}$

_____ 9. $\frac{2}{9} = \frac{}{27}$

_____10. $\frac{2}{5} = \frac{}{500}$

ADDING FRACTIONS

If the fractions have the same bottom numbers, just add the top numbers together and write the total over the bottom number.

Examples: $\frac{2}{9} + \frac{4}{9} = \frac{2+4}{9} = \frac{6}{9}$ Reduce the sum: $\frac{2}{3}$

$\frac{5}{8} + \frac{7}{8} = \frac{12}{8}$ Change the sum to a mixed number: $1\frac{4}{8}$; then reduce: $1\frac{1}{2}$

There are a few extra steps to add mixed numbers with the same bottom numbers, say $2\frac{3}{5} + 1\frac{4}{5}$:

1. Add the fractions: $\frac{3}{5} + \frac{4}{5} = \frac{7}{5}$
2. Change the improper fraction into a mixed number: $\frac{7}{5} = 1\frac{2}{5}$
3. Add the whole numbers: $2 + 1 = 3$
4. Add the results of steps 2 and 3: $1\frac{2}{5} + 3 = 4\frac{2}{5}$

Finding the Least Common Denominator

If the fractions you want to add don't have the same bottom number, you'll have to raise some or all of the fractions to higher terms so that they all have the same bottom number, called the **common denominator.** All of the original bottom numbers divide evenly into the common denominator. If it is the smallest number that they all divide evenly into, it is called the **least common denominator (LCD).**

Here are a few tips for finding the LCD, the smallest number that all the bottom numbers evenly divide into:

- See if all the bottom numbers divide evenly into the biggest bottom number.
- Check out the multiplication table of the largest bottom number until you find a number that all the other bottom numbers evenly divide into.

- When all else fails, multiply all the bottom numbers together.

> **Example:** $\frac{2}{3} + \frac{4}{5}$

1. Find the LCD. Multiply the bottom numbers: $\qquad\qquad\qquad\qquad\qquad\qquad\qquad$ $3 \times 5 = 15$

2. Raise each fraction to 15ths: $\qquad\qquad\qquad\qquad\qquad\qquad\qquad\qquad\qquad$ $\frac{2}{3} = \frac{10}{15}$

$$+\frac{4}{5} = \frac{12}{15}$$
$$\frac{22}{15}$$

3. Add as usual:

Try these addition problems:

_____ **11.** $\frac{3}{4} + \frac{1}{6}$

_____ **12.** $\frac{7}{8} + \frac{2}{3} + \frac{3}{4}$

_____ **13.** $4\frac{1}{3} + 2\frac{3}{4} + \frac{1}{6}$

SUBTRACTING FRACTIONS

If the fractions have the same bottom numbers, just subtract the top numbers and write the difference over the bottom number.

> **Example:** $\frac{4}{9} - \frac{3}{9} = \frac{4-3}{9} = \frac{1}{9}$

If the fractions you want to subtract don't have the same bottom number, you'll have to raise some or all of the fractions to higher terms so that they all have the same bottom number, or LCD. If you forgot how to find the LCD, just read the section on adding fractions with different bottom numbers.

> **Example:** $\frac{5}{6} - \frac{3}{4}$

1. Raise each fraction to 12ths because 12 is the LCD, the smallest number $\qquad$ $\frac{5}{6} = \frac{10}{12}$
that 6 and 4 both divide into evenly: $\qquad\qquad\qquad\qquad\qquad\qquad\qquad\qquad$ $-\frac{3}{4} = \frac{9}{12}$

2. Subtract as usual: $\qquad\qquad\qquad\qquad\qquad\qquad\qquad\qquad\qquad\qquad\qquad\qquad\qquad$ $\frac{1}{12}$

Subtracting mixed numbers with the same bottom number is similar to adding mixed numbers.

> **Example:** $4\frac{3}{5} - 1\frac{2}{5}$

1. Subtract the fractions: $\qquad\qquad\qquad\qquad\qquad\qquad\qquad\qquad\qquad\qquad$ $\frac{3}{5} - \frac{2}{5} = \frac{1}{5}$

2. Subtract the whole numbers: $\qquad\qquad\qquad\qquad\qquad\qquad\qquad\qquad\qquad$ $4 - 1 = 3$

3. Add the results of steps 1 and 2: $\qquad\qquad\qquad\qquad\qquad\qquad\qquad$ $\frac{1}{5} + 3 = 3\frac{1}{5}$

Sometimes there is an extra "borrowing" step when you subtract mixed numbers with the same bottom numbers, say $7\frac{3}{5} - 2\frac{4}{5}$:

1. You can't subtract the fractions the way they are because $\frac{4}{5}$ is bigger than $\frac{3}{5}$.

So you borrow 1 from the 7, making it 6, and change that 1 to $\frac{5}{5}$ because

5 is the bottom number: $\qquad 7\frac{3}{5} = 6\frac{5}{5} + \frac{3}{5}$

2. Add the numbers from step 1: $\qquad 6\frac{5}{5} + \frac{3}{5} = 6\frac{8}{5}$

3. Now you have a different version of the original problem: $\qquad 6\frac{8}{5} - 2\frac{4}{5}$

4. Subtract the fractional parts of the two mixed numbers: $\qquad \frac{8}{5} - \frac{4}{5} = \frac{4}{5}$

5. Subtract the whole number parts of the two mixed numbers: $\qquad 6 - 2 = 4$

6. Add the results of the last 2 steps together: $\qquad 4 + \frac{4}{5} = 4\frac{4}{5}$

Try these subtraction problems:

_____**14.** $\frac{4}{5} - \frac{2}{3}$

_____**15.** $\frac{7}{8} - \frac{1}{4} - \frac{1}{2}$

_____**16.** $4\frac{1}{3} - 2\frac{3}{4}$

Now let's put what you've learned about adding and subtracting fractions to work in some real-life problems.

_____**17.** Patrolman Peterson drove $3\frac{1}{2}$ miles to the police station. Then he drove $4\frac{3}{4}$ miles to his first assignment. When he left there, he drove 2 miles to his next assignment. Then he drove $3\frac{2}{3}$ miles back to the police station for a meeting. Finally, he drove $3\frac{1}{2}$ miles home. How many miles did he travel in total?

    a. $17\frac{5}{12}$ **b.** $16\frac{5}{12}$ **c.** $15\frac{7}{12}$ **d.** $15\frac{5}{12}$ **e.** $13\frac{11}{12}$

_____**18.** Before leaving the fire station, Firefighter Sorensen noted that the mileage gauge on Engine 2 registered $4{,}357\frac{4}{10}$ miles. When he arrived at the scene of the fire, the mileage gauge then registered $4{,}400\frac{1}{10}$ miles. How many miles did he drive from the station to the fire scene?

    a. $42\frac{3}{10}$ **b.** $42\frac{7}{10}$ **c.** $43\frac{7}{10}$ **d.** $47\frac{2}{10}$ **e.** $57\frac{3}{10}$

MULTIPLYING FRACTIONS

Multiplying fractions is actually easier than adding them. All you do is multiply the top numbers and then multiply the bottom numbers.

Examples: $\qquad \frac{2}{3} \times \frac{5}{7} = \frac{2 \times 5}{3 \times 7} = \frac{10}{21} \qquad \frac{1}{2} \times \frac{3}{5} \times \frac{7}{4} = \frac{1 \times 3 \times 7}{2 \times 5 \times 4} = \frac{21}{40}$

Sometimes you can *cancel* before multiplying. Cancelling is a shortcut that makes the multiplication go faster because you're multiplying with smaller numbers. It's very similar to reducing: if there is a number that divides evenly into a top number and bottom number, do that division before multiplying. If you forget to cancel, you'll still get the right answer, but you'll have to reduce it.

Example: $\frac{5}{6} \times \frac{9}{20}$

1. Cancel the 6 and the 9 by dividing 3 into both of them: $6 \div 3 = 2$ and $9 \div 3 = 3$. Cross out the 6 and the 9.

$$\frac{5}{\overset{}{\underset{2}{6}}} \times \frac{9}{20}^{3}$$

2. Cancel the 5 and the 20 by dividing 5 into both of them: $5 \div 5 = 1$ and $20 \div 5 = 4$. Cross out the 5 and the 20.

$$\frac{^{1}5}{\underset{2}{6}} \times \frac{9}{20}_{4}^{3}$$

3. Multiply across the new top numbers and the new bottom numbers:

$$\frac{1 \times 3}{2 \times 4} = \frac{3}{8}$$

Try these multiplication problems:

_____**19.** $\frac{1}{5} \times \frac{2}{3}$

_____**20.** $\frac{2}{3} \times \frac{4}{7} \times \frac{3}{5}$

_____**21.** $\frac{3}{4} \times \frac{8}{9}$

To multiply a fraction by a whole number, first rewrite the whole number as a fraction with a bottom number of 1:

Example: $5 \times \frac{2}{3} = \frac{5}{1} \times \frac{2}{3} = \frac{10}{3}$ (Optional: convert $\frac{10}{3}$ to a mixed number: $3\frac{1}{3}$)

To multiply with mixed numbers, it's easier to change them to improper fractions before multiplying.

Example: $4\frac{2}{3} \times 5\frac{1}{2}$

1. Convert $4\frac{2}{3}$ to an improper fraction:

$$4\frac{2}{3} = \frac{4 \times 3 + 2}{3} = \frac{14}{3}$$

2. Convert $5\frac{1}{2}$ to an improper fraction:

$$5\frac{1}{2} = \frac{5 \times 2 + 1}{2} = \frac{11}{2}$$

3. Cancel and multiply the fractions:

$$\frac{^{7}14}{3} \times \frac{11}{\underset{1}{2}} = \frac{77}{3}$$

4. Optional: convert the improper fraction to a mixed number:

$$\frac{77}{3} = 25\frac{2}{3}$$

Now try these multiplication problems with mixed numbers and whole numbers:

_____**22.** $4\frac{1}{3} \times \frac{2}{5}$

_____**23.** $2\frac{1}{2} \times 6$

_____**24.** $3\frac{3}{4} \times 4\frac{2}{5}$

Here are a few more real-life problems to test your skills:

_____**25.** After driving $\frac{2}{3}$ of the 15 miles to work, Mr. Stone stopped to make a phone call. How many miles had he driven when he made his call?

   a. 5   **b.** $7\frac{1}{2}$ **c.** 10   **d.** 12   **e.** $15\frac{2}{3}$

_____**26.** If Henry worked $\frac{3}{4}$ of a 40-hour week, how many hours did he work?

   a. $7\frac{1}{2}$ **b.** 10   **c.** 20   **d.** 25   **e.** 30

_____**27.** Technician Chin makes \$14.00 an hour. When she works more than 8 hours a day, she gets over-time pay of $1\frac{1}{2}$ times her regular hourly wage for the extra hours. How much did she earn for working 11 hours in one day?

   a. \$77   **b.** \$154   **c.** \$175   **d.** \$210   **e.** \$231

DIVIDING FRACTIONS

To divide one fraction by a second fraction, invert the second fraction (that is, flip the top and bottom numbers) and then multiply. That's all there is to it!

   Example: $\frac{1}{2} \div \frac{3}{5}$

1. Invert the second fraction ($\frac{3}{5}$): $\frac{5}{3}$

2. Change the division sign ($\div$) to a multiplication sign ($\times$)

3. Multiply the first fraction by the new second fraction: $\frac{1}{2} \times \frac{5}{3} = \frac{1 \times 5}{2 \times 3} = \frac{5}{6}$

   To divide a fraction by a whole number, first change the whole number to a fraction by putting it over 1. Then follow the division steps above.

   Example: $\frac{3}{5} \div 2 = \frac{3}{5} \div \frac{2}{1} = \frac{3}{5} \times \frac{1}{2} = \frac{3 \times 1}{5 \times 2} = \frac{3}{10}$

   When the division problem has a mixed number, convert it to an improper fraction and then divide as usual.

   Example: $2\frac{3}{4} \div \frac{1}{6}$

1. Convert $2\frac{3}{4}$ to an improper fraction: $2\frac{3}{4} = \frac{2 \times 4 + 3}{4} = \frac{11}{4}$

2. Divide $\frac{11}{4}$ by $\frac{1}{6}$: $\frac{11}{4} \div \frac{1}{6} = \frac{11}{4} \times \frac{6}{1}$

3. Flip $\frac{1}{6}$ to $\frac{6}{1}$, change $\div$ to $\times$, cancel and multiply: $\frac{11}{\underset{2}{4}} \times \frac{\overset{3}{6}}{1} = \frac{11 \times 3}{2 \times 1} = \frac{33}{2}$

Here are a few division problems to try:

_____**28.** $\frac{1}{3} \div \frac{2}{3}$

_____**29.** $2\frac{3}{4} \div \frac{1}{2}$

_____**30.** $\frac{3}{5} \div 3$

_____**31.** $3\frac{3}{4} \div 2\frac{1}{3}$

Let's wrap this up with some real-life problems.

_____**32.** If four friends evenly split $6\frac{1}{2}$ pounds of candy, how many pounds of candy does each friend get?

    a. $\frac{8}{13}$ **b.** $1\frac{5}{8}$ **c.** $1\frac{1}{2}$ **d.** $1\frac{5}{13}$ **e.** 4

_____**33.** How many $2\frac{1}{2}$-pound chunks of cheese can be cut from a single 20-pound piece of cheese?

    a. 2   **b.** 4   **c.** 6   **d.** 8   **e.** 10

_____**34.** Ms. Goldbaum earned $36.75 for working $3\frac{1}{2}$ hours. What was her hourly wage?

    a. $10.00   **b.** $10.50   **c.** $10.75   **d.** $12.00   **e.** $12.25

DECIMALS

WHAT IS A DECIMAL?

A decimal is a special kind of fraction. You use decimals every day when you deal with money—$10.35 is a decimal that represents 10 dollars and 35 cents. The decimal point separates the dollars from the cents. Because there are 100 cents in one dollar, 1¢ is $\frac{1}{100}$ of a dollar, or $.01.

Each decimal digit to the right of the decimal point has a name:

Example: .1 = 1 tenth = $\frac{1}{10}$

                  .02 = 2 hundredths = $\frac{2}{100}$

                  .003 = 3 thousandths = $\frac{3}{1000}$

                  .0004 = 4 ten-thousandths = $\frac{4}{10,000}$

When you add zeroes after the rightmost decimal place, you don't change the value of the decimal. For example, 6.17 is the same as all of these:

6.170

6.1700

6.17000000000000000

If there are digits on both sides of the decimal point (like 10.35), the number is called a mixed decimal. If there are digits only to the right of the decimal point (like .53), the number is called a decimal. A whole number (like 15) is understood to have a decimal point at its right (15.). Thus, 15 is the same as 15.0, 15.00, 15.000, and so on.

CHANGING FRACTIONS TO DECIMALS

To change a fraction to a decimal, divide the bottom number into the top number after you put a decimal point and a few zeroes on the right of the top number. When you divide, bring the decimal point up into your answer.

Example: Change $\frac{3}{4}$ to a decimal.

1. Add a decimal point and 2 zeroes to the top number (3):

3.00

2. Divide the bottom number (4) into 3.00:

Bring the decimal point up into the answer:

$$\begin{array}{r} .75 \\ 4\overline{)3.00} \\ \underline{2\ 8} \\ 20 \\ \underline{20} \\ 0 \end{array}$$

3. The quotient (result of the division) is the answer:

.75

Some fractions may require you to add many decimal zeroes in order for the division to come out evenly. In fact, when you convert a fraction like $\frac{2}{3}$ to a decimal, you can keep adding decimal zeroes to the top number forever because the division will never come out evenly! As you divide 3 into 2, you'll keep getting 6's:

$$2 \div 3 = .6666666666 \text{ etc}$$

This is called a *repeating decimal* and it can be written as $.66\overline{6}$ or as $.66\frac{2}{3}$. You can approximate it as .67, .667, .6667, and so on.

CHANGING DECIMALS TO FRACTIONS

To change a decimal to a fraction, write the digits of the decimal as the top number of a fraction and write the decimal's name as the bottom number of the fraction. Then reduce the fraction, if possible.

Example: .018

1. Write 18 as the top of the fraction:

$\frac{18}{}$

2. Three places to the right of the decimal means *thousandths*, so write 1000 as the bottom number:

$\frac{18}{1000}$

3. Reduce by dividing 2 into the top and bottom numbers:

$\frac{18 \div 2}{1000 \div 2} = \frac{9}{500}$

Change these decimals or mixed decimals to fractions:

_____**35.** .005

_____**36.** 3.48

_____**37.** 123.456

COMPARING DECIMALS

Because decimals are easier to compare when they have the same number of digits after the decimal point, tack zeroes onto the end of the shorter decimals. Then all you have to do is compare the numbers as if the decimal points weren't there:

     Example: Compare .08 and .1

1. Tack one zero at the end of .1:   .10
2. To compare .10 to .08, just compare 10 to 8.
3. Since 10 is larger than 8, .1 is larger than .08.

ADDING AND SUBTRACTING DECIMALS

To add or subtract decimals, line them up so their decimal points are even. You may want to tack on zeroes at the end of shorter decimals so you can keep all your digits lined up evenly. Remember, if a number doesn't have a decimal point, then put one at the right end of the number.

     Example: $1.23 + 57 + .038$

1. Line up the numbers like this:

$$\begin{array}{r} 1.230 \\ 57.000 \\ +.038 \\ \hline \end{array}$$

2. Add: 58.268

     Example: $1.23 - .038$

1. Line up the numbers like this:

$$\begin{array}{r} 1.230 \\ -.038 \\ \hline \end{array}$$

2. Subtract: 1.192

Try these addition and subtraction problems:

_____**38.** $.905 + .02 + 3.075$

_____**39.** $.005 + 8 + .3$

_____**40.** $3.48 - 2.573$

_____**41.** $123.456 - 122$

_____**42.** Officer Peterson drove 3.7 miles to the state park. He then walked 1.6 miles around the park to make sure everything was all right. He got back into the car, drove 2.75 miles to check on a broken traffic light and then drove 2 miles back to the police station. How many miles did he drive in total?

a. 8.05   b. 8.45   c. 8.8   d. 10   e. 10.05

_____**43.** The average number of emergency room visits at City Hospital fell from 486.4 per week to 402.5 per week. By how many emergency room visits per week did the average fall?

a. 73.9   b. 83   c. 83.1   d. 83.9   e. 84.9

MULTIPLYING DECIMALS

To multiply decimals, ignore the decimal points and just multiply the numbers. Then count the total number of decimal digits (the digits to the *right* of the decimal point) in the numbers you're multiplying. Count off that number of digits in your answer beginning at the right side and put the decimal point to the *left* of those digits.

Example: 215.7×2.4

1. Multiply 2157 times 24:

$$
\begin{array}{r}
2157 \\
\times\ \ 24 \\
\hline
8628 \\
4314\ \ \\
\hline
51768 \\
\end{array}
$$

2. Because there are a total of 2 decimal digits in 215.7 and 2.4, count off 2 places from the right in 51768, placing the decimal point to the *left* of the last 2 digits: 517.68

If your answer doesn't have enough digits, tack zeroes on to the left of the answer.

Example: $.03 \times .006$

1. Multiply 3 times 6: $3 \times 6 = 18$

2. You need 5 decimal digits in your answer, so tack on 3 zeroes: 00018

3. Put the decimal point at the front of the number (which is 5 digits in from the right):   .00018

You can practice multiplying decimals with these:

_____**44.** $.05 \times .6$

_____**45.** $.053 \times 6.4$

_____**46.** $38.1 \times .0184$

_____ **47.** Joe earns $14.50 per hour. Last week he worked 37.5 hours. How much money did he earn that week?

    a. $518.00   **b.** $518.50   **c.** $525.00   **d.** $536.50   **e.** $543.75

_____ **48.** Nuts cost $3.50 per pound. Approximately how much will 4.25 pounds of nuts cost?

    a. $12.25   **b.** $12.50   **c.** $12.88   **d.** $14.50   **e.** $14.88

DIVIDING DECIMALS

To divide a decimal by a whole number, set up the division ($8\overline{).256}$) and immediately bring the decimal point straight up into the answer ($8\overline{).256}$). Then divide as you would normally divide whole numbers:

Example:
$$
\begin{array}{r}
.032 \\
8\overline{).256} \\
\underline{0} \\
25 \\
\underline{24} \\
16 \\
\underline{16} \\
0
\end{array}
$$

To divide any number by a decimal, there is an extra step to perform before you can divide. Move the decimal point to the very right of the number you're dividing by, counting the number of places you're moving it. Then move the decimal point the same number of places to the right in the number you're dividing into. In other words, first change the problem to one in which you're dividing by a whole number.

Example: $.06\overline{)1.218}$

1. Because there are 2 decimal digits in .06, move the decimal point 2 places to the right in both numbers and move the decimal point straight up into the answer:

    $.06.\overline{)1.21.8}$

2. Divide using the new numbers:

$$
\begin{array}{r}
20.3 \\
6\overline{)121.8} \\
\underline{12} \\
01 \\
\underline{00} \\
18 \\
\underline{18} \\
0
\end{array}
$$

Under certain conditions, you have to tack on zeroes to the right of the last decimal digit in number you're dividing into:

- If there aren't enough digits for you to move the decimal point to the right, or
- If the answer doesn't come out evenly when you do the division, or
- If you're dividing a whole number by a decimal. Then you'll have to tack on the decimal point as well as some zeroes.

Try your skills on these division problems:

_____**49.** $7\overline{)9.8}$

_____**50.** $.0004\overline{).0512}$

_____**51.** $.05\overline{)28.6}$

_____**52.** $.14\overline{)196}$

_____**53.** If James Worthington drove his truck 92.4 miles in 2.1 hours, what was his average speed in miles per hour?

a. 41   b. 44   c. 90.3   d. 94.5   e. 194.04

_____**54.** Mary Sanders walked a total of 18.6 miles in 4 days. On average, how many miles did she walk each day?

a. 4.15   b. 4.60   c. 4.65   d. 22.60   e. 74.40

PERCENTS

WHAT IS A PERCENT?

A percent is a special kind of fraction or part of something. The bottom number (the *denominator*) is always 100. For example, 17% is the same as $\frac{17}{100}$. Literally, the word *percent* means *per 100 parts*. The root *cent* means 100: a *cent*ury is 100 years, there are 100 *cents* in a dollar, etc. Thus, 17% means 17 parts out of 100. Because fractions can also be expressed as decimals, 17% is also equivalent to .17, which is 17 hundredths.

You come into contact with percents every day. Sales tax, interest, and discounts are just a few common examples.

If you're shaky on fractions, you may want to review the fraction section before reading further.

CHANGING A DECIMAL TO A PERCENT AND VICE VERSA

To change a decimal to a percent, move the decimal point two places to the **right** and tack on a percent sign (%) at the end. If the decimal point moves to the very right of the number, you don't have to write the decimal point. If there aren't enough places to move the decimal point, add zeroes on the **right** before moving the decimal point.

To change a percent to a decimal, drop off the percent sign and move the decimal point two places to the **left**. If there aren't enough places to move the decimal point, add zeroes on the **left** before moving the decimal point.

Try changing these decimals to percents:

_____**55.** .45

_____**56.** .008

_____**57.** .16$\frac{2}{3}$

Now change these percents to decimals:

_____**58.** 12%

_____**59.** 87$\frac{1}{2}$%

_____**60.** 250%

CHANGING A FRACTION TO A PERCENT AND VICE VERSA

To change a fraction to a percent, there are two techniques. Each is illustrated by changing the fraction $\frac{1}{4}$ to a percent:

Technique 1:   Multiply the fraction by 100%.
Multiply $\frac{1}{4}$ by 100%:

$$\frac{1}{\underset{1}{4}} \times \frac{\overset{25}{\cancel{100}}\%}{1} = 25\%$$

Technique 2:   Divide the fraction's bottom number into the top number; then move the decimal point two places to the **right** and tack on a percent sign (%).
Divide 4 into 1 and move the decimal point 2 places to the right:

$$4\overline{)1.00}^{\;.25} \qquad .25 = 25\%$$

To change a percent to a fraction, remove the percent sign and write the number over 100. Then reduce if possible.

Example: Change 4% to a fraction

1. Remove the % and write the fraction 4 over 100: $\frac{4}{100}$

2. Reduce: $\frac{4 \div 4}{100 \div 4} = \frac{1}{25}$

Here's a more complicated example: Change 16$\frac{2}{3}$% to a fraction

1. Remove the % and write the fraction 16$\frac{2}{3}$ over 100: $\frac{16\frac{2}{3}}{100}$

2. Since a fraction means "top number divided by bottom number," rewrite the fraction as a division problem: $16\frac{2}{3} \div 100$

3. Change the mixed number ($16\frac{2}{3}$) to an improper fraction ($\frac{50}{3}$): $\frac{50}{3} \div \frac{100}{1}$

4. Flip the second fraction ($\frac{100}{1}$) and multiply: $\overset{1}{\cancel{\frac{50}{3}}} \times \frac{1}{\underset{2}{\cancel{100}}} = \frac{1}{6}$

Try changing these fractions to percents:

_____**61.** $\frac{1}{8}$

_____**62.** $\frac{13}{25}$

_____**63.** $\frac{7}{12}$

Now change these percents to fractions:

_____**64.** 95%

_____**65.** $37\frac{1}{2}$%

_____**66.** 125%

Sometimes it is more convenient to work with a percentage as a fraction or a decimal. Rather than have to *calculate* the equivalent fraction or decimal, consider memorizing the equivalence table below. Not only will this increase your efficiency on the math test, but it will also be practical for real life situations.

CONVERSION TABLE

Decimal	%	Fraction
.25	25%	$\frac{1}{4}$
.50	50%	$\frac{1}{2}$
.75	75%	$\frac{3}{4}$
.10	10%	$\frac{1}{10}$
.20	20%	$\frac{1}{5}$
.40	40%	$\frac{2}{5}$
.60	60%	$\frac{3}{5}$
.80	80%	$\frac{4}{5}$
$.33\overline{3}$	$33\frac{1}{3}$%	$\frac{1}{3}$
$.66\overline{6}$	$66\frac{2}{3}$%	$\frac{2}{3}$

PERCENT WORD PROBLEMS

Word problems involving percents come in three main varieties:

- Find a percent of a whole.

    Example: What is 30% of 40?

- Find what percent one number is of another number.

    Example: 12 is what percent of 40?

- Find the whole when the percent of it is given.

    Example: 12 is 30% of what number?

While each variety has its own approach, there is a single shortcut formula you can use to solve each of these:

$$\frac{is}{of} = \frac{\%}{100}$$

The *is* is the number that usually follows or is just before the word *is* in the question.

The *of* is the number that usually follows the word *of* in the question.

The **%** is the number that in front of the **%** or *percent* in the question.

Or you may think of the shortcut formula as:

$$\frac{part}{whole} = \frac{\%}{100}$$

To solve each of the three varieties, we're going to use the fact that the **cross-products** are equal. The cross-products are the products of the numbers diagonally across from each other. Remembering that *product* means *multiply*, here's how to create the cross-products for the percent shortcut.

$$\frac{part}{whole} = \frac{\%}{100}$$
$$part \times 100 = whole \times \%$$

Here's how to use the shortcut with cross-products:

- Find a percent of a whole.

    What is 30% of 40?

    30 is the % and 40 is the *of* number: $\frac{is}{40} = \frac{30}{100}$

    Cross-multiply and solve for *is*: $is \times 100 = 40 \times 30$

    $is \times 100 = 1200$

    $\mathbf{12 \times 100 = 1200}$

    Thus, **12** *is* 30% of 40.

- Find what percent one number is of another number.

    12 is what percent of 40?

    12 is the *is* number and 40 is the *of* number: $\frac{12}{40} = \frac{\%}{100}$

    Cross-multiply and solve for %: $12 \times 100 = 40 \times \%$

    $1200 = 40 \times \%$

    $1200 = 40 \times \mathbf{30}$

    Thus, 12 is **30%** of 40.

- Find the whole when the percent of it is given.
  12 is 30% of what number?
  12 is the *is* number and 30 is the %: $\frac{12}{of} = \frac{30}{100}$
  Cross-multiply and solve for the *of* number: $12 \times 100 = of \times 30$
  $$1200 = of \times 30$$
  $$1200 = 40 \times 30$$

Thus 12 is 30% *of* 40.

You can use the same technique to find the percent increase or decrease. The *is* number is the actual increase or decrease, and the *of* number is the original amount.

Example: If a merchant puts his $20 hats on sale for $15, by what percent does he decrease the selling price?

1. Calculate the decrease, the *is* number: $\$20 - \$15 = \$5$
2. The *of* number is the original amount, $20
3. Set up the equation and solve for *of* by cross-multiplying: $\frac{5}{20} = \frac{\%}{100}$
$$5 \times 100 = 20 \times \%$$
$$500 = 20 \times \%$$
$$500 = 20 \times 25$$

4. Thus, the selling price is decreased by **25%**.

If the merchant later raises the price of the hats from $15 back to $20, $\frac{5}{15} = \frac{\%}{100}$
don't be fooled into thinking that the percent increase is also 25%! It's $5 \times 100 = 15 \times \%$
actually more, because the increase amount of $5 is now based on a lower $500 = 15 \times \%$
original price of only $15: $500 = 15 \times 33\frac{1}{3}$
Thus, the selling price is increased by **33%**.

Find a percent of a whole:

_____**67.** 1% of 25

_____**68.** 18.2% of 50

_____**69.** $37\frac{1}{2}$% of 100

_____**70.** 125% of 60

Find what percent one number is of another number.

_____**71.** 10 is what % of 20?

_____**72.** 4 is what % of 12?

_____**73.** 12 is what % of 4?

Find the whole when the percent of it is given.

_____**74.** 15% of what number is 15?

_____**75.** $37\frac{1}{2}$% of what number is 3?

_____**76.** 200% of what number is 20?

Now try your percent skills on some real life problems.

_____**77.** Last Monday, 20% of the 140-member nursing staff was absent. How many nurses were absent that day?
a. 14   b. 20   c. 28   d. 112   e. 126

_____**78.** 40% of Vero's postal service employees are women. If there are 80 women in Vero's postal service, how many men are employed there?
a. 32   b. 112   c. 120   d. 160   e. 200

_____**79.** Of the 840 crimes committed last month, 42 involved petty theft. What percent of the crimes involved petty theft?
a. .5%   b. 2%   c. 5%   d. 20%   e. 50%

_____**80.** Sam's Shoe Store put all of its merchandise on sale for 20% off. If Jason saved $10 by purchasing one pair of shoes during the sale, what was the original price of the shoes before the sale?
a. $12   b. $20   c. $40   d. $50   e. $70

ANSWERS TO MATH PROBLEMS

WORD PROBLEMS

1. a
2. d
3. d
4. e

FRACTIONS

5. $\frac{1}{4}$
6. $\frac{2}{5}$
7. $\frac{3}{8}$
8. 10
9. 6
10. 200
11. $\frac{11}{12}$
12. $\frac{55}{24}$ or $2\frac{7}{24}$
13. $7\frac{1}{4}$
14. $\frac{2}{15}$
15. $\frac{1}{8}$
16. $\frac{19}{12}$ or $1\frac{7}{12}$
17. a
18. b
19. $\frac{2}{15}$
20. $\frac{8}{35}$
21. $\frac{2}{3}$
22. $\frac{26}{15}$ or $1\frac{11}{15}$
23. 15
24. $\frac{33}{2}$ or $16\frac{1}{2}$
25. c
26. e
27. c
28. $\frac{1}{2}$
29. $5\frac{1}{2}$
30. $\frac{1}{5}$
31. $\frac{45}{28}$ or $1\frac{17}{28}$
32. b
33. d
34. b

DECIMALS

35. $\frac{5}{1000}$ or $\frac{1}{200}$
36. $3\frac{12}{25}$
37. $123\frac{456}{1000}$ or $123\frac{57}{125}$
38. 4
39. 8.305
40. .907
41. 1.456
42. b
43. d
44. .03
45. .3392
46. .70104
47. e
48. c
49. 1.4
50. 128
51. 572
52. 1400
53. b
54. c

PERCENTS

55. 45%
56. .8%
57. 16.67% or $16\frac{2}{3}$%
58. .12
59. .875
60. 2.5
61. 12.5% or $12\frac{1}{2}$%
62. 52%
63. 58.33% or $58\frac{1}{3}$%
64. $\frac{19}{20}$
65. $\frac{3}{8}$
66. $\frac{5}{4}$ or $1\frac{1}{4}$
67. $\frac{1}{4}$ or .25
68. 9.1
69. $37\frac{1}{2}$ or 37.5
70. 75
71. 50%
72. $33\frac{1}{3}$%
73. 300%
74. 100
75. 8
76. 10
77. c
78. c
79. c
80. d

C·H·A·P·T·E·R

WRITING

9

CHAPTER SUMMARY

This chapter gives vital help on writing an essay or a report for law enforcement exams, as well as on multiple-choice tests where you have to choose the most clearly written paragraph. Even if the exam you have to take doesn't test writing skills in these ways, your career as a law enforcement officer will require these skills.

 ost people would be stunned to learn that law enforcement officers spend up to a third of their duty time writing reports. Other professionals, such as lawyers and judges, base their actions and decisions on the data in these reports. Because of this, law enforcement candidates need solid writing skills.

KINDS OF WRITING QUESTIONS ON CIVIL SERVICE EXAMS

A civil service exam might test your writing skills in one of three ways:

- By asking you to write an essay from scratch
- By asking you to view a video (perhaps a dramatization of officers responding to a call) or listen to an interview, take notes, and write an incident report

- By asking you to choose from among several sentences the one that most clearly and accurately presents the facts

No matter which of the three methods is used, learning and applying a few basic principles will help you do well on this section of your test.

WRITING AN ESSAY

Your exam may actually have you write an essay not that different from the kinds of essays you might have written in school. This is the best way to tell whether you can use written language to express your ideas clearly. The most important thing to remember is to keep your writing simple and straightforward. You're writing to express yourself so that others can read and understand what you write. You're *not* writing to impress your high school English teacher. Use words most people will understand, and avoid long, drawn-out sentences that might confuse a reader.

CHOOSING A TOPIC

It's impossible to predict the questions, but chances are you'll be allowed to choose a general interest question most people could answer, such as:

- What events in your life caused you to choose law enforcement as a profession?
- Describe a person or event that has influenced your life.
- Describe a significant accomplishment in your life.
- Describe yourself.

Whatever the question, answer it by writing about something you know well. If you would enjoy having a conversation about the topic you're considering, it's probably a good choice.

Your time to write this essay will undoubtedly be limited. Start quickly and don't get too fancy. Starting is sometimes the hardest part, but if you begin with a thesis, you'll find writing much easier. A thesis is simply a sentence that *tells what the essay is about* and *forecasts how you will present your information.* The easiest way to write a thesis is to turn the question into a statement and add the main ideas. Take a look at these examples.

Question

How did you develop self-discipline?

Thesis

I learned self-discipline from taking music lessons and by caring for my younger siblings.

This thesis answers the question by suggesting the two ways the writer will present the information: writing about music lessons and writing about caring for siblings.

Question

Describe an event that taught you an important lesson.

Thesis

The car accident I had when I was 22 taught me that I was not immortal and that life is a precious gift.

This thesis tells specifically what the essay is going to be about—a car accident at age 22. It also forecasts how the writer will present the information: as a lesson about being mortal and as a lesson about the value of life. You may have noticed that the "question" isn't in the form of a question. That's common on tests.

Now try writing your own thesis statements for these two questions.

Question

Describe an event that taught you an important lesson.

Your Thesis
_____

Question

How did you develop self-discipline?

Your Thesis
_____

Do your thesis statements answer the question and forecast what your essay will cover? If so, you have written a thesis statement that will make the actual essay easier to write.

ORGANIZING YOUR IDEAS

The thesis establishes the destination and the direction for your essay; the essay will be easier to write when you know where you're going and how you're going to get there. Before you actually write the essay, take a few minutes to organize your thoughts and to make a quick outline. Choose two or three main ideas to write about in support of your thesis. Make a list of what you will write concerning each main idea. Once you've jotted down the ideas so you can see how they look, it's easier to consider the order. When you have to write an essay under timed testing conditions, it's best to begin with the strongest point first. Try to arrange the ideas in such a way that they can be easily hooked together, so your

essay will flow smoothly from one idea to another. This brief outline will make your essay easier to write.

Organize your ideas in paragraphs—units of thought that fully develop a single idea. Each paragraph should begin with a topic sentence that states the subject of the paragraph. The rest of the sentences in the paragraph should support, illustrate, or prove the topic sentence. These sentences can offer examples, narrate a sequence of events, explain an idea, or describe something.

WRITING THE ESSAY

You have a thesis, you have an outline, now all you need to do is write. Start with the topic sentence for your first paragraph, then follow it with several sentences that prove or develop the idea presented in the topic sentence.

Remember the purpose behind the essay. You're trying to show that you can **express** your ideas clearly. You're *not* out to impress anyone with your huge vocabulary or your ability to write long, involved, "intellectual-sounding" sentences. Just keep it simple. Write using complete sentences. Each sentence should present just one point in support of the topic sentence. If you keep your sentences short and specific, you're less likely to muddle your facts or make other mistakes that might distort the meaning or confuse the reader.

The topics you're given will most likely ask you to write about yourself. Use the "I, me" point of view as you write the essay to give it a natural, informal tone. The tone or attitude of your essay is important. You don't want your writing to be filled with slang or street language, but you don't want it to sound formal and stuffy either. It should sound like an educated person speaking in an informal situation, like a conversation. Think through each sentence before you write it. If it would sound awkward in a conversation, think of a way to rephrase the sentence before you write it.

Write using active verbs to make your essay more interesting. In a sentence with an active verb, the person or thing that performs the action is named before the verb, or the action word(s), in a sentence. The following examples illustrate the difference between active and passive verbs. The italicized words show who is performing the action. The underlined words are verbs.

Passive Verbs

I *was taken* to my first horse show by my *grandfather*.

I *was taught* to fish by my *mother* almost before *I was taught* to walk.

Active Verbs

My *grandfather took* me to my first horse show.

My *mother taught* me to fish almost before *I learned* to walk.

In each of the active verb sentences, the person performing the action is named first. If you look more closely at these examples, you'll notice that the active verb versions are shorter and clearer. They sound more like natural conversation. Strive for these qualities in your essay.

Finally, be concise and specific when you write. The best writing is that which clearly says the most using the fewest words. Avoid *general* statements that don't really say anything. Instead, write *specific* statements that give the reader a clear picture of what you have in mind. Detailed, *specific* language keeps readers interested and makes your ideas easier to remember. The following examples illustrate the difference.

General

My sister and I enjoyed each other's company as we were growing up. We had a lot of fun, and I will always remember her. We did interesting things and played fun games.

Specific

As children, my sister and I built rafts out of old barrels and tires, then tried to float them on the pond behind our house. I'll never forget playing war or hide-and-seek in the grove beside the pond.

The idea behind both of these versions is similar, but the specific example is more interesting and memorable. Be specific when you write.

Tips for Writing an Essay

- Keep it simple. Express, not impress.
- Start with a thesis. State the idea and forecast the direction.
- Organize first!
- Present ideas in paragraphs.
- Use the "I, me" point of view.
- Use active verbs.
- Be concise and specific.

LearningExpress

20 Academy Street, P.O. Box 7100, Norwalk, CT 06852-9879

To provide you with the best test prep, basic skills, and
career materials, we would appreciate your help.
Please answer the following questions and return this postage paid piece.
Thank you for your time!

Name : _____

Address : _____

_____

Age : _____   Sex : ☐ Male   ☐ Female

Highest Level of School Completed : ☐ High School ☐ College

1) I am currently :

    A student — Year/level: _____

    Employed — Job title: _____

    Other — Please explain: _____

2) Jobs/careers of interest to me are :

    1. _____

    2. _____

    3. _____

3) If you are a student, did your guidance/career counselor provide
you with job information/materials? _____

4) What newspapers and/or magazines do you subscribe to or
read regularly? _____

_____

5) Do you own a computer? _____

    If so, do you have Internet access? _____

    How often do you go on-line? _____

6) The last time you visited a bookstore, did you make a purchase?

_____

Have you purchased career-related materials from bookstores?

_____

7) Do you subscribe to cable TV? _____

    Which channels to you watch regularly (please give network
letters rather than channel numbers)?

_____

_____

8) Which radio stations do you listen to regularly (please give call
letters and city name)?

_____

_____

9) How did you hear about the book you just purchased from
LearningExpress?

    An ad? _____

    If so, where? _____

    An order form in the back of another book? _____

    A recommendation? _____

    A bookstore? _____

    Other? _____

10) Title of the book this card came from:

_____

LearningExpress books are also available in the test prep/study guide section of your local bookstore.

LEARNINGEXPRESS

The leading publisher of customized career and test preparation books!

LearningExpress is an affiliate of Random House, Inc.

Examine the sample question, thesis, and outline below to see this plan in action.

Question

Describe a well-known personality whom you admire.

Thesis

I admire Larry King because he is interesting to watch, because he handles controversial subjects well, and because he has staying power in a high-profile occupation.

I. Interesting to watch

   A. timely topics

   B. interesting guests

   C. humor

II. Handles controversial topics well

   A. straightforward and informative:

      doesn't gloss over tough issues

      doesn't "beat around the bush"

      probes for ideas behind opinions

   B. fair:

      tries to represent both sides of an issue equally

      steers callers and guests away from prejudicial assumptions

III. Staying power

   A. hasn't become sensational or extreme

   B. more impressed with his guests than with himself

   C. manages to stay fresh and enthusiastic night after night

Following the thesis in this essay, the writer would develop the essay in three paragraphs: one about how interesting Larry King is, one about how well he handles controversial issues, and one about the reasons behind his staying power as a media personality. The first sentence of each paragraph would be a complete sentence stating the main idea. Each subheading could be turned into a sentence supporting the topic sentence. The writer would give examples for each point.

You may want to write the essay outlined here for practice. Better yet, write your own thesis, outline, and essay about a personality you admire.

WRITING FROM VIDEO OR INTERVIEW NOTES

This kind of written exam most nearly represents the kind of writing law enforcement officers do in their jobs. You may see a video of officers responding to a call, or you may listen to a dramatization of an interview an officer might conduct. You'll be asked to take notes from which you'll write an incident report. This exercise tests your ability to record facts and events accurately and write about them clearly.

TAKING NOTES

Taking good notes is a vital first step. First, make sure you accurately record the most important information (who, what, when, where). Clearly identify the people involved and record all of the data the officers request: name, date of birth, address, age, etc. List every event, no matter how small or insignificant it may seem, in chronological order. If a time is mentioned, record the time next to the event.

When you write your report, you'll include "just the facts"—no conclusions, assumptions or predictions—so be sure to record specific data rather than the judgments you might make. For example, rather than writing, "violent suspect," record the specific behavior from which you drew that conclusion: "threw a bottle, knocked over a lamp and end table, said 'I'm gonna strangle you.'" Include as much specific detail as you can. Write clearly so you can decipher your notes later when it's time to write.

WRITING THE INCIDENT REPORT

The purpose of an incident report is to create a permanent record that clearly and accurately represents the facts. The same advice you read earlier about writing an essay applies to an incident report. Use plain English. Rather than trying to make your report sound "official" by writing jargon, use the ordinary language you would use in a conversation. Here, too, write short sentences with active verbs. Write in past tense (*asked, drove, went, escaped*) reporting action that has already happened. Keep your writing clear and crisp.

Begin with the most important information (who, what, when, where). Below are two versions of a beginning sentence. Which one is a better beginning for an incident report?

- On or approximately at 0335 hours on the date of February 5, 1996, Officer Barrett was dispatched to go to 628 Elm to investigate a noise disturbance complaint allegedly called in by one Andrea Jones, a resident at the above-stated address (date of birth January 18, 1971).
- At 3:35 a.m. on February 5, 1996, Officer Barrett arrived at 628 Elm and interviewed Andrea Jones (date of birth January 18, 1971), the resident who had called with a noise complaint.

If you chose the second option, you were correct. Although both sentences include identical information, the second one is shorter and easier to read. All of the important data appears in the first line. The writer uses active verbs and avoids unnecessary words. On the other hand, the first option is long and difficult to read. It contains unnecessary words (*On or approximately at, the date of, go to*). The writer uses passive verbs (*was dispatched*) and jargon (*allegedly, above-stated address*) probably in an attempt to sound "official." The effect is to make the writing cumbersome and unclear. The report should begin with the most important information stated clearly and concisely.

After you've recorded the vital information, write about what happened in chronological order. Remember to keep your sentences and paragraphs clear and concise. Record only the facts, not your interpretations or assumptions, and write in such a way that others who read what you have written will draw the same conclusions you did. Don't state the conclusions for them; let the facts speak for themselves. Facts take longer to record than conclusions, but they are infinitely more valuable in an incident report. The examples below illustrate the difference.

Conclusion

Strader was drunk.

Facts

Strader smelled strongly of alcohol, slurred his words when he spoke, and stumbled often as he walked.

Tips for Writing from Notes

- Take thorough, accurate notes.
- Begin with the most important information first.
- Use plain English.
- Use active verbs in past tense.
- Report events in chronological order.
- Include just the facts, not conclusions or assumptions.

CHOOSING THE BEST OPTION

Your writing skills may be tested in yet another way. You may be asked to read two or more written versions of the same information and to choose the one that most clearly presents accurate information. Check for accuracy first. If the facts are wrong, the answer is wrong, no matter how well-written the answer choice is. If the facts are accurately represented in several of the answer choices, then you must evaluate the writing itself. Here are a few tips for choosing the **best** answer.

1. The **best** answer will be written in plain English in such a way that most readers can understand it the first time through. If you read through an answer choice and find you need to reread it to understand what it says, look for a better option.
2. The **best** option will present the information in logical order, usually chronological order. If the order seems questionable or is hard to follow, look for a better option.
3. The **best** option will be written with active rather than passive verbs. Answer choices written with

passive verbs sound formal and stuffy. Look for an option that sounds like normal conversation. Here's an example.

Passive Voice

At 8:25 p.m., Officer Sanchez was dispatched to 18 Grand, an apartment complex, where a burglary had been reported by Milo Andrews, the manager.

Active Voice

At 8:25 p.m., Officer Sanchez responded to a burglary reported by Milo Andrews, the manager of an apartment complex at 18 Grand.

The first version uses the passive verbs "was dispatched" and "had been reported" rather than active verbs. Example 2 uses the active verb "responded."

4. The **best** answer contains clearly identified pronouns (*he, she, him, her, them,* etc.) that match the number of nouns they represent. First, the pronouns should be clearly identified.

Unclear

Ann Dorr and the officer went to the precinct house, where she made her report.
Bob reminded his father that he had an appointment.

Clear

Ann Dorr and the officer went to the precinct house, where the officer made her report.
Bob reminded his father that Bob had an appointment.

An answer choice with clearly identified pronouns is a better choice than one with uncertain pronoun references. Sometimes the noun must be repeated to make the meaning clear.

In addition, the pronoun must match the noun it represents. If the noun is singular, the pronoun must be singular. Similarly, if the noun is plural, the pronoun must match.

Mismatch

I stopped the driver to tell them a headlight was burned out.

Match

I stopped the driver to tell him a headlight was burned out.

In the first example, *driver* is singular but the pronoun *them* is plural. In the second, the singular pronoun *him* matches the word it refers to.

5. The **best** option is one in which the verb tense is consistent. Look for answer choices that describe the action as though it has already happened, using past tense verbs (mostly *-ed* forms). The verb tense must remain consistent throughout the passage.

Inconsistent

I searched the cell and find nothing unusual.

Consistent

I searched the cell and found nothing unusual.

The verbs *opened* and *found* are both in the past tense in the second version. In the first, *find*, in the present tense, is inconsistent with *opened*.

6. The **best** option will use words clearly. Watch for unclear modifying words or phrases such as the ones in the following sentences. Misplaced and dangling modifiers can be hard to spot because your brain tries to make sense of things as it reads. In the case of misplaced or dangling modifiers, you may make a logical connection that is not present in the words.

Dangling Modifiers

Nailed to the tree, Cedric saw a "No Hunting" sign.
Waddling down the road, we saw a skunk.

Clear Modifiers

Cedric saw a "No Hunting" sign nailed to a tree.
We saw a skunk waddling down the road.

In the first version of the sentences, it sounds like *Cedric* was nailed to a tree and *we* were waddling down the road. The second version probably represents the writer's intentions: the *sign* was nailed to a tree and the *skunk* was waddling.

Misplaced Modifier

A dog followed the boy who was growling and barking.
George told us about safe sex in the kitchen.

Clear Modifiers

A dog who was growling and barking followed the boy.
In the kitchen, George told us about safe sex.

Do you think the boy was growling and barking? Did George discuss avoiding sharp knives and household poisons? The second version of each sentence represents the real situation.

7. Finally, the **best** option will use words efficiently. Avoid answer choices that are redundant (repeat unnecessarily) or wordy. Extra words take up valuable time and increase the chances that facts will be misunderstood. In the following examples, the italicized words are redundant or unnecessary. Try reading the sentences without the italicized words.

Redundant

They refunded our money *back to us*.

We can proceed *ahead* with the plan we made *ahead of time*.

The car was red *in color*.

Wordy

The reason he pursued the car *was* because it ran a stoplight.

We didn't know what *it was* we were doing.

There are many citizens *who* obey the law.

In each case, the sentence is simpler and easier to read without the italicized words. When you find an answer choice that uses unnecessary words, look for a better option.

The BEST Option:

- Is ACCURATE
- Is written in plain English
- Presents information in a logical order
- Uses active verbs
- Has clearly identified pronouns that match the number of the nouns they represent
- Has a consistent verb tense
- Uses words clearly
- Uses words efficiently

Here are four sample multiple-choice questions. By applying the principles explained in this section, choose the best version of each of the four sets of sentences. The answers and a short explanation for each question are at the end of the chapter.

1.
   a. Vanover caught the ball. This was after it had been thrown by the shortstop. Vanover was the first baseman who caught the double-play ball. The shortstop was Hennings. He caught a line drive.
   b. After the shortstop Hennings caught the line drive, he threw it to the first baseman Vanover for the double play.
   c. After the line drive was caught by Hennings, the shortstop, it was thrown to Vanover at first base for a double play.
   d. Vanover the first baseman caught the flip from shortstop Hennings.

2.
   a. This writer attended the movie *Casino* starring Robert DeNiro.
   b. The movie *Casino* starring Robert DeNiro was attended by me.
   c. The movie *Casino* starring Robert DeNiro was attended by this writer.
   d. I attended the movie *Casino* starring Robert DeNiro.

3.

  a. They gave cereal boxes with prizes inside to the children.

  b. They gave cereal boxes to children with prizes inside.

  c. Children were given boxes of cereal by them with prizes inside.

  d. Children were given boxes of cereal with prizes inside by them.

4.

  a. After playing an exciting drum solo, the crowd rose to its feet and then claps and yells until the band plays another cut from their new album.

  b. After playing an exciting drum solo, the crowd rose to its feet and then clapped and yelled until the band played another cut from their new album.

  c. After the drummer's exciting solo, the crowd rose to its feet and then claps and yells until the band plays another cut from their new album.

  d. After the drummer's exciting solo, the crowd rose to its feet and then clapped and yelled until the band played another cut from their new album.

Whether you write an essay yourself or choose the **best** option written by someone else, remember the basic principles of good writing. Use them in your writing and look for them in the writing you read.

ANSWERS

1. **b.** Answer **a** is unnecessarily wordy and the order is not logical. Answer **c** is written using passive voice verbs. Answer **d** omits a piece of important information.

2. **d.** Both Answers **a** and **c** use the stuffy-sounding *this writer.* Answer **d** is best because it uses an active verb.

3. **a.** In both Answers **b** and **c** the modifying phrase *with prizes inside* is misplaced. Both Answers **c** and **d** are written in passive rather than active voice.

4. **d.** Both Answers **a** and **b** contain a dangling modifier, stating that the crowd played an exciting drum solo. Both Answers **b** and **c** mix past and present verb tense. Only Answer **d** has clearly written modifiers and a consistent verb tense.

ADDITIONAL RESOURCES

This chapter has touched on only a few aspects of learning to write clearly. If you need more assistance to prepare for the exam, or if you want to improve your writing skills for your career, you might want additional help. Many high schools and community colleges offer inexpensive writing courses for adults in their continuing education departments, or you may be able to find a teacher who is willing to tutor you for a modest fee. In addition, you might consult one of the following books.

- *The Handbook of Good English* by Edward D. Johnson (Washington Square Press)
- *Writing Skills in 20 Minutes a Day* by Judith Olson (LearningExpress, order information at the back of this book)
- *Smart English* by Anne Francis (Signet)
- *Writing Smart* by Marcia Lerner (Princeton Review)

VOCABULARY AND SPELLING

10

CHAPTER SUMMARY

Vocabulary and spelling are tested, at least indirectly, on most law enforcement exams. This chapter provides tips and exercises to help you improve your score in both areas.

 person's vocabulary is seen as a measure of an ability to express ideas clearly and precisely. Law enforcement officers must know the working vocabulary of the profession or have the tools for acquiring that vocabulary quickly. Spelling is regarded as a measure of a person's accuracy in presenting information. Law enforcement officers must be able to write correctly in order to communicate clearly. In addition, accurate spelling and a wide and flexible vocabulary are seen as the marks of thoughtful and well-educated people.

VOCABULARY

Many civil service exams test vocabulary. There are three basic kinds of questions.

■ Synonyms and antonyms: Identifying words that mean the same or the opposite of given words

- Context: Determining the meaning of a word or phrase by noting how it is used in a sentence or paragraph
- Word parts: Choosing the meaning suggested by a part of the word, such as a prefix or suffix

SYNONYM AND ANTONYM QUESTIONS

A word is a *synonym* of another word if it has the same or nearly the same meaning as the other word. *Antonyms* are words with opposite meanings. Test questions often ask you to find the synonym or antonym of a word. If you're lucky, the word will be surrounded by a sentence that helps you guess what the word means. If you're less lucky, you'll just get the word, and then you have to figure out what the word means without any help.

Questions that ask for synonyms and antonyms can be tricky because they require you to recognize the meaning of several words that may be unfamiliar—not only the words in the questions but also the answer choices. Usually the best strategy is to *look* at the structure of the word and to *listen* for its sound. See if a part of a word looks familiar. Think of other words you know that have similar key elements. How could those words be related?

Synonym Practice

Try your hand at identifying the word parts and related words in these sample synonym questions. Circle the word that means the same or about the same as the underlined word. Answers and explanations appear right after the questions.

1. a set of <u>partial</u> prints
   a. identifiable
   b. incomplete
   c. visible
   d. enhanced

2. <u>substantial</u> evidence
   a. inconclusive
   b. weighty
   c. proven
   d. alleged

3. <u>corroborated</u> the statement
   a. confirmed
   b. negated
   c. denied
   d. challenged

4. <u>ambiguous</u> questions
   a. meaningless
   b. difficult
   c. simple
   d. vague

Answers to Synonym Questions

The explanations are just as important as the answers, because they show you how to go about choosing a synonym if you don't know the word.

1. **b.** *Partial* means *incomplete*. The key part of the word here is *part*. A partial print is only part of the whole.
2. **b.** *Substantial* evidence is *weighty*. The key part of the word here is *substance*. Substance has weight.
3. **a.** *Corroboration* is *confirmation*. The key part of the word here is the prefix *co-*, which means *with* or *together*. Corroboration means that one statement fits with another.
4. **d.** *Ambiguous* questions are *vague* or uncertain. The key part of this word is *ambi-*, which means *two* or *both*. An ambiguous question can be taken two ways.

Antonym Practice

The main danger in answering questions with antonyms is forgetting that you are looking for *opposites* rather than synonyms. Most questions will include one or more synonyms as answer choices. The trick is to keep your mind on the fact that you are looking for the opposite of the word. If you're allowed to mark in the books or on the test papers, circle the word *antonym* or *opposite* in the directions to help you remember.

Otherwise, the same tactics that work for synonym questions work for antonyms as well: try to determine the meaning of part of the word or to remember a context where you've seen the word before.

Circle the word that means the *opposite* of the underlined word in the sentences below. Answers are immediately after the questions.

5. zealous pursuit
    a. envious
    b. eager
    c. idle
    d. comical

6. inadvertently left
    a. mistakenly
    b. purposely
    c. cautiously
    d. carefully

7. exorbitant prices
    a. expensive
    b. unexpected
    c. reasonable
    d. outrageous

8. compatible workers
    a. comfortable
    b. competitive
    c. harmonious
    d. experienced

9. belligerent attitude
    a. hostile
    b. reasonable
    c. instinctive
    d. ungracious

Answers to Antonym Questions

Be sure to read the explanations as well as the right answers.

5. **c.** *Zealous* means *eager*, so *idle* is most nearly opposite. Maybe you've heard the word *zeal* before. One trick in this question is not to be misled by the similar sounds of *zealous* and *jealous*. The other is not to choose the synonym, *eager*.

6. **b.** *Inadvertently* means *by mistake*, so *purposely* is the antonym. The key element in this word is the prefix *in-*, which usually means *not, the opposite of*. As usual, one of the answer choices (a) is a synonym.

7. **c.** The key element here is *ex-*, which means *out of* or *away from*. *Exorbitant* literally means "out of orbit." The opposite of an *exorbitant* or *outrageous* price would be a *reasonable* one.

8. **b.** The opposite of *compatible* is *competitive*. Here you have to distinguish among three words that contain the same prefix, *com-*, and to let the process of elimination work for you. The other choices are too much like synonyms.

9. **b.** The key element in this word is the root *belli-*, which means *warlike*. The synonym choices, then, are *hostile* and *ungracious*; the antonym is *reasonable*.

CONTEXT QUESTIONS

Context is the surrounding text in which a word is used. Most people use context to help them determine the meaning of an unknown word. A vocabulary question that gives you a sentence around the vocabulary word is usually easier to answer than one with little or no context. The surrounding text can help you as you look for synonyms for the specified words in the sentences.

The best way to take meaning from context is to look for key words in sentences or paragraphs that convey the meaning of the text. If nothing else, the context will give you a means to eliminate wrong answer choices that clearly don't fit. The process of elimination will often leave you with the correct answer.

Context Practice

Try these sample questions. Circle the word that best describes the meaning of the underlined word in the sentence.

10. The members of the jury were underlined appalled by the wild and uncontrolled behavior of the witness in the case.
    a. horrified
    b. amused
    c. surprised
    d. dismayed

11. Despite the fact that he appeared to have financial resources, the defendent claimed to be destitute.
    a. wealthy
    b. ambitious
    c. solvent
    d. impoverished

12. Though she was distraught over the disappearance of her child, the woman was calm enough to give the officer her description.
    a. punished
    b. distracted
    c. composed
    d. anguished

13. The unrepentant criminal expressed no remorse for his actions.
    a. sympathy
    b. regret
    c. reward
    d. complacency

Some tests may ask you to fill in the blank by choosing a word that fits the context. In the following questions, circle the word that best completes the sentence.

14. Professor Washington was a very_____ man known for his reputation as a scholar.
    a. stubborn
    b. erudite
    c. illiterate
    d. disciplined

15. His_____was demonstrated by his willingness to donate large amounts of money to worthy causes.
    a. honesty
    b. loyalty
    c. selfishness
    d. altruism

Answers to Context Questions

Check to see whether you were able to pick out the key words that help you define the target word, as well as whether you got the right answer.

10. a. The key words *wild* and *uncontrolled* signify *horror* rather than the milder emotions described by the other choices.

11. d. The key words here are *financial resources,* but this is a clue by contrast. The introductory *Despite the fact* signals that you should look for the opposite of the idea of having financial resources.

12. d. The key words here are *though* and *disappearance of her child,* signalling that you are looking for an opposite of *calm* in describing how the mother spoke to the officer. The only word strong enough to match the situation is *anguish.*

13. b. *Remorse* means *regret* for one's action. The part of the word here to beware of is the prefix *re-*. It doesn't signify anything in this word, though it often means *again* or *back*. Don't be confused by the two choices which also contain the prefix *re-*. The strategy here is to see which word sounds better in the sentence. The key words are *unrepentant* and *no,* indicating that you're looking for something that shows no repentance.

14. b. The key words here are *professor* and *scholarly.* Even if you don't know the word *erudite,* the other choices don't fit the description of the professor.

15. d. The key words here are *large amounts of money to worthy causes.* They give you a definition of the word you're looking for. Again, even if you don't know the word *altruism,* the other choices seem inappropriate to describe someone so generous.

For Non-Native Speakers of English

Be very careful not to be confused by the sound of words that may mislead you. Be sure you look at the word carefully, and pay attention to the structure and appearance of the word as well as its sound. You may be used to hearing English words spoken with an accent. The sounds of those words may be misleading in choosing a correct answer.

QUESTIONS ABOUT WORD PARTS

Some tests may ask you to find the meaning of a part of a word: roots, which are the main part of the word; prefixes, which go before the root word; or suffixes, which go after. Any of these elements can carry meaning or change the use of a word in a sentence. For instance, the suffix *-s* or *-es* can change the meaning of a noun from singular to plural: *boy, boys.* The prefix *un-* can change the meaning of a root word to its opposite: *necessary, unnecessary.*

To identify most parts of words, the best strategy is to think of words you already know which carry the same root, suffix, or prefix. Let what you know about those words help you to see the meaning in words that are less familiar.

Word Part Practice

Circle the word or phrase below that best describes the meaning of the underlined portion of the word. Answers appear after the questions.

16. <u>pro</u>active
   a. after
   b. forward
   c. toward
   d. behind

17. <u>re</u>cession
   a. against
   b. see
   c. under
   d. back

18. <u>con</u>temporary
   a. with
   b. over
   c. apart
   d. time

19. etymo<u>logy</u>
   a. state of
   b. prior to
   c. study of
   d. quality of

20. vanda<u>lize</u>
   a. to make happen
   b. to stop

   c. to fill
   d. to continue

Answers to Word Part Questions

Even if the word in the question was unfamiliar, you might have been able to guess the meaning of the prefix or suffix by thinking of some other word that has the same prefix or suffix.

16. b. Think of *propeller*. A propeller sends an airplane *forward*.

17. d. Think of *recall*: Manufacturers *recall* or *bring back* cars that are defective; people *recall* or *bring back* past events in memory.

18. a. Think of *congregation*: a group of people gather *with* each other in a house of worship.

19. c. Think of *biology*, the *study of* life.

20. a. Think of *scandalize*: to *make* something shocking *happen*.

WORDS THAT ARE EASILY CONFUSED

Vocabulary tests of any kind often contain words that are easily confused with each other. A smart test taker will be aware of these easily mixed up words or phrases:

accept: to receive willingly	**except:** exclude or leave out
complement: to complete	**compliment:** to say something flattering
council: a group that makes decisions	**counsel:** to give advice
contemptuous: having an attitude of contempt	**contemptible:** worthy of contempt
continuous: without interruption	**continual:** from time to time
emigrate: to move from	**immigrate:** to move to
ingenious: something clever	**ingenuous:** guileless or naive
oral: pertaining to the mouth	**verbal:** pertaining to language
persecute: to oppress someone	**prosecute:** to bring a legal action against someone

How to Answer Vocabulary Questions

- The key to answering vocabulary questions is to **notice and connect** what you do know to what you may not recognize.
- **Know your word parts**. You can recognize or make a good guess at the meanings of words when you see some suggested meaning in a root word, prefix, or suffix.
- **Note directions very carefully**. Remember when you are looking for opposites rather than synonyms.
- **Use a process of elimination**. Think of how the word makes sense in the sentence.
- **Don't be confused by words that sound like other words**, but may have no relation to the word you need.

A List of Word Parts

On the next page are some of the word elements seen most often in vocabulary tests. Simply reading them and their examples five to ten minutes a day will give you the quick recognition you need to make a good association with the meaning of an unfamiliar word.

SPELLING

Generally spelling tests are in a multiple-choice format. You will be given several possible spellings for a word and asked to identify the one that is correct. Thus, you must be able to see very fine differences between word spellings. The best way to prepare for a spelling test is to have a good grasp of the spelling fundamentals and be able to recognize when those rules don't apply.

Remember that English is full of exceptions in spelling. You have to develop a good eye to spot the errors.

Even though there are so many variant spellings for words in English, civil service tests generally are looking to make sure that you know and can apply the basic rules. Here are some of those rules to review:

- *i* before *e*, except after *c*, or when *ei* sounds like *a*
  Examples: piece, receive, neighbor
- *gh* can replace *f* or be silent
  Examples: enough, night
- Double the consonant when you add an ending
  Examples: forget/forgettable, shop/shopping
- Drop the *e* when you add *ing*
  Example: hope/hoping
- The spelling of prefixes and suffixes generally doesn't change
  Examples: project, propel, proactive

SPELLING PRACTICE

Here are some examples of how spelling would appear on a civil service test. Choose the word that is spelled correctly in the following sentences. This time there's no answer key. Instead, use your dictionary to find the right answers.

21. We went to an _____ of early Greek art.
    a. exibition
    b. exhibition
    c. excibition
    d. exebition

word element	meaning	example
ama	love	amateur
ambi	both	ambivalent, ambidextrous
aud	hear	audition
bell	war	belligerent, bellicose
bene	good	benefactor
cid/cis	cut	homicide, scissor
cogn/gno	know	knowledge, recognize
curr	run	current
flu/flux	flow	fluid, fluctuate
gress	to go	congress, congregation
in	not, in	ingenious
ject	throw	inject, reject
luc/lux	light	lucid, translucent
neo	new	neophyte
omni	all	omnivorous
pel/puls	push	impulse, propeller
pro	forward	project
pseudo	false	pseudonym
rog	ask	interrogate
sub	under	subjugate
spec/spic	look, see	spectator
super	over	superfluous
temp	time	contemporary, temporal
un	not, opposite	uncoordinated
viv	live	vivid

22. We will _____ go to the movies tonight.
   a. probly
   b. probbaly
   c. probely
   d. probably

23. We took _____ of pictures on our vacation.
   a. allot
   b. alot
   c. a lot
   d. alott

24. The high scorer had the greatest number of
_____ answers.
a. accurate
b. acurate
c. accuret
d. acccurit

25. He was warned not to use
_____ force.
a. exessive
b. excesive
c. excessive
d. excesive

USING SPELLING LISTS

Some test makers will give you a list to study before you take the test. If you have a list to work with, here are some suggestions.

- Divide the list into groups of three, five, or seven to study. Consider making flash cards of the words you don't know.
- Highlight or circle the tricky elements in each word.
- Cross out or discard any words that you already know for certain. Don't let them get in the way of the ones you need to study.
- Say the words as you read them. Spell them out in your mind so you can "hear" the spelling.

Here's a sample spelling list. These words are typical of the words that appear on exams. If you aren't given a list by the agency that's testing you, study this one.

achievement	doubtful	ninety
allege	eligible	noticeable
anxiety	enough	occasionally
appreciate	enthusiasm	occurred
asthma	equipped	offense
arraignment	exception	official
autonomous	fascinate	pamphlet
auxiliary	fatigue	parallel
brief	forfeit	personnel
ballistics	gauge	physician
barricade	grieve	politics
beauty	guilt	possess
beige	guarantee	privilege
business	harass	psychology
bureau	hazard	recommend
calm	height	referral
cashier	incident	recidivism
capacity	indict	salary
cancel	initial	schedule
circuit	innocent	seize
colonel	irreverent	separate
comparatively	jeopardy	specific
courteous	knowledge	statute
criticism	leisure	surveillance
custody	license	suspicious
cyclical	lieutenant	tentative
debt	maintenance	thorough
definitely	mathematics	transferred
descend	mortgage	warrant

How to Answer Spelling Questions

- **Sound out the word in your mind.** Remember that long vowels inside words usually are followed by single consonants: *sofa, total.* Short vowels inside words usually are followed by double consonants: *dribble, scissors.*
- **Give yourself auditory (listening) clues when you learn words.** Say *"Wed-nes-day"* or *"lis-ten"* or *"bus-i-ness"* to yourself so that you remember to add letters you do not hear.
- **Look at each part of a word.** See if there is a root, prefix or suffix that will always be spelled the same way. For example, in *uninhabitable, un-, in-,* and *-able* are always spelled the same. What's left is *habit,* a self-contained root word that's pretty easy to spell.

MORE PRACTICE IN VOCABULARY AND SPELLING

Here is a second set of practice exercises with samples of each kind of question covered in this chapter. Answers to all questions except spelling questions are at the end of the chapter. For spelling questions, use a dictionary.

Circle the word that means the same or nearly the same as the underlined word.

26. convivial company
    a. lively
    b. dull
    c. tiresome
    d. dreary

27. conspicuous behavior
    a. secret
    b. notable
    c. visible
    d. boorish

28. meticulous record-keeping
    a. dishonest
    b. casual
    c. painstaking
    d. careless

29. superficial wounds
    a. life-threatening
    b. bloody
    c. severe
    d. shallow

30. impulsive actions
    a. cautious
    b. imprudent
    c. courageous
    d. cowardly

Circle the word that is most nearly opposite in meaning to the underlined word.

31. amateur athlete
    a. professional
    b. successful
    c. unrivaled
    d. former

32. lucid opinions
    a. clear
    b. strong
    c. hazy
    d. heartfelt

33. traveling <u>incognito</u>
   a. unrecognized
   b. alone
   c. by night
   d. publicly

34. <u>incisive</u> reporting
   a. mild
   b. sharp
   c. dangerous
   d. insightful

35. <u>tactful</u> comments
   a. rude
   b. pleasant
   c. complimentary
   d. sociable

Using the context, choose the word that means the same or nearly the same as the underlined word.

36. Though he had little time, the student took <u>copious</u> notes in preparation for the test.
   a. limited
   b. plentiful
   c. illegible
   d. careless

37. Though flexible about homework, the teacher was <u>adamant</u> that papers be in on time.
   a. liberal
   b. casual
   c. strict
   d. pliable

38. The condition of the room after the party was <u>deplorable</u>.
   a. regrettable
   b. pristine
   c. festive
   d. tidy

Choose the word that best completes the following sentences.

39. Her position as a(n) _____ teacher took her all over the city.
   a. primary
   b. secondary
   c. itinerant
   d. permanent

40. Despite her promise to stay in touch, she remained _____ and difficult to locate.
   a. steadfast
   b. stubborn
   c. dishonest
   d. elusive

Choose the word or phrase closest in meaning to the underlined part of the word.

41. <u>uni</u>verse
   a. one
   b. three
   c. under
   d. opposite

42. <u>re</u>entry
   a. back
   b. push
   c. against
   d. forward

43. <u>bene</u>fit
   a. bad
   b. suitable
   c. beauty
   d. good

44. educat<u>ion</u>
   a. something like
   b. state of
   c. to increase
   d. unlike

45. urban<u>ite</u>
   a. resident of
   b. relating to
   c. that which is
   d. possessing

Circle the correct spelling of the word that fits in the blank.

46. The information was _____ to the action.
   a. irelevent
   b. irrevelent
   c. irrelevant
   d. irrevelent

47. He made no _____ to take the job.
   a. comittment
   b. commitment
   c. comitment
   d. comittmint

48. He made an income _____ to meet his needs.
   a. adaquate
   b. adequate
   c. adiquate
   d. adequet

49. We went to eat at a fancy new _____.
   a. restarant
   b. restaraunt
   c. restaurant
   d. resteraunt

50. The vote was _____ to elect the chairman.
   a. unannimous
   b. unanimous
   c. unanimus
   d. unaminous

ADDITIONAL RESOURCES

One of the best resources for any adult student is the public library. Many libraries have sections for adult learners or for those preparing to enter or change careers. Those sections contain skill books and review books on a number of subjects, including spelling and vocabulary. Here are some books you might consult:

- *504 Absolutely Essential Words* by Murray Bromberg et al. (Barron's)
- *All About Words: An Adult Approach to Vocabulary Building* by Maxwell Nurnberg and Morris Rosenblum (Mentor Books)
- *Checklists for Vocabulary Study* by Richard Yorkey (Longman)

- *Vocabulary and Spelling in 20 Minutes a Day* by Judith Meyers (LearningExpress, order information at the back of this book)
- *Word Watcher's Handbook* by Phyllis Martin (St. Martin's)
- *Spelling Made Simple* by Stephen V. Ross (Doubleday)
- *Spelling the Easy Way* by Joseph Mersand and Francis Griffith (Barron's)
- *Word Smart Revised* by Adam Robinson (The Princeton Review)

ANSWERS TO PRACTICE QUESTIONS

26. a.	**33.** d.	**40.** d.
27. c.	**34.** a.	**41.** a.
28. c.	**35.** a.	**42.** a.
29. d.	**36.** b.	**43.** d.
30. b.	**37.** c.	**44.** b.
31. a.	**38.** a.	**45.** a.
32. c.	**39.** c.	

MASSACHUSETTS STATE POLICE PRACTICE EXAM 2

11

CHAPTER SUMMARY

This is the second practice exam in this book based on the areas that the State of Massachusetts wants to see tested on the Massachusetts State Police written exam. After working through the instructional material in the previous chapters, take this test to see how much your score has improved since you took the first exam.

The exam that follows is based on the skills that the State of Massachusetts plans to assess. Although the actual exam may differ somewhat from the exam you're about to take, you should find that most of the same skills are tested. The test includes 100 multiple-choice questions on memorization, reading comprehension, logic and reasoning, basic mathematics, and writing skills.

For this practice exam, simulate the actual test-taking experience as much as possible. Find a quiet place to work where you won't be interrupted. Tear out the answer sheet on the next page, get out your number 2 pencils to fill in the circles with, and set a timer or stopwatch for ten minutes to study the memorization material. When your ten minutes are up, reset your timer for two and a half hours for taking the entire exam.

After the exam, use the answer key that follows it to see how you did and to find out why the correct answers are correct. The answer key is followed by a section on how to score your exam.

1.	(a)	(b)	(c)	(d)		36.	(a)	(b)	(c)	(d)		71.	(a)	(b)	(c)	(d)
2.	(a)	(b)	(c)	(d)		37.	(a)	(b)	(c)	(d)		72.	(a)	(b)	(c)	(d)
3.	(a)	(b)	(c)	(d)		38.	(a)	(b)	(c)	(d)		73.	(a)	(b)	(c)	(d)
4.	(a)	(b)	(c)	(d)		39.	(a)	(b)	(c)	(d)		74.	(a)	(b)	(c)	(d)
5.	(a)	(b)	(c)	(d)		40.	(a)	(b)	(c)	(d)		75.	(a)	(b)	(c)	(d)
6.	(a)	(b)	(c)	(d)		41.	(a)	(b)	(c)	(d)		76.	(a)	(b)	(c)	(d)
7.	(a)	(b)	(c)	(d)		42.	(a)	(b)	(c)	(d)		77.	(a)	(b)	(c)	(d)
8.	(a)	(b)	(c)	(d)		43.	(a)	(b)	(c)	(d)		78.	(a)	(b)	(c)	(d)
9.	(a)	(b)	(c)	(d)		44.	(a)	(b)	(c)	(d)		79.	(a)	(b)	(c)	(d)
10.	(a)	(b)	(c)	(d)		45.	(a)	(b)	(c)	(d)		80.	(a)	(b)	(c)	(d)
11.	(a)	(b)	(c)	(d)		46.	(a)	(b)	(c)	(d)		81.	(a)	(b)	(c)	(d)
12.	(a)	(b)	(c)	(d)		47.	(a)	(b)	(c)	(d)		82.	(a)	(b)	(c)	(d)
13.	(a)	(b)	(c)	(d)		48.	(a)	(b)	(c)	(d)		83.	(a)	(b)	(c)	(d)
14.	(a)	(b)	(c)	(d)		49.	(a)	(b)	(c)	(d)		84.	(a)	(b)	(c)	(d)
15.	(a)	(b)	(c)	(d)		50.	(a)	(b)	(c)	(d)		85.	(a)	(b)	(c)	(d)
16.	(a)	(b)	(c)	(d)		51.	(a)	(b)	(c)	(d)		86.	(a)	(b)	(c)	(d)
17.	(a)	(b)	(c)	(d)		52.	(a)	(b)	(c)	(d)		87.	(a)	(b)	(c)	(d)
18.	(a)	(b)	(c)	(d)		53.	(a)	(b)	(c)	(d)		88.	(a)	(b)	(c)	(d)
19.	(a)	(b)	(c)	(d)		54.	(a)	(b)	(c)	(d)		89.	(a)	(b)	(c)	(d)
20.	(a)	(b)	(c)	(d)		55.	(a)	(b)	(c)	(d)		90.	(a)	(b)	(c)	(d)
21.	(a)	(b)	(c)	(d)		56.	(a)	(b)	(c)	(d)		91.	(a)	(b)	(c)	(d)
22.	(a)	(b)	(c)	(d)		57.	(a)	(b)	(c)	(d)		92.	(a)	(b)	(c)	(d)
23.	(a)	(b)	(c)	(d)		58.	(a)	(b)	(c)	(d)		93.	(a)	(b)	(c)	(d)
24.	(a)	(b)	(c)	(d)		59.	(a)	(b)	(c)	(d)		94.	(a)	(b)	(c)	(d)
25.	(a)	(b)	(c)	(d)		60.	(a)	(b)	(c)	(d)		95.	(a)	(b)	(c)	(d)
26.	(a)	(b)	(c)	(d)		61.	(a)	(b)	(c)	(d)		96.	(a)	(b)	(c)	(d)
27.	(a)	(b)	(c)	(d)		62.	(a)	(b)	(c)	(d)		97.	(a)	(b)	(c)	(d)
28.	(a)	(b)	(c)	(d)		63.	(a)	(b)	(c)	(d)		98.	(a)	(b)	(c)	(d)
29.	(a)	(b)	(c)	(d)		64.	(a)	(b)	(c)	(d)		99.	(a)	(b)	(c)	(d)
30.	(a)	(b)	(c)	(d)		65.	(a)	(b)	(c)	(d)		100.	(a)	(b)	(c)	(d)
31.	(a)	(b)	(c)	(d)		66.	(a)	(b)	(c)	(d)						
32.	(a)	(b)	(c)	(d)		67.	(a)	(b)	(c)	(d)						
33.	(a)	(b)	(c)	(d)		68.	(a)	(b)	(c)	(d)						
34.	(a)	(b)	(c)	(d)		69.	(a)	(b)	(c)	(d)						
35.	(a)	(b)	(c)	(d)		70.	(a)	(b)	(c)	(d)						

MASSACHUSETTS STATE POLICE EXAM 2

You have 10 minutes to study the following Wanted Posters. When the 10 minutes are up, turn the page and proceed with taking the exam.

MISSING
Leonard Prescott Smith

DESCRIPTION:

> Age: 78
> Race: White
> Height: 6'0"
> Weight: 185 lb.
> Hair: Bald
> Eyes: Green

REMARKS: Alzheimer's patient last seen in lobby of Hillside Nursing Home on Christmas Day. Has been found wandering in Red Rock Park on other occasions.

IF LOCATED: Call Barnstable Police Department, Barnstable, Massachusetts, at 508-555-8000.

WANTED
Denise Gibbons

ALIASES: Dipsey Gibbons; Dee Gibbs

WANTED BY: Hays County Parole Board

CHARGES: Violation of Parole

DESCRIPTION:

     Age: 26

     Race: White

     Height: 5'5"

     Weight: 125 lb.

     Hair: Blond

     Eyes: Hazel

IDENTIFYING SCARS OR MARKS: Six-inch surgical scar on front left knee; needle marks on inner right arm.

REMARKS: Known prostitute. Frequents Shady Grove area. Is thought to be active heroin addict. Last seen with short, purple-tinted hair. May head for sister's home in Bangor, Maine.

CAUTION: Has been known to carry knives and will fight police. Handle with caution.

WANTED
Jamil Hassid

ALIASES: Jay Hassid
WANTED BY: FBI
CHARGES: Kidnapping
DESCRIPTION:

       Age: 22
       Race: White
       Height: 5'10"
       Weight: 165 lb.
       Hair: Black
       Eyes: Black

IDENTIFYING SCARS OR MARKS: Thin scar along left cheek.
REMARKS: Last known employer, Lucky Limo Service in Quincy, Massachusetts. Frequently seen with full black beard and mustache. Speaks with thick mid-Eastern accent.
CAUTION: Hassid is known to carry a .45 mm Browning.

WANTED
Louis James Serna

ALIASES: L. J. Serna

WANTED BY: Boston Police Department

CHARGES: Assault

DESCRIPTION:

> Age: 17
>
> Race: Hispanic
>
> Height: 5'6"
>
> Weight: 120 lb.
>
> Hair: Black
>
> Eyes: Black

IDENTIFYING SCARS OR MARKS: Tattoos of a tear drop at base of left eye, "Angie" on right upper shoulder, and snake curling around left wrist.

REMARKS: Latino Riders gang member. Limps heavily on right leg.

WANTED
Alice Faye Bunn

ALIASES: Allie Jones

WANTED BY: Coal County Sheriff's Department

CHARGES: Abuse of the Elderly

DESCRIPTION:

> Age: 40
>
> Race: White
>
> Height: 5'7"
>
> Weight: 170 lb.
>
> Hair: Brunette
>
> Eyes: Blue

IDENTIFYING SCARS OR MARKS: Burn scars along top of right hand.

REMARKS: Frequently works as a nurse's aide. Last seen in Tempe, Arizona, but is believed to be en route to New Haven, Connecticut.

PART ONE: MEMORIZATION

Questions 1–20 are based on the Wanted Posters you have just studied. **Do not turn back to the Wanted posters to answer these questions.** When you finish Part One, continue with the rest of the exam.

1. Denise Gibbons is wanted for
   a. armed robbery
   b. fraud
   c. sexual assault
   d. violation of parole

2. Leonard Prescott Smith is
   a. Middle Eastern
   b. white
   c. Hispanic
   d. black

3. Leonard Prescott Smith has
   a. a mostly bald head
   b. a tattoo near his eye
   c. missing front teeth
   d. a scar on his cheek

4. Louis James Serna also goes by the name
   a. A.J. Serna
   b. Allie Jones
   c. L.J. Serna
   d. Louie Serna

5. Jamil Hassid's last known employer was
   a. L.J.'s Limo Service
   b. Lucky Limo Service
   c. Smith's Limo Service
   d. Hillside Limo Service

6. Alice Faye Bunn is wanted for
   a. kidnapping
   b. violation of parole
   c. abuse of the elderly
   d. assault

7. Denise Gibbons' hair is
   a. spiked on top
   b. curly
   c. dyed blond
   d. wavy

8. Louis Serna's snake tattoo is located on his
   a. right shoulder
   b. chest
   c. forehead
   d. left wrist

9. Alice Bunn is believed to be en route to
   a. Quincy, Massachusetts
   b. Tempe, Arizona
   c. Barnstable, Massachusetts
   d. New Haven, Connecticut

10. Hassid's scar runs
    a. vertically down his chin
    b. vertically down his right cheek
    c. horizontally along his left cheek
    d. horizontally along his forehead

11. Which of the following is true of Smith?
    a. He is wanted for violation of parole.
    b. He is an Alzheimer's patient.
    c. He is armed and dangerous.
    d. He is a former nursing home employee.

12. Serna has been seen wearing
    a. a scarf around his head
    b. a t-shirt
    c. a heavy jacket
    d. a cross around his neck

13. Which two suspects are known to carry weapons?
   a. Hassid and Bunn
   b. Gibbons and Serna
   c. Serna and Bunn
   d. Gibbons and Hassid

14. Which suspect walks with a limp?
   a. Smith
   b. Hassid
   c. Serna
   d. Bunn

15. Which two suspects are in their twenties?
   a. Smith and Hassid
   b. Gibbons and Hassid
   c. Bunn and Hassid
   d. Gibbons and Bunn

16. Which two suspects have black hair and black eyes?
   a. Gibbons and Bunn
   b. Hassid and Bunn
   c. Serna and Gibbons
   d. Hassid and Serna

17. Of the people listed below, which is tallest?
   a. Smith
   b. Hassid
   c. Bunn
   d. Serna

18. Which suspect is known to carry a gun?
   a. Serna
   b. Gibbons
   c. Hassid
   d. Bunn

19. Based on the information in the wanted posters, which of the following is TRUE?
   a. Bunn is the only suspect with blue eyes.

   b. Serna is the only suspect with brown eyes.
   c. Bunn and Gibbons both have blue eyes.
   d. Smith and Gibbons both have hazel eyes.

20. Based on the information in the wanted posters, which of the following is FALSE?
   a. Gibbons wears a nose ring.
   b. Serna has a tattoo of the name "Angie."
   c. Serna and Hassid both have beards.
   d. Bunn wears glasses.

PART TWO: READING COMPREHENSION

Following are several reading passages. Answer the questions that come after each, based solely on the information in the passage.

The rules for obtaining evidence, set down in state and federal law, usually come to our attention when they work to the advantage of defendants in court, but these laws were not created with the courtroom in mind. They were formulated with the pragmatic intent of shaping police procedure before the arrest, in order to ensure justice, thoroughness, and the preservation of civil liberties. A good law enforcement officer must be as well schooled in the rules for properly obtaining evidence as is a defense lawyer, or risk losing a conviction. When a case is thrown out of court or a defendant is released because of these evidentiary "technicalities," we are often angered and mystified, but we are not always aware of how these rules of evidence shape police procedure in positive ways every day.

21. The main idea of this passage is that
   a. the rules of evidence protect the rights of defendants at trial
   b. police officers should know the rules of evidence

   c. rules of evidence help shape police proce-
     dure

   d. the rules of evidence have more positive than
     negative effects

22. According to the passage, rules of evidence are
designed to ensure all of the following EXCEPT
   a. meticulousness in gathering evidence
   b. proof of guilt
   c. protection of individual rights
   d. fairness of treatment

23. According to the passage, why should a law
enforcement officer know the rules of evidence?
   a. The rules protect the rights of the accused.
   b. The public does not appreciate the rules'
     importance.
   c. An officer must follow the rules to obtain a
     conviction.
   d. Following the rules protects officers from
     accusations of misconduct.

24. In saying that the intent of rules of evidence is
"pragmatic," the author most likely means that
   a. the focus of the rules is on police procedures
     in the field rather than on legal maneuvers in
     court
   b. the practical nature of the rules enables
     lawyers to use them in court to protect
     defendants
   c. the framers of these rules designed them to
     maintain idealistic standards of fairness
   d. the rules are often misused in court because
     of their limited scope

Evidence concerning the character of a witness
must be limited to questions of truthfulness. The credibility of a witness can be attacked by any party, and by
evidence of a prior conviction for a felony, so long as
the relevance of the conviction to the question of truthfulness is deemed by the court to outweigh the prejudicial damage caused to the witness. If, for example, the
witness is guilty of some crime which the jury might
find repugnant but which is not relevant to the witness's
credibility, this would be deemed unacceptably prejudicial. The elements of credibility which can be
impeached are perception, memory, clarity, and sin-
cerity. Law enforcement officers should not base an
arrest on the testimony of an untruthful or otherwise
unreliable witness—a witness who is mentally unsta-
ble, senile, or intoxicated, for example. Officers should
recognize that any case based on the testimony of a witness with prior felony convictions is vulnerable to dis-
missal.

25. What is the primary purpose of the passage?
   a. to review the criteria for impeaching the
     credibility of a witness
   b. to argue for the importance of determining
     the credibility of a witness before arresting a
     suspect
   c. to raise questions concerning the reliability
     of witnesses with prior convictions.
   d. to teach law enforcement officers proper wit-
     ness interrogation techniques

26. Which of the following would not be admissible to impeach the credibility of a witness testifying at an embezzlement trial?
   a. proof of a felony conviction
   b. a psychiatric evaluation
   c. a neighbor's claim that the witness is a liar
   d. a claim that the witness is prone to spousal
     abuse

27. According to the passage, why shouldn't the police base their case on the testimony of an untruthful witness?

a. The accused might be innocent.

b. The case might be dismissed.

c. The police will be embarrassed in court.

d. The police will be vulnerable to a lawsuit.

28. Which of the following witnesses would be LEAST likely to be vulnerable to having their credibility impeached, according to the criteria set forth in the passage?

a. a nearsighted person who wasn't wearing glasses

b. an alcoholic

c. a petty thief

d. a person with a psychiatric history

Law enforcement officers must read suspects their Miranda rights upon taking them into custody. When a suspect who is merely being questioned incriminates himself, he might later claim to have been in custody, and seek to have the case dismissed on the grounds of having been unapprised of his Miranda rights. In such cases, a judge must make a determination as to whether or not a reasonable person would have believed himself to have been in custody, based on certain criteria. The judge must determine whether the suspect was questioned in a threatening manner (for example, if the suspect was seated while both officers remained standing) and whether the suspect was aware that he or she was free to leave at any time. Officers must be aware of these criteria and take care not to give suspects grounds for later claiming they believed themselves to be in custody.

29. What is the main idea of the passage?

a. Officers must remember to read suspects their Miranda rights.

b. Judges, not law enforcement officers, make the final determination as to whether or not a suspect was in custody.

c. Officers who are merely questioning a suspect must not give the suspect the impression that he or she is in custody.

d. Miranda rights needn't be read to all suspects before questioning.

30. When is a suspect not in custody?

a. when free to refuse to answer questions

b. when free to leave the police station

c. when apprised of his or her Miranda rights

d. when not apprised of his or her Miranda rights

31. When must police officers read Miranda rights to a suspect?

a. while questioning the suspect

b. before taking the suspect to the police station

c. while placing the suspect under arrest

d. before releasing the suspect

32. An officer who is questioning a suspect who is not under arrest must

a. read the suspect his Miranda rights

b. inform the suspect that he is free to leave

c. advise the suspect of his right to a lawyer

d. allow the suspect a phone call

Hearsay evidence, which is the secondhand reporting of a statement, is allowed in court only when the truth of the statement is irrelevant. Hearsay that depends on the statement's truthfulness is inadmissible because the witness does not appear in court and swear an oath to tell the truth, his or her demeanor when making the statement is not visible to the jury, the accuracy of the statement cannot be tested under cross-examination, and to introduce it would be to deprive the accused of the constitutional right to confront the accuser. Hearsay is admissible, however, when the truth of the statement is unimportant. If, for example, a defendant claims to have been unconscious at a certain time, and a witness claims that the defendant actually spoke to her at that time, this evidence would be admissible because the truth of what the defendant actually said is irrelevant.

33. The main purpose of the passage is to
   a. explain why hearsay evidence abridges the rights of the accused
   b. question the truth of hearsay evidence
   c. argue that rules about the admissibility of hearsay evidence should be changed
   d. specify which use of hearsay evidence is inadmissible and why

34. Which of the following is NOT a reason given in the passage for the inadmissibility of hearsay evidence?
   a. Rumors are not necessarily credible.
   b. The person making the original statement was not under oath.
   c. The jury should be able to watch the gestures and facial expressions of the person making the statement.
   d. The person making the statement cannot be cross-examined.

35. How does the passage explain the proper use of hearsay evidence?
   a. by listing a set of criteria
   b. by providing a hypothetical example
   c. by referring to the Constitution
   d. by citing case law

36. The passage suggests that the criterion used for deciding that most hearsay evidence is inadmissible was most likely
   a. the unreliability of most hearsay witnesses
   b. the importance of physical evidence to corroborate witness testimony
   c. concern for discerning the truth in a fair manner
   d. doubt about the relevance of hearsay testimony

Most criminals do not suffer from anti-social personality disorder; however, nearly all persons with this disorder have been in trouble with the law. Sometimes labeled "sociopaths," they are a grim problem for society. Their crimes range from con games to murder, and they are set apart by what appears to be a complete lack of conscience. Often attractive and charming, and always inordinately self-confident, they nevertheless demonstrate a disturbing emotional shallowness, as if they had been born without a faculty as vital as sight or hearing. These individuals are not legally insane, nor do they suffer from the distortions of thought associated with mental illness; however, some experts believe they are mentally ill. If so, it is an illness that is exceptionally resistant to treatment, particularly since these individuals have a marked inability to learn from the past. It is this latter trait that makes them a special problem for law enforcement officials. Their ability to mimic true emotion enables them to convince prison officials, judges, and psychiatrists that they feel remorse. When released from incarceration, however, they go back to their old tricks, to their con games, their impulsive destructiveness, and their sometimes lethal deceptions.

37. Based on the passage, which of the following is likely NOT a characteristic of the person with anti-social personality disorder?
   a. delusions of persecution
   b. feelings of superiority
   c. inability to suffer deeply
   d. inability to feel joy

38. Which of the following careers would probably best suit the person with anti-social personality?
   a. soldier with ambition to make officer
   b. warden of a large penitentiary
   c. loan officer in a bank
   d. salesperson dealing in non-existent real estate

39. Based on the passage, which of the following words best sums up the inner emotional life of the person with anti-social personality?
   a. angry
   b. empty
   c. anxious
   d. repressed

40. According to the passage, which of the following characteristics is most helpful to the person with anti-social personality in getting out of trouble with the law?
   a. inability to learn from the past
   b. ability to mimic the emotions of others
   c. attractiveness and charm
   d. indifference to the suffering of others

Stalking—the "willful, malicious, and repeated following and harassing of another person"—is probably as old as human society. But in the United States, until 1990, no substantive law existed to protect the stalking victim. The most that law enforcement officials could do was arrest the stalker for a minor offense or suggest the victim obtain a restraining order, a civil remedy often ignored by the offender. (One of the Orange County victims mentioned below was shot by her husband while carrying a restraining order in her purse.) Frightened victims had their worst fears confirmed: They would have to be harmed—or killed—before anything could be done

In 1990, however, partly because of the 1989 stalker-murder of television star Rebecca Schaeffer, and partly because of the 1990 stalker-murders of four Orange County women in a single six-week period, California drafted the first anti-stalking law. Now most states have similar laws.

The solution is not perfect: Some stalkers are too mentally deranged or obsessed to fear a prison term. There is danger, however small, of abuse of the law, particularly in marital disputes. Most importantly, both police and society need better education about stalking, especially about its often sexist underpinnings. (The majority of stalking victims are women terrorized by former husbands or lovers.)

But the laws are a start, carrying with them felony penalties of up to ten years in prison for those who would attempt to control or possess others through intimidation and terror.

41. Which of the following best expresses the main idea of the passage?
   a. More education is needed about sexism, as it is the most important element in the crime of stalking.

b. Stalking is thought of as a new kind of crime, but has probably existed throughout human history.

c. The new anti-stalking legislation is an important weapon against the crime of stalking, though it is not the complete answer.

d. Today almost every state in the U.S. has an effective, if not perfect, anti-stalking law.

42. Based on the passage, which of the following is likely the most common question asked of police by stalking victims prior to 1990?
    a. How can I get a restraining order?
    b. Does he have to hurt me before you'll arrest him?
    c. Why is this person stalking me?
    d. Is it legal for me to carry a weapon in my purse?

43. Which of the following is NOT mentioned in the passage as a weakness in the new anti-stalking legislation?
    a. The laws alone might not deter some stalkers.
    b. A person might be wrongly accused of being a stalker.
    c. Neither the police nor the public completely understand the crime.
    d. Victims do not yet have adequate knowledge about anti-stalking laws.

44. Based on the passage, which of the following is the main reason restraining orders are ineffective in preventing stalking?
    a. No criminal charges can be leveled against the violator.
    b. Until 1990, restraining orders could not be issued against stalkers.

c. Law enforcement officials do not take such orders seriously.

d. Restraining orders apply only to married couples.

45. Based on the information in the passage, which of the following did the murders of Rebecca Schaeffer and the Orange County woman mentioned in the first paragraph have in common?
    a. Both murders provided impetus for anti-stalking laws.
    b. Both victims sought, but could not obtain, legal protection.
    c. Both victims were stalked and killed by a husband or lover.
    d. Both murders were the result of sexism.

PART THREE: LOGIC AND REASONING

46. State troopers are in pursuit of a stolen vehicle. Trooper Baker is directly behind the stolen car. Trooper Lopez is behind Baker; Trooper O'Malley is behind Lopez. Trooper Reinhart is ahead of the stolen car and coming from the opposite direction. Trooper Reinhart makes a U-turn and joins the pursuit. He pulls in behind Trooper Lopez. Trooper Baker pulls up on the driver's side of the stolen vehicle and Trooper Lopez pulls up on the other side. Which officer is directly behind the vehicle?
    a. Baker
    b. Lopez
    c. Reinhart
    d. O'Malley

47. Citizens living near Route 1 in Foxboro have been complaining about drag racers in the area, and Trooper Yang has noticed an increase in traffic fatalities along this roadway. Which situation would most likely cause her to investigate possible drag racing?
   a. Two vehicles, exceeding the speed limit, come toward her cruiser at a high rate of speed, side-by-side.
   b. Two trucks, driving at the speed limit, come toward her cruiser, one passing the other with two wheels on the shoulder.
   c. Two cars full of teenagers, driving at the speed limit, pass her cruiser; then immediately one car passes the other, honking its horn.
   d. A red sports car passes her cruiser driving slightly below the speed limit, but the driver honks the horn and speeds up as the car goes by.

Answer question 48 on the basis of the following definition.

It's a crime to harm or threaten to harm someone who is about to report a crime. This is called **Intimidation of a Witness.**

48. Which situation below is the best example of Intimidation of a Witness?
   a. Sally tells Larry she is going to hire someone to beat him up if he tells anyone her secret.
   b. Ernie breaks Alfonso's nose with his fist, and then tells Alfonso he will break his legs if he reports the incident to the police.
   c. The man Sue will testify against in a robbery trial bumps her shoulder in the crowded courthouse hallway and walks on.

   d. A robbery suspect comments to his cellmate that he intends to do everything he can to keep a witness from testifying against him in court.

49. Captain Forest likes to let her officers choose who their partners will be; however, no pair of officers may patrol together more than seven shifts in a row. Officers Adams and Baxter patrolled together seven shifts in a row. Officers Carver and Dennis have patrolled together three shifts in a row. Officer Carver does not want to work with Officer Adams. Who should Officer Baxter be assigned with?
   a. Adams
   b. Dennis
   c. Forest
   d. Carver

50. Four eyewitnesses give descriptions of the car involved in a hit-and-run accident. Which description is probably right?
   a. dark green with a gray roof
   b. dark blue with a white roof
   c. black with a gray roof
   d. dark green with a tan roof

Answer question 51 on the basis of the following definition.

Larceny under $100 occurs when a person unlawfully takes property valued under $100 with the intent of depriving the owner of it.

51. Which situation below is the best example of Larceny under $100?
   a. Bill borrows his brother's calculator without asking, and his brother, thinking it stolen, calls the police.

b. Tran watches an elderly man place an umbrella on the bus seat next to him. Tran grabs the umbrella and dashes off the bus.

c. Jean borrows her best friend's dress and still has possession of it four months later.

d. Frederico rents a video from a video store and cannot find it when it's time to return it.

52. The new governor has decreed that one-quarter of all inmates in the state prison system must be released, due to overcrowding. She has directed police officials to release the inmates that have been held the longest. Weston has been in prison longer than Papak, but not as long as Gomez. Rashad has been in prison less time than Weston, but more time than Papak. Which one prisoner should be released?

a. Gomez

b. Weston

c. Papak

d. Rashad

Answer question 53 on the basis of the following definition.

A person commits **Driving to Endanger** if that person, while driving a motor vehicle, recklessly engages in conduct that places another in danger of bodily injury.

53. Which situation below is the best example of Driving to Endanger?

a. Cheryl drives her car at a high rate of speed in the parking lot at the mall, narrowly missing a number of pedestrians.

b. Clarence takes Selena for a drive in rush hour traffic in Boston, driving below the speed limit.

c. Manuela is stopped for exceeding the speed limit on the interstate by 10 miles an hour with her one-year-old baby in the car.

d. Jack backs out of his driveway one morning and absent-mindedly fails to look both ways.

54. Burrows County has a higher crime rate than Kirk County. Kirk County has a higher crime rate than Madison County, but lower than Rogers County. Which county has the lowest crime rate?

a. Burrows County

b. Kirk County

c. Madison County

d. Rogers County

55. Taylor, Hudson, Xavier, and Muller are on the security detail for the governor's visit. Taylor is in front of the stage, Hudson is behind the stage, Xavier is near the exit door, and Muller is at the back of the auditorium. If Hudson switches places with Xavier and Xavier then switches places with Muller, where is Muller?

a. near the exit

b. in front of the stage

c. at the back of the auditorium

d. behind the stage

Use the following information to answer questions 56 and 57.

State troopers are expected to follow departmental policy regarding the use of vacation time. Departmental policy states that before a trooper can take vacation the trooper must properly fill out a Leave Request Form. To complete this task the trooper must:

1. Place his/her name on the form with the last name first, followed by first name and then middle initial.

2. List the date and time the leave is to begin.

3. List the date and time he/she expects to return to regular duty.

4. Sign and date the form.

5. Turn the form into his/her supervisor a minimum of 48 hours before the leave is due to begin.

56. Trooper Broshnack decides he needs a day off. He picks up a Leave Request Form and fills it out, listing his last name first, then first name and middle initial. He lists the date and time the leave is to begin, and the date and time he expects to return to duty, and then he signs and dates the form. He puts the form in his briefcase to turn in at the end of the day. Several days pass, and soon it is the evening before his day off is to begin. He turns in the form at the end of the day and does not report for duty the next morning. Under these circumstances the actions taken by Trooper Broshnack were
    a. proper, because he filled out the form exactly as required
    b. improper, because he did not check with the Colonel before requesting a day off
    c. proper, because he turned in the form before taking off
    d. improper, because he did not turn in the form 48 hours ahead of time

57. Late one afternoon Trooper LaJoya realizes that she must turn in a Leave Request Form within the hour or she will miss the 48-hour deadline. She grabs a Leave Request Form, writes her last name first, followed by her first name and middle initial. She lists the date and time she wants her leave to begin, and includes the time and date she will return to regular duty, signs and dates the form, then rushes in to leave the form on her supervisor's desk, barely making the deadline. Under these circumstances the actions taken by Trooper LaJoya were
    a. improper, because she did not list the reason why she wanted to take off
    b. proper, because she turned the form in 24 hours ahead of time
    c. improper, because she did not list the date and time she expected to return
    d. proper, because she followed all the steps in the procedure

58. Abraham has been arrested one more time than Jolson. Kirk has been arrested one less time than Jolson and one more time than Sanchez. Jolson has been arrested seven times. How many times has Sanchez been arrested?
    a. six times
    b. five times
    c. four times
    d. eight times

59. Upon conviction, Jackson was sentenced to two more years than Williams, but three less than Hobbes. Richards was sentenced to one more year than Hobbes. Williams was sentenced to twelve years. How long was Richards' sentence?
    a. eighteen years
    b. seventeen years

c. sixteen years

d. nineteen years

60. While operating a speed trap on the interstate, Officer Hamin is running the radar in the east-bound lane and Officer Firth is posted further down that lane to pursue speeders that Hamin identifies. Officer Wong is running the radar in the west-bound lane and Officer Kelly is further down that lane to pursue speeders. If Kelly switches with Wong, who then switches with Hamin, where is Wong now posted?

a. running the radar in the west-bound lane

b. pursuing speeders in the east-bound lane

c. running the radar in the east-bound lane

d. pursuing speeders in the west-bound lane

61. Traffic stops can be stressful situations for both trooper and violator. All troopers are expected to handle themselves in a professional, safe manner even if the violator does not. Trooper McDaniel pulls a vehicle over for driving in the breakdown lane. The driver tells Trooper McDaniel that he saw the sign prohibiting the use of the breakdown lane for normal traffic but that he didn't care because there's hardly any traffic at all right now and the rule is senseless. Which reaction is most appropriate for Trooper McDaniel?

a. She should recognize the driver has a good argument, apologize for disturbing him, and allow him to go on his way with a warning.

b. She should ignore his comments, issue the citation, and allow him to sign it and be on his way.

c. She should arrest him and place him in handcuffs because as a peace officer she doesn't have to take that kind of treatment.

d. She should find a way to drag out the traffic stop as long as possible so that the driver will know who is in control and learn his lesson.

62. Extortion is a less serious crime than burglary. Breaking and entering is more serious than extortion, but less serious than assault. Assault is more serious than burglary. Which crime is the most serious?

a. burglary

b. breaking and entering

c. assault

d. extortion

63. Officer Phelps has been on the force two years longer than Officer Smith and three years less than Officer London. Officer London has been on the force nine years. How long has Smith been on the force?

a. five years

b. six years

c. four years

d. three years

64. In the K-9 Corps, Officer Thomas is partnered with Ranger. Officer Cain is partnered with Scout, and Officer Stern is partnered with Laddie. Officer Walker is partnered with Astro. If Officer Thomas switches partners with Officer Stern and Officer Stern then switches with Officer Cain, who is Officer Stern's new partner?

a. Ranger

b. Scout

c. Laddie

d. Astro

65. The alarm goes off at the State National Bank. Officer Manson is patrolling in his cruiser ten miles away. Officer Fromme is patrolling five miles away, Officer Smith, seven miles away. Officer Sexton is farther away than Fromme, but closer than Smith. About how far away from the bank is Officer Sexton?
   a. nine miles
   b. seven miles
   c. eight miles
   d. six miles

PART FOUR: BASIC MATHEMATICS

Choose the correct solution to problems 66–80.

66. Studies have shown that automatic sprinkler systems save about $5,700 in damages per arson fire in stores and offices. If a particular community has on average 14 store and office fires every year, about how much money is saved each year if these buildings have sprinkler systems?
   a. $28,500
   b. $77,800
   c. $79,800
   d. $87,800

67. If an officer weighs 168 pounds, what is the approximate weight of that officer in kilograms? (1 kilogram = about 2.2 pounds)
   a. 76
   b. 77
   c. 149
   d. 150

68. State police officers must report the mileage on their cruisers each week. The mileage reading of Officer Gutierrez's vehicle was 20,907 at the beginning of one week, and 21,053 at the end of the same week. What was the total number of miles driven that week?
   a. 46
   b. 145
   c. 146
   d. 156

69. Department regulations require state police vehicles to have transmission maintenance every 13,000 miles. Trooper Moy's vehicle last had maintenance on its transmission at 12,398 miles. The mileage gauge now reads 22,003. How many more miles can the cruiser be driven before it must be brought in for transmission maintenance?
   a. 3,395
   b. 4,395
   c. 9,003
   d. 9,605

70. If it takes two workers 2 hours 40 minutes to complete a particular task, about how long will it take one worker to complete the same task alone?
   a. 1 hour 20 minutes
   b. 4 hours 40 minutes
   c. 5 hours
   d. 5 hours 20 minutes

71. A street sign reads "Loading Zone 15 Minutes." If a truck pulls into this zone at 11:46 a.m., by what time must it leave?
   a. 11:59 a.m.
   b. 12:01 p.m.
   c. 12:03 p.m.
   d. 12:06 p.m.

72. If a vehicle is driven 21 miles on Monday, 18 miles on Tuesday, and 24 miles on Wednesday, what is the average number of miles driven each day?
   a. 19
   b. 21
   c. 22
   d. 23.5

73. The directions on an exam allow $2\frac{1}{2}$ hours to answer 50 questions. If you want to spend an equal amount of time on each of the 50 questions, about how much time should you allow for each one?
   a. 45 seconds
   b. $1\frac{1}{2}$ minutes
   c. 2 minutes
   d. 3 minutes

74. If a worker is given a salary increase of $1.25 per hour, what it the total amount of the salary increase for one 40-hour week?
   a. $49.20
   b. $50.20
   c. $50.25
   d. $51.75

75. An elevator sign reads "Maximum weight 600 pounds." Which of the following may ride the elevator?
   a. three people: one weighing 198 pounds, one weighing 185 pounds, one weighing 200 pounds
   b. one person weighing 142 pounds with a load weighing 500 pounds
   c. one person weighing 165 pounds with a load weighing 503 pounds

   d. three people: one weighing 210 pounds, one weighing 101 pounds, one weighing 298 pounds.

76. Which of these is equivalent to 35°C? ($F = \frac{9}{5}C + 32$)
   a. 105°F
   b. 95°F
   c. 63°F
   d. 19°F

77. A piece of tape 3 feet 4 inches long was divided in 5 equal parts. How long was each part?
   a. 1 foot 2 inches
   b. 10 inches
   c. 8 inches
   d. 6 inches

78. What is 0.716 rounded to the nearest tenth?
   a. 0.7
   b. 0.8
   c. 0.72
   d. 1.0

79. Which of these has a 9 in the thousandths place?
   a. 3.0095
   b. 3.0905
   c. 3.9005
   d. 3.0059

80. Out of 100 citizens polled, 80 said they believed street crime was on the rise. How many citizens out of 30,000 could be expected to say they believe street crime is on the rise?
   a. 2,400
   b. 6,000
   c. 22,000
   d. 24,000

PART FIVE: WRITING SKILLS

81. State Troopers Gutterez and Forbes respond to a radio dispatch concerning a person in need of assistance. At the scene, they obtain the following information.

Date of incident: May 4, 1997
Time of incident: 3:20 p.m.
Place of incident: 10 Mayfield Road
Reporter: Mary Campbell
Person Aided: Confused, unidentified woman reported by Mary Campbell to be wandering on foot
Disposition: Victim transported by police to Mt. Pilot Community Hospital

Trooper Gutterez is writing a report of the incident. Which of the following expresses the above information *most clearly and accurately?*

a. On May 4, 1997, at 3:20 p.m., a confused, unidentified woman was found wandering on foot at 10 Mayfield Road, when Mary Campbell drove past and was transported by police to Mt. Pilot Hospital.

b. On May 4, 1997, at 3:20 p.m., Mary Campbell drove past 10 Mayfield Road and found a confused, unidentified woman wandering on foot. The woman was transported by police to Mt. Pilot Hospital.

c. Mary Campbell reported that, driving past 10 Mayfield Road, a confused, unidentified woman was found wandering on foot on May 4, 1997, at 3:20 p.m.. She was transported by police to Mt. Pilot Hospital.

d. Confused and unidentified, Mary Campbell found a woman wandering on foot at 10 Mayfield Road, who was transported by

police to Mt. Pilot Hospital on May 4, 1997, at 3:20 p.m.

82. Officers Karayan and Walker are asked to investigate a report of stalking. They obtain the following information.

Dates of occurrence: Between July 3 and 14
Victim: Rachel Goode
Suspect: Melvin Redding, former coworker at Robinson's Dry Cleaners
Disposition: Order of Protection issued by the court

Officer Karayan is writing a report of the investigation. Which of the following expresses the above information *most clearly and accurately?*

a. Stalked by former coworker at Robinson's Dry Cleaners, Melvin Redding, an Order of Protection was issued to Rachel Goode, between July 3–14, by the court.

b. A former coworker at Robinson's Dry Cleaners, Melvin Redding stalked Rachel Goode, and an Order of Protection was issued by the court. This occurred between July 3 and 14.

c. Between July 3–14, stalked by Melvin Redding, a former coworker at Robinson's Dry Cleaners, the court issued an Order of Protection to Ms. Rachel Goode.

d. Between July 3 and 14, Ms. Rachel Goode was stalked by Melvin Redding, a former coworker at Robinson's Dry Cleaners. An Order of Protection was issued by the court.

83. Trooper Guebers responds to a radio dispatch concerning a nursing home resident who has wandered off. The trooper obtains the following information.

Date of occurrence: June 2, 1997

Time of occurrence: Approximately 4:30 p.m.

Place of occurrence: Cedar Manor Nursing Home

Resident: Marguerite Aznar

Disposition: Ms. Aznar found at Mirror Lake and transported back to Cedar Manor

Trooper Guebers is making a memo book entry of the occurrence. Which of the following expresses the above information *most clearly and accurately?*

a. On June 2, 1997, at approximately 4:30 p.m., resident Marguerite Aznar wandered away from the Cedar Manor Nursing Home. She was found at Mirror Lake and transported back to Cedar Manor.

b. A resident, Marguerite Aznar, was found at Mirror Lake and transported back to Cedar Manor Nursing Home, where she wandered away on June 2, 1997, at approximately 4:30 p.m.

c. Found at Mirror Lake and transported back to Cedar Manor Nursing Home, Marguerite Aznar was a resident who wandered away. This was on June 2, 1997, at approximately 4:30 p.m.

d. Wandering away on June 2, 1997, at approximately 4:30 p.m., Marguerite Aznar was found at Mirror Lake. A resident of Cedar Manor Nursing Home, she was transported back.

84. Officer Spanheimer responds to a report of a person having been bitten by a cat. At the scene, the officer obtains the following information.

Date of incident: July 4, 1997

Place of incident: Backyard at 907 Willow Lane

Victim: Peter Mims

Injury: Ankle bitten after kicking cat belonging to his ex-wife

The officer is making a memo book entry regarding the incident. Which of the following expresses the above information *most clearly and accurately?*

a. On July 4, 1997, Peter Mims was bitten on the ankle by his ex-wife's cat in the backyard at 907 Willow Lane. This occurred just after being kicked.

b. On July 4, 1997, after kicking it, Peter Mims' ankle was bitten by his ex-wife's cat in the backyard at 907 Willow Lane.

c. On July 4, 1997, in the backyard at 907 Willow Lane, Peter Mims was bitten on the ankle by his ex-wife's cat, which he had just kicked.

d. On July 4, 1997, after being kicked, Peter Mims' ex-wife's cat bit his ankle in the backyard at 907 Willow Lane.

85. State Troopers Yamuna and Rand respond to a 911 call regarding an automobile accident. At the scene, they obtain the following information.

Date of accident: July 2, 1996

Type of accident: Hit-and-run

Victim: Pedestrian Harry Sales

Type of car: Light blue Ford

Driver of car: Unknown

Trooper Yamuna is writing a report of the incident. Which of the following expresses the above information *most clearly and accurately*?

a. On July 2, 1996, pedestrian Harry Sales was the victim of a hit-and-run accident. He was struck by a light blue Ford, driver unknown.

b. Hit-and-run victim and pedestrian Harry Sales was struck by the unknown driver of a light blue Ford on July 2, 1996.

c. A light blue Ford struck Harry Sales, a hit-and-run pedestrian, on July 2, 1996. The driver is unknown.

d. Harry Sales, a pedestrian, was hit-and-run by a light blue Ford on July 2, 1996, driver unknown.

Answer questions 86–88 by choosing the sentence that best combines the underlined sentences into one.

86. This rural area is known for its high crime rate. Many criminals have been apprehended here.

a. Many criminals have been apprehended here, while this rural area is known for its high crime rate.

b. Many criminals have been apprehended here, but this rural area is known for its high crime rate.

c. Many criminals have been apprehended here; therefore, this rural area is known for its high crime rate.

d. This rural area is known for its high crime rate; meanwhile, many criminals have been apprehended here.

87. The owl parrot looks like a bird of prey. The owl parrot feeds on vegetable matter.

a. The owl parrot looks like a bird of prey; however, it feeds on vegetable matter.

b. Feeding on vegetable matter, the owl parrot looks like a bird of prey.

c. Looking like a bird of prey, the owl parrot feeds on vegetable matter.

d. The owl parrot feeds on vegetable matter, and it looks like a bird of prey.

88. Mr. Markley has an unpleasant personality. Mr. Markley is a crook.

a. Mr. Markley has an unpleasant personality, although he is a crook.

b. Mr. Markley has an unpleasant personality, and furthermore he's a crook.

c. While he is a crook, Mr. Markley has an unpleasant personality.

d. Being a crook, Mr. Markley has an unpleasant personality.

Answer questions 89–90 by choosing the sentence that is correctly written from among the four choices.

89. a. Peace of mind, caused by owning a good security system.

b. Owning a good security system, for one to have peace of mind.

c. To have peace of mind by one's owning a good security system.

d. Owning a good security system can help one have peace of mind.

90. a. One of the first modern detectives in literature were created by Edgar Allen Poe.

b. One of the first modern detectives in literature was created by Edgar Allen Poe.

c. Edgar Allen Poe having created one of the first modern detectives in literature.

d. In literature, one of the first modern detectives, created by Edgar Allen Poe.

Answer questions 91–95 by choosing the word or phrase that means the same or nearly the same as the underlined word.

91. The officers <u>inferred</u> that the prisoner was planing to escape, because of the bed-sheets tied together in her cell.
   a. guessed
   b. imagined
   c. implied
   d. surmised

92. State Trooper Martinez presented an <u>ultimatum</u> to the motorist regarding exceeding the speed limit—next time, she would be issued a ticket.
   a. earnest plea
   b. formal petition
   c. solemn promise
   d. non-negotiable demand

93. The documentation of her infractions of the rules was <u>meticulous</u>.
   a. delicate
   b. painstaking
   c. responsible
   d. objective

94. The <u>prerequisite</u> training for state police should include a course in basic psychology.
   a. required
   b. optional
   c. preferred
   d. advisable

95. The state police computer system in our area is <u>outmoded</u>.
   a. worthless
   b. unusable
   c. obsolete
   d. unnecessary

Answer questions 96–100 by choosing the word that is spelled correctly and best completes the sentence.

96. The Healthy Living Vitamins Corporation is soon to be _____ for fraud.
   a. prosecuted
   b. prossecuted
   c. prosecutted
   d. proseccuted

97. Trooper Martin's uniform was quite _____ among all the gray suits.
   a. conspiccuous
   b. connspicuous
   c. conspicuous
   d. conspicious

98. The broccoli you bought will _____ up unless you put it in the refrigerator.
   a. shrivel
   b. shrivvel
   c. shrivell
   d. shrival

99. I just don't know what I'd do in her _____.
   a. sittuation
   b. situation
   c. situachun
   d. sitiation

100. Our surveillance site in that basement is so damp that my skin constantly feels _____.
   a. clamby
   b. clamy
   c. clammy
   d. clammby

ANSWERS

PART ONE: MEMORIZATION

1. **d.** Refer to Charges section on Gibbons.
2. **b.** Refer to the Description of Smith.
3. **a.** Refer to the drawing of Smith.
4. **c.** Refer to Serna's Aliases.
5. **b.** Refer to the Remarks on Hassid.
6. **c.** Refer to the Charges on Bunn.
7. **a.** Refer to the drawing of Gibbons.
8. **d.** Refer to Serna's Identifying Scars or Marks.
9. **d.** Refer to Remarks on Bunn.
10. **c.** Refer to the drawing of Hassid, as well as the section on Identifying Scars or Marks.
11. **b.** Refer to Remarks on Smith.
12. **d.** Refer to the drawing of Serna.
13. **d.** Refer to the Caution section for both Gibbons and Hassid.
14. **c.** Refer to the Remarks on Serna.
15. **b.** Refer to the Descriptions of Gibbons and Hassid.
16. **d.** Refer to the Descriptions of Hassid and Serna.
17. **a.** The Description of Smith says that he is six feet tall, taller than any of the suspects.
18. **c.** Refer to the Caution on Hassid.
19. **a.** Refer to Description sections.
20. **c.** Both Serna and Hassid are clean-shaven. Don't miss the part of this question that asks you which statement is *false*.

PART TWO: READING COMPREHENSION

21. **c.** This idea is stated in the second sentence and discussed throughout the passage.
22. **b.** Proof of guilt is the whole point of gathering evidence, but this is never referred to in the passage.
23. **c.** This is stated in the third sentence. Choice **a** is incorrect because, while rules of evidence protect the accused, that is not the reason the passage gives that an officer must know them.
24. **a.** The pragmatic, or practical, intent the author refers to in the third sentence is the purpose of shaping police procedure before arrest.
25. **a.** The criteria for using information about a witness to cast doubt on his or her testimony is the subject of the whole passage.
26. **d.** An accusation of spousal abuse would be prejudicial but not relevant to the question of the witness's truthfulness.
27. **b.** This prospect is raised in the last sentence.
28. **c.** A petty thief is not a felon.
29. **c.** While choices **b** and **d** are also true, they are not the main idea, which is supported by the whole passage and spelled out in the last sentence.
30. **b.** This is implied in the next-to-last sentence.
31. **c.** See the first sentence of the passage.
32. **b.** Choice **a** is incorrect because Miranda rights are read only when the suspect is taken into custody. The right to call a lawyer (choice **c**) and the right to a phone call (choice **d**) are included in the Miranda rights.
33. **d.** Although the last sentence expands on the main point, the rest of the passage explains why hearsay evidence is only admissible when it doesn't matter whether or not the statement is true.
34. **a.** This statement may be true, but it isn't in the passage.
35. **b.** See the last sentence of the passage.
36. **c.** The passage mentions the truthfulness of testimony several times.

37. a. The discussion of the traits of a person with anti-social personality disorder in the middle of the passage specifies that such a person does not have distortions of thought. The passage speaks of the anti-social person as being *inordinately self-confident* (choice **b**) and of the person's *emotional shallowness* (choices **c** and **d**).

38. d. The third sentence of the passage speaks of *con games*. None of the other professions would suit an impulsive, shallow person who has been in trouble with the law.

39. b. The passage mentions *emotional shallowness*. The other choices hint at the capability to feel meaningful emotion.

40. b. The passage says that a person with anti-social personality disorder can mimic real emotion, thereby conning prison officials, judges, and psychiatrists. The other choices are mentioned in the passage, but not in connection with getting out of trouble with the law.

41. c. See paragraphs 3 and 4. The other answer choices are mentioned in the passage but are not the central argument.

42. b. See the last sentences of paragraph 1, which discusses the stalking victim's *worst fear*.

43. d. All of the other choices are mentioned in the third paragraph. The victim's knowledge or lack of knowledge about anti-stalking laws is not discussed in the passage.

44. a. As discussed in the first paragraph, a restraining order is a civil remedy that is often not taken seriously by the stalker.

45. a. See the second paragraph. Choices **b** and **c** apply only to the Orange Country woman; choice **d** cannot be shown to apply to either woman.

PART THREE: LOGIC AND REASONING

46. c. After all the switches were made, Reinhart is directly behind the vehicle, Baker is on the driver's side of the vehicle, Lopez on the passenger side, and O'Malley is behind Reinhart.

47. a. The other three situations appear to be a bit ill-advised but ordinary, involving no violation of traffic laws. The situation in choice **a** appears to be exactly what has citizens in Foxboro concerned and is a dangerous situation as well.

48. b. In the other situations there is no crime involved and no action threatened or taken to keep anyone from reporting a crime.

49. d. Baxter should be assigned to patrol with Carver. Baxter cannot be assigned with Adams, because they have already been together for seven shifts. If Baxter is assigned to Dennis, that would leave Carver with Adams. Adams does not want to work with Carver.

50. a. *Dark green* and *gray roof* are the elements repeated most often by the eyewitnesses and are therefore most likely correct.

51. b. Tran appears to have an obvious desire to deprive the old man of his umbrella here in choice **b**. In the other options there seems to be no intent to deprive anyone of property.

52. a. Gomez has been in prison longer than Weston, who has been in longer than Rashad, who has been in longer than Papak.

53. a. This situation has more of the element of recklessness than any of the other situations. It is also the most likely situation to place someone else besides the driver in danger of bodily injury.

54. c. From lowest to highest, the county crime rates are Madison, Kirk, and then Burrows and Rogers. Not enough information is given to determine whether Burrows or Rogers has the highest crime rate.

55. d. After all the switches are made, Muller is behind the stage. Hudson is near the exit, Xavier is at the back of the auditorium, and Taylor is in front of the stage.

56. d. Remember, the strategy for answering these questions is make sure the steps in the procedure are followed. Trooper Broshnack did not follow step 5, so his actions are improper.

57. d. Trooper LaJoya followed all the steps correctly.

58. b. Sanchez has been arrested five times. Jolson has been arrested seven times, and Kirk has been arrested one less time (six). Sanchez has been arrested one less time than Kirk.

59. a. Richards' sentence was eighteen years. Williams was sentenced to twelve years, Jackson was sentenced to two more (fourteen), and Hobbes to three more than Jackson (seventeen). Richards was sentenced to one more than Hobbes.

60. c. After all the switches were made, Officer Wong was running the radar in the east-bound lane. Officer Firth was pursuing speeders in the east-bound lane, Officer Kelly was running the radar in the west-bound lane, and Officer Hamin was pursuing speeders in the west-bound lane.

61. b. The driver is violating a law, so he shouldn't be let go. Still, even though he is being a jerk, he is not violating any laws other than the one for which he was stopped. Trooper McDaniel should handle herself professionally by writing out the citation in a normal manner so that they both can move on.

62. c. Assault is the most serious crime, followed, in descending order, by burglary, breaking and entering, and extortion.

63. c. Officer Smith has been on the force four years. Officer London has been on the force nine years, Officer Phelps has been on the force three less years

(six), and Officer London has been on two less than Phelps (four).

64. b. After all the switches were made, Officer Stern's partner was Scout. Officer Thomas' partner was Laddie, Officer Cain's was Ranger, and Officer Walker's was Astro.

65. d. Sexton is farther away than Fromme, who is five miles away, and closer than Smith, who is seven miles away. Therefore, Officer Sexton is about six miles from the bank.

PART FOUR: BASIC MATHEMATICS

66. c. To solve this problem, multiply the amount saved per fire, $5,700, by the average number of fires: 5,700 times 14 is 79,800.

67. a. To solve this problem, divide the number of pounds (168) by the number of kilograms in a pound (2.2): 168 divided by 2.2 is 76.36. Now round to the nearest unit, which is 76.

68. c. You must subtract the reading at the beginning of the week from the reading at the end of the week. 21,053 minus 20,907 is 146.

69. a. This is a two-step subtraction problem. First you must find out how many miles the cruiser has traveled since its last maintenance. To do this, subtract 12,398 from 22,003. Then, take the answer, 9,605, and subtract that from 13,000 to find out how many more miles the cruiser can travel before it must have another maintenance: 3,395.

70. d. It will take one worker about twice as long. First add the hours and minutes. Four hours 80 minutes is equal to 5 hours 20 minutes.

71. b. If it is 11:46 a.m., in 14 minutes it will be noon. In 15 minutes, then, it will be 12:01.

72. b. This is a two-step problem. First, add the three numbers; then divide the sum by 3 to find the average. 22 + 18 + 24 = 63. 63 divided by 3 is 21.

73. d. First convert the $2\frac{1}{2}$ hours to minutes. Then divide the answer by 50. 2 hours 30 minutes is 150 minutes. 150 divided by 50 is 3.

74. b. This is a multiplication problem. $1.25 times 40 is $50.20.

75. a. It is easy to see by rounding off the numbers that choice **a** is less than 600 and choices **b**, **c**, and **d** are all over 600 pounds.

76. b. Use 35 for C. $F = (\frac{9}{5} \times 35) + 32$. Therefore, $F = 63 + 32$, or 95.

77. c. Three feet 4 inches equals 40 inches; 40 divided by 5 is 8.

78. a. Choice **b** is rounded up instead of down. Choice **c** is rounded to the thousandths place. Choice **d** is rounded to the nearest whole number.

79. a. In **b**, the 9 is in the hundredths place. In **c**, it is in the tenths place; in **d**, the ten thousandths place.

80. d. Eighty out of 100 is 80 percent. Eighty percent of 30,000 is 24,000.

PART FIVE: WRITING SKILLS

81. b. Choices **a** and **c** do not make clear who was transported. Choice **d** implies it was Mary Campbell who was confused and unidentified.

82. d. Choices **a** and **c** do not make clear who was stalked. Choice **b** does not make clear what occurred between July 3–14.

83. a. In choices **b** and **c**, the chronological order is wrong; choice **d** does not make clear where Ms. Aznar was wandering away from.

84. c. Choices **a** and **b** do not make clear who or what was kicked; choice **d** implies that the cat bit its own ankle.

85. a. Choice **b** implies that Harry Sales was struck by a driver rather than by a car. Choices **c** and **d** are illogical—there's no such thing as a *hit-and-run pedestrian*, nor can anyone be *hit-and-run*.

86. c. This choice establishes the causal relationship between the two sentences, through use of the word *therefore*.

87. a. The transitional word *however* correctly establishes a contrast.

88. b. The transitional word *furthermore* correctly indicates the addition of one unpleasant trait to another. Choice **d** is wrong because not all crooks have unpleasant personalities.

89. d. This is a complete sentence; the others are fragments.

90. b. This is a complete sentence; choices **c** and **d** are fragments; in choice **a**, the verb does not agree in number with its subject, *one*.

91. d. To *infer* is to conclude from the evidence or to *surmise*.

92. d. An *ultimatum* is a final statement of terms or a *non-negotiable demand*.

93. b. To be *meticulous* is to be extremely careful or *painstaking*.

94. a. Something that is *prerequisite* is needed or *required*.

95. c. When something is *outmoded* it is out of date or *obsolete*.

96. a. The correct spelling is *prosecuted*.

97. c. The correct spelling is *conspicuous*.

98. a. The correct spelling is *shrivel*.

99. b. The correct spelling is *situation*.

100. c. The correct spelling is *clammy*.

SCORING

As noted before, 70 percent is a passing score on the Massachusetts State Police exam; however, you need a much higher score than that to have a good chance of getting the job. You have probably seen improvement between your first practice exam score and this one. Here are some options, based on your score:

- **If you scored below 70 percent,** you should do some serious thinking about whether you're really ready to take the Massachusetts State Police Exam. An adult education course in reading comprehension at a high school or community college would be a very good strategy. If you don't have time for a course, you should at least try to get some private tutoring.
- **If your score is in the 70 to 80 percent range,** you need to work as hard as you can in the time you have left to boost your skills. Consider the LearningExpress book *Reading Comprehension in 20 Minutes a Day* (order information at the back of this book) or other books from your public library. Also, re-read Chapters 5–10 of this book, and make sure you take *all* of the advice there for improving your score. Enlist friends and family to help you by making up mock test questions and quizzing you on them.
- **If your score is between 70 and 90 percent,** you could still benefit from additional work to help improve your score. Go back to Chapters 5–10

and study them diligently between now and test day. Follow the suggestions in those chapters for Additional Resources to improve your score.
- **If you scored above 90 percent,** congratulations! Your score should be high enough to make you an attractive candidate to the Massachusetts State Police Department. Make sure you don't lose your edge; keep studying this book up to the day before the exam.

If you didn't score as well as you would like, try to analyze the reasons why. Did you run out of time before you could answer all the questions? Did you go back and change your answer from the right one to a wrong one? Did you get flustered and sit staring at a hard question for what seemed like hours? If you had any of these problems, go back and review the test-taking strategies in Chapter 3 to learn how to avoid them.

You should also look at how you did on each kind of question on the test. You may have done very well on reading comprehension questions and poorly on mathematics questions, or vice versa. If you can figure out where your strengths and weaknesses lie, you'll know where to concentrate your efforts in the time you have left before the exam. Go to the self-evaluation table at the end of Chapter 4 to help you decide which chapters you need to study hardest.

Finally, one of the biggest factors in your success on the exam is your self-confidence. Remember, because you're using this book, you're better prepared than most of the other people who are taking the exam with you.

C·H·A·P·T·E·R

THE PHYSICAL ABILITY TEST

12

CHAPTER SUMMARY

This chapter presents an overview of what to expect on the physical test you'll take on the way to becoming a state trooper. It also offers specific advice on how to get in shape for this often-demanding exam—and how to stay in shape.

P hysical fitness testing, otherwise known as the physical ability or physical agility test, is a staple in the law enforcement selection process. In an attempt to measure your ability to successfully perform the duties of a law enforcement officer or to complete the training to perform those duties, an agency will in all probability require you to perform a test or series of tests that will physically challenge you. The timing as well as the make-up of the test are dictated to a certain extent by legislation that protects against potentially discriminatory practices. The goal of this chapter is to identify the types of tests you are likely to encounter and to provide you with some instruction—so that you can run and jump and push and pull your way through the selection test.

Tests to measure your physical ability to be a law enforcement officer generally take one of two forms: what's known as "job task simulation" and physical fitness. Physical fitness tests are widely used and favored for their validity and predictability. A battery of tests measure your physiological parameters, such as body composition, aerobic capacity, muscular strength and endurance, and flexibility. Physical fitness tests also hint at your medical status and, perhaps more important, they reveal your ability to perform the potentially hundreds of physical tasks required of a law enforcement officer.

Job task simulation tests, on the other hand, while they may tax your physiological fitness, are designed for the most part to illustrate your ability in a handful of job areas. Typically these tests also challenge your motor skills: balance, coordination, power, speed, reaction time, and agility.

Physical Fitness Tests

Physical fitness testing typically takes place in a group setting, most often in a gymnasium, field house, or athletic field—remember, these are "field tests." Attire for a day of testing is usually casual—sweats and sneakers—unless it occurs on the same day as other screening activities, such as a written exam. The time between events and the duration of the test vary according to the number of candidates and the number of test events.

Be prepared for the test. Bring water, nonperishable, easily digested "fuel foods" such as fruits and grains (bagels or bread), and a change of clothes in the event locker and shower facilities are available. At least one positive picture identification, black pens, and writing paper should also be in your bag.

Physical fitness test events typically include some *aerobic capacity test*, which measures your cardiorespiratory system's ability to take in and use oxygen to sustain activity. A field test, such as a one and one-half mile run or a 12-minute run, give an indication of your ability to participate in sustained activities such as walking a patrol, foot pursuits, and subject control and restraint. The most common standards here are "time to complete the distance" and "distance covered in the allotted time."

Flexibility, the ability to freely use the range of motion available at a given joint in your body, is fre-

quently tested because it impacts upon many movements and activities. Sitting for long periods at a dispatching center or behind the wheel of a patrol car or bending over to lift a handcuffed subject—all will affect or be affected by your flexibility. *Sit and reach tests* to evaluate low back and hamstring flexibility require you to sit with straight legs extended and to reach as far forward as possible. The performance standard for this commonly used test is to touch or to go beyond your toes.

Another staple of fitness tests are muscular strength and endurance measures. Muscular strength, the ability to generate maximum force, is indicative of your potential in a "use-of-force" encounter, subject control, or other emergency situation. *Bench press* and *leg press tests* to measure upper and lower body strength are commonly used and require you to lift a percentage of your present body weight. A maximum effort is required after a warm-up on the testing machine/apparatus.

Dynamic muscular endurance, on the other hand, is the ability to sustain effort over time. This very common element of fitness tests is related to sitting or standing for long periods of time as well as to the incidence of low back pain and disability. *Sit-up* and *push-up tests* are frequently timed events lasting one to two minutes that involve military push-ups and traditional or hands-across-the-chest sit-ups.

Finally, it is not uncommon to encounter a test that estimates the amount of fat compared to lean tissue or total body weight. *Body composition* is an indication of health risk status, and the results are usually expressed as a percent. Normal ranges for healthy young adults are 18-24% for females and 12-18% for males. A skinfold technique that measures the thickness of the skin and subcutaneous fat at sex-specific sites is the most common field test to estimate overall percentage of body fat.

Job Task Simulation Tests

Job task simulation tests use a small sample of actual or simulated job tasks to evaluate your ability to do the job of a law enforcement officer. This type of test is used because of its realistic relationship to the job and law enforcement training and because of its defensibility as a fair measure of a candidate's physical abilities.

Because courts of law have found it unreasonable to evaluate skills that require prior training, general job-related skills are tested at the applicant level. It's unlikely that you will be required to demonstrate competency with a firearm or handcuffs, for example. But climbing through a window, over barriers, and up stairs and use-of-force situations, such as a takedown or simulated application of handcuffs, are common tasks.

Simulation tests are often presented as obstacle courses, with the events performed one after another and linked by laps around the gymnasium or athletic field. Frequently, the requirement is to successfully complete the course or each event in a given amount of time. The test may be given on an individual or small group basis. Candidates performing a job task simulation test may be walked or talked through the first run or allowed to practice certain events prior to actual testing.

A job task simulation test is typically held during one of two periods, subject to labor and anti-discrimination legislation. Testing can legally occur at the very beginning of the process, alone or in combination with a written test, to establish an applicant's rank. Or it can take place after a written test but before a conditional offer of employment. In some cases, it may also occur following a conditional offer of employment. If this is the case you can reasonably expect a medical examination prior to participating in the test, which may also serve as an academy selection test. Due to the variability in the timing of the test, it is advisable to ask about physical standards as early in the selection process as possible.

IMPORTANT:
Regardless of the type of physical test you take, you need to be reasonably fit to successfully complete the test. Because the selection process, law enforcement training, and lifestyle of law enforcement officers are all stressful, it is essential to achieve fitness early and to maintain it for the duration of your law enforcement career.

Training Tips

In preparing for a physical fitness test, you must plan ahead, taking into account both the timing and the content of the test. The short-term objective, of course, is to pass the test. But your greater goal is to integrate fitness into your lifestyle so that you can withstand the rigors of the career you want in law enforcement.

The first order of business is to determine the type of fitness test you'll have to complete. What you have to accomplish on the test naturally will guide your training program. You can tailor your training to simulate the test and to train for the test events. Even if you're facing a job task test, you may want to include physical fitness test events, such as push-ups and sit-ups, in your training regimen. It's unsafe and inadequate to use skill events as your only training mode. If you're unfit it won't allow for a slow progression and if you are fit it may not represent enough of a challenge for you.

Following some basic training principles will help you create a safe and effective training program. Steady progress is the name of the game. Remember, you didn't get into or out of shape overnight, so you won't be able to change your condition overnight. To avoid injury while achieving overall fitness, balance in fitness training is essential. Work opposing muscle groups when doing strength or flexibility training and include aerobic conditioning as well as proper nutrition in your total fitness program.

To achieve continued growth in fitness you must overload the body's systems. The body makes progress by adapting to increasing demands. With adaptation, your systems are able to overcome the physical challenge, resulting in a higher level of fitness.

Finally, don't forget rest. It allows the body and the mind to recover from the challenges of training—and to prepare for another day.

12 Weeks to the Test Date

Your primary goal when faced with a short window of preparation is to meet a given standard, either physical fitness or job task simulation. Therefore, "specificity of training"—training for what you will actually be asked to do on the test—is the rule.

If you're training for a physical fitness test, then the performance standards are your training goals. You should make every attempt to use or to build up to the standards as the training intensity level. If you

STAYING "FITT"

FITT stands for Frequency, Intensity, Type, and Time. FITT simplifies your training by helping you plan what to do, when, how hard, and for how long. Because the four FITT "variables" are interrelated, you need to be careful in how you exercise. For example, intensity and time have an inverse relationship: as the intensity of your effort increases, the length of time you can maintain that effort decreases. A good rule of thumb when adjusting your workout variables to achieve optimum conditioning is to modify one at a time, increasing by 5-10%. Be sure to allow your body to adapt before adjusting up again.

The following presents some FITT guidelines to help you plan your training program.

Frequency
- 3-5 times a week

Intensity
- Aerobic training—60-85% of maximum effort
- Resistance training—8-12 repetitions
- Flexibility training—Just to slight tension

Type
- Aerobic—Bike, walk, jog, swim
- Resistance—Free weights, weight machines, calisthenics
- Flexibility—Static stretching

Time
- Aerobic—20-60 minutes
- Resistance—1-3 sets, 2-4 exercises/body part
- Flexibility—Hold stretched position 8-30 seconds

are unable to reach the standards right away, approximate them and increase the intensity 5% per week until you achieve them.

If you're training for a pre-academy test, try to determine what the academy's "PT" curriculum entails, use these as your modes of training, and test yourself with the standards every two to three weeks.

On the other hand, if the short-term goal is to meet a job task simulation test standard, particularly one that is used for pre-academy selection, you should determine the content of the PT curriculum and use it as the training model. At the same time, practice the skills required on the test once every two weeks in lieu of a training day.

Six or More Months to Go

The training program when there are six or more months to prepare is essentially similar to the one described above. However, the longer timeframe means that your goal can become making permanent, positive changes in your lifestyle rather than simply applying training principles to pass a test. Reasonable and gradual changes in your lifestyle will help to ensure that the behavioral and physical changes are permanent.

This extended timetable also reduces the likelihood of injury and allows for more diversity and balance in your training program and lifestyle. If you're preparing for a physical fitness test, you have the opportunity to set (and meet) performance goals that may be 25-50% greater than the standards themselves. On the other hand, if you have more than six months to prepare for a job task simulation test, you may want to avoid practicing any of the skills required for the first three months to avoid injury. Instead, consider incorporating sports activities into your conditioning routine; this will provide an enjoyable opportunity to train the necessary motor skills. After three months, you could begin practicing the physical test skills one day every two to four weeks.

A Sample Exercise Program

All of the information in this chapter about training principles and practices is put into action on the gym floor. A page taken from the academy physical fitness training book will help to get you fit and ready to excel in the physical test.

Physical training begins with a warm-up to increase your core body temperature and to prepare you for the more intense conditioning to follow. Brisk walking or jogging, in place or around a gymnasium, or jumping rope are good start-up options and should be conducted for three to five minutes. This is followed immediately by a period of active head-to-toe stretching to prevent injury.

Basic conditioning in the academy frequently is achieved with calisthenic exercises. Beginners can do sets of 10 on a "two count" and those of intermediate or advanced fitness can begin on a "four count" (1,2,3,1; 1,2,3,2; etc.). Running in formation typically follows 'cals' and is done at about a 9-10 minute per mile pace. Marine Corps cadences played on a Walkman may help to put you in the mood for academy runs! For those who are just beginning to prepare for the fitness test, 8-12 minutes of running is a safe start; those more fit may begin with 25 or more minutes. A three to five minute cooldown period to recover and some gentle, static stretching from the floor, focusing on the lower legs, will complete your workout and prepare you for the showers!

SAMPLE CALISTHENICS

Here are some recommended calisthenics to help get you in shape:

- Side straddle hop (jumping jacks)
- Half squats
- Heel raises
- Push-ups
- Stomach crunches

And for the more advanced:

- Diamond push-ups
- Bent leg raises

C·H·A·P·T·E·R

THE PERSONAL HISTORY STATEMENT

13

CHAPTER SUMMARY

Paperwork tells the tale—and you only get one shot at this document. This chapter explores the quirks, subtleties, and realities of the most critical phase of the application process. Ignore the advice here and chances are you'll be reading a letter of rejection!

The Personal History Statement is exactly that—a detailed personal statement of your life history. You may hear it called many things—the Application and the Applicant History Statement being the other common terms. No doubt you will come up with a few of your own by the time you finish this project. Although the paperwork may go by different names, the reason for jumping through these hoops is the same. The purpose of the statement is to provide law enforcement background investigators with the material for a panel, an individual, or a personnel department to make a sound decision about hiring you.

Not For The Faint of Heart

When you take your first look at the Personal History Statement, you might want to be sitting down. Or at least have a chair handy. This document can be a black hole for the unprepared. All of your precious time, energy, and resources will be sucked into the void if you aren't prepared to be asked for the tiniest details of your life. Although not all departments require the same level of detail, don't be surprised to find yourself madly hunting for the address of that kindergarten you once attended.

Some agencies aren't so demanding. They'll ask you to start out this tale of your life with your high school days and work forward. It's best to expect the worst, though. As one investigator told an applicant in Austin, Texas, "By the time I'm through going through the information in this document, I'll know whether or not you were breast fed as a child." He was.

This Size Fits All

No matter where you choose to apply, this chapter may be the helping hand you need to make your background investigation go as smoothly as possible. It will serve as a guide to help you present an accurate, HONEST summary of your past and present life. After all, the Personal History Statement—how you complete it, what you reveal and what you don't reveal—can determine whether or not you get the opportunity to convince an oral board you are worth hiring.

You may not make the connection between the oral interview board and the Personal History Statement at first. The connection is there and it's strong. What you reveal—and what you fail to reveal—in your Personal History Statement will come back around to help or haunt you at your oral board. Background investigators will rustle around in your life's basement using this document as a flashlight. They'll illuminate the good things and the bad things for all the oral board members to see and to use in their questioning. You're forewarned, however, and you are ready.

Different Methods—Same Results

One of the more frustrating aspects of searching for that perfect state police job is realizing that every state has

its own way of doing business. Yes, you may have applied yesterday to the New Jersey State Police, but today you may be filling out paperwork for the California Highway Patrol. Law enforcement agencies rarely have the same priorities, budgets, or staffing so the process, right down to the people they may want to hire, won't match up.

Be flexible. No matter how the application process is designed, no matter what order you handle each task given you, information you will need to supply each department remains the same. They all want to know about your past, present, and potential.

No Need To Wait

Even if you haven't decided which departments you will grace with your applications, you can start work now. Beginning with the day you were born, make a list of every address where you've lived up to the present. If you are 34 years old and normally change addresses twice a year you can pause a moment now to groan aloud. Make this list and keep plenty of copies. You'll only need to do this once instead of every time you apply to a different department if you are careful to keep copies of your efforts. Since your crystal ball works about like everyone else's, you can't be too sure what's in the future. The CIA, FBI, or other agency may lure you from your dream department one day and you'll wish you'd kept up the list.

Addresses aren't the only project you can work on ahead of time. Create a list of every part-time, full-time, some-time job you've had since your working life began. Once again, not every agency will use the same jump-off point to investigate your job history. Many forms ask you to list the jobs you've held during the past ten years, some during the past five years, and the others want your history from the moment you received your first check.

And There's Always . . .

Tickets. Here's yet another project to work on before applying to be a state police officer. Research your driving history. You'll be asked by some agencies to list every traffic ticket you've ever received in any state or country, whether on a military post or on civilian roadways. Some may ask you to list only the moving violations (these include speeding, running red lights, unsafe lane changes, etc.) while other agencies want to see moving violations and tickets for things like expired license plates, failure to wear seat belts, and most certainly expired automobile insurance.

One agency may ask for you to tell them about the tickets you've received in the past five years while others want to know your driving history from the moment your foot first touched an accelerator. Do your homework. And don't leave off tickets you think they won't find out about, because that kind of ticket doesn't exist. Tickets leave paper trails and paper trails are the easiest kinds to follow.

Dig These Up ASAP

Your pre-application preparations wouldn't be complete without a list of documents you'll need to have handy. This list does not include *every* form you may have to cough up, but it's almost a dead certainty you will need:

- Birth Certificate
- Social Security Card
- DD 214 (if you are a veteran)
- Naturalization papers (if applicable)
- High School Diploma or G.E.D. Certificate
- High School Transcripts
- College Transcripts
- Current Driver's License(s)
- Current Copies of Driving Records
- Current Consumer Credit Reports

If you don't have certified copies of these above-listed documents, start calling or writing the proper authorities *now* to find out what you need to do to get them. If you've sucked your social security card up in the vacuum cleaner and haven't seen it since, run down to the social security office in your community and arrange for a new one. Legal documents often take anywhere from six to eight weeks for delivery, but you probably won't be able to wait that long if you have already received and started on your Personal History Statement. Most agencies have a deadline for filling out and returning Personal History Statements so you may have to tap dance a bit.

If time runs out and you realize you won't be able to turn the Personal History Statement in with all the required documents, *ask* the powers-that-be what you should do. Many agencies will tell you to attach a memo to your application outlining your problem and what you have done about it. For example, you've ordered a copy of your birth certificate but either the postal service is using it for scratch paper or your request is mired in the bureaucratic process. Attach a letter of explanation to your application detailing when you requested a copy of your birth certificate, where you asked for the copy to be sent, and when you expect to receive the document. If you have it, attach all copies of correspondence you sent out requesting a copy of your certificate. That'll show that you are making all the right moves.

Check First

You have a little homework to do before rounding up all of these documents. Check with as many agencies as you can to find out what rules they have for how certain documents are submitted—like college transcripts, for instance. Agency officials may require you to have the school send the documentation directly to their recruiting office instead of to you at home via regular mail. The same goes for credit reports or copies of driving records. It's best to call the recruiting department, explain to them that you are trying to round up all of your documentation, and ask them how they accept these documents so you'll know what to do.

Other questions you need to ask are:

- Do you need photocopies or original documents?
- Will you return my original if I send it?
- How recent does the credit history have to be?
- What's the most recent copy you will accept of my college transcript?

The answers to these questions can save you lots of money on antacids and postage. You'd be surprised at the number of ways each agency can come up with for you to chase paper.

READY FOR ACTION

So, you're as prepared as you can be. You've made your decision on where you are applying and let's even assume you are at the point in the application process where you've received the Personal History Statement. *Before* you set pen to paper, make a copy of this form. Do not write on it, breathe on it, or dare to set it down on the coffee table without having a copy made FIRST. After you have a copy, then put away the original for now. (You'll be using the photocopy as a working draft and a place to make mistakes.) Eventually you will transfer all the information you have on your practice copy onto the original. You may be spending lots of time on this project and using more than a few dimes in the copy machine before this is all over, but it'll be time and money well spent. Especially if the *unthinkable* happens. And the unthinkable usually goes like this:

Your phone rings. It's your recruiter. "Gee, Fred, this is Trooper Jones in recruiting and I have a little bad news. We can't seem to put a finger on that application you sent. Isn't that the darndest thing? Could you make us a copy from the one you have at home and send it out right away?"

Don't think it doesn't happen. Be sure to make copies of the application and accompanying documentation you submit and keep them in a safe place. And hold on to these copies! You need to review this document before the oral board gets ahold of you, not to mention the possibility that you may need this information to complete other applications for other adventures years down the road.

Personal History Statements may vary from agency to agency, but the questions most applicants ask about these tedious documents have not changed over the years. The following are a few questions and comments made by actual applicants as they went through application processes across the U.S. The responses made to these questions and comments will allow you to learn from someone else's mistakes, thereby giving you an advantage over the competition—and having an advantage in this highly competitive field can never hurt!

"What do you mean you don't accept resumes? It cost me $60 to get this one done!"

A formal resume like one you may prepare for a civilian job is usually not much good to a law enforcement agency. Although criminal justice instructors in many colleges suggest to their students to have a resume made, it's always best to call and ask a recruiter whether or not to bother. Why go to the expense if the agency is going to throw away the resume upon receipt? Most agencies will rely upon their Personal History Statements to get the details of your life, education, and experience, so save yourself time and dimes when you can.

Those dimes will come in handy at the copy machine when you make backup copies of your Personal History Statement!

"I didn't realize the Personal History Statement would take so long to complete and the deadline for turning it in caught me by surprise. I got in a hurry and left some things blank."

The letter this applicant received in the mail disqualifying her from further consideration probably caught her by surprise as well. As you know from reading this chapter so far, a Personal History Statement requires planning, efficiency, and attention to detail. Most agencies demand accuracy, thoroughness, and timeliness. There are entirely too many applicants to choose from who have taken the time necessary to properly fill out an application for a busy background investigator to bother with an applicant who has left half of the form blank and isn't quite sure what should go in the other half. In fact, many agencies will tell you up front in their application instructions that failing to respond to questions or failure to provide requested information can result in disqualification.

"I read *most* of the instructions. I didn't see the part that said I had to print."

Read *all* of the instructions. Every sentence. Every word. And please do so before you begin filling out your practice copy of the Personal History Statement. In fact, you need to read the entire document from the first page to the last page before you tackle this project. Have a note pad next to you and as you read make notes of everything you do not understand. You'll be making a phone call to your recruiter AFTER reading the entire document to ask questions. It's important to read the whole document because the questions on your pad may be answered as you read along. It's a bit embar-

rassing to call with a question that the recruiter answers by saying "Well, as you would have found out by reading the next sentence, you should . . . ."

"No one is going to follow up on all this stuff anyway. It'd take way too long and it's way too involved."

A good background investigator lives for the opportunity to follow up on the details of your life. That's their job. When all is said and done, they must sign their name at the bottom of the report documenting their investigation. It's not wise to assume someone will put their career at risk by doing a sloppy job on your background investigation. A thorough investigator will take as much time as it takes to do a good job. The good news is that you can earn brownie points by making that investigator's job as simple as possible. Give them as much information as you possibly can and make that information RIGHT. When you write down a phone number, make sure it's correct. For example, if you used to work at Jumpin' Jacks Coffee Parlor four years ago and you still remember the phone number, CALL that number to make sure it's correct before you write it down. Nothing is more irritating to a busy investigator than dialing wrong number after wrong number. If that's the only number you have and you discover it's no longer in service, make a note of this so the investigator doesn't assume you are being sloppy. Phone numbers get changed and businesses go under every day.

When you turn in a Personal History Statement you are building on the reputation you began forming from the moment you first made contact with recruiting staff. An application that is turned in on time, is filled out neatly and meticulously, and that has *correct*, detailed information that is easily verified says a lot about the person who filled it out. Not only will an investigator have warm fuzzy thoughts for anyone who makes his/her job easier, they will come to the conclusion that you will probably carry over these same traits into your work as a state police officer.

The investigator, the oral board, and the staff psychologist all will be looking at HOW you filled out the application as well as what information is contained in the application. Investigators will build a case for hiring you (or *not* hiring you) based on facts, impressions, and sometimes even intuition. With this in mind, *every detail is worth a second look* before you call your Personal History Statement complete. Ask yourself:

- Is my handwriting as neat as it can be?
- Did I leave off answers or skip blanks?
- Do my sentences make sense?
- Is my spelling accurate?
- Are my dates and times consistent?

"I figured you could find out that information easier than I could. That's why I didn't look up that information. After all, you're the investigator."

And this applicant is probably *still* looking for a job. The Personal History Statement is a prime opportunity for you to showcase your superb organizational skills, knack for detail, and professionalism. Do as much of the work as you can for the background investigator. Make your extra credit points where you can. For example, let's say you worked for Grace's High Heels and Muffler Emporium. The business went under after a few months, much to everyone's surprise, and you moved on to other employment. You're not sure what happened to Grace, your immediate supervisor and owner of the business, but you do know a friend of hers. Contact that friend, find out Grace's address and phone number, and give this information to your investigator. Yes, the investigator probably would find her on his/her own, but you went the extra mile, you showed the initiative, and you are going to get the brownie points.

It's not uncommon for state public safety agencies to get thousands of applications per year. Most of the applicants have the same credentials to offer as you do. Do all you can do to stand out from the crowd. Nothing gets noticed faster than efficiency, professionalism, and accuracy. Well, that's not quite right. Inaccuracies, sloppiness, and laziness usually win first notice.

"I know I got disqualified, but it's only because I misunderstood the question. I didn't want to ask about it because I didn't want to look dumb."

If you do not understand a question—ASK someone. By not making sure you know how to properly answer a question you run the risk of answering it incorrectly, incompletely, or not at all. Any one of these mistakes can lead to your disqualification if an investigator thinks you are not telling the truth, or that you are unwilling to provide the information requested. Don't take chances when a simple question will clear up the problem.

"You know, I didn't have any idea what that question meant so I just guessed."

Never guess. Never assume. This advice can never be repeated too often—if you don't know, find out. ASK QUESTIONS. Answering them is part of the job for recruiters or background investigators.

"I lied because I thought if I told the truth, I'd look bad."

Never lie about *anything*. As far as law enforcement professionals are concerned, there is no such thing as a harmless lie. Supervisors don't want people working for them who cannot tell the truth, other troopers don't want to work with partners whom they can't trust, and citizens expect *criminals* to lie, not state police officers. Your credibility must be beyond reproach.

Let's look at an example. One applicant told his recruiter that the reason he didn't admit to getting a ticket for failing to have his car registered was because he thought the agency would think he wasn't organized and couldn't take care of business. Which would you prefer for a potential employer to know about you—that you lie instead of admitting to mistakes, or that you make mistakes and admit to them readily? The fact is, telling the truth is crucial if you want to be a state police officer.

"I listed John Doe as a personal reference because he's the mayor and I worked on his campaign. Why did my investigator call and make me give another reference?"

Choose your personal references carefully. Background investigators do not want to talk to people because they have impressive credentials. They want to talk to them so they can get a feel for how you are as a person. Investigators will know within minutes whether or not a reference knows you well. Personal references are important enough to warrant their own in-depth discussion later in this chapter, so read on.

HOW TO READ AND ANSWER QUESTIONS

Reading questions and instructions carefully is critical to successfully completing the Personal History Statement. Certain words should leap off the page at you. These are the words you should key in on:

- All
- Every
- Any
- Each

If you see these words in a question, you are being asked to include all the information you know. For example,

you may see the following set of instructions in your Personal History Statement:

List **any** and **all** pending criminal charges against you.

This doesn't mean list only the charges facing you in Arizona, but not the ones from that incident in Nevada last week. This agency wants to know about every single criminal charge that may be pending against you no matter what city, county, parish, village, country, or planet may be handling the case(s). Do not try to tap dance your way around instructions like these for any reason. If your fear is that the information you list might make you look bad, you may have some explaining to do. And you may have perfectly good explanations for your past and your present. If you lie or try to make yourself look good, chances are you'll be disqualified in short order and no one will get the opportunity to consider those explanations.

Another question you may see is:

Have you **ever** been arrested or taken into police custody for **any** reason?

The key words are **ever** and **any**. This agency means at any time in your life, beginning at your moment of birth, up to and including the split second that just went by. If you don't know what is meant by the term "arrested," then call your recruiter or investigator and ASK. Do not play the well-no-one-put-handcuffs-on-me-so-I-wasn't-really-under-arrest game. When in doubt, list any situation you think has a ghost of a chance of falling into the category you are working on. The best advice, though, is ASK IF YOU DON'T KNOW!

Here's a request for information that includes several eye-catching words.

List **all** traffic citations you received in the past five (5) years, in this or **any** other state (moving and non-moving) **excluding** parking tickets.

In this example, the agency leaves little doubt that what you should do here is make a complete list of every kind of violation you've been issued a citation for, no matter where you got it and no matter what the traffic violation was for within the past five years. They even let you know the one kind of citation they don't need to know about—parking tickets. If you aren't sure what a moving violation is or what a non-moving violation is, call the department and have them explain. Keep in mind that when the officer issued you a citation on a single piece of paper, you may have been cited for more than one violation. Most citations have blanks for at least three violations, sometimes more. For example, last year you were pulled over for speeding. The officer discovered you had no insurance and your car license plates were expired. She told you she was writing you three tickets for these violations, but handed you only one piece of paper. Did you get one citation or three? You got three.

Once again, ASK if you don't know. No one will make fun of you if you are unfamiliar with terminology such as "moving violation."

PERSONAL REFERENCES

Your personal references are the people who will be able to give the background investigator the best picture of you as a whole person. Some Personal History Statements ask you to list at least five people as references and some only ask for three. You also may be given a specific time limit for how long you may have known these people before listing them. Your instructions may direct you to list only those individuals whom you've known for a minimum of two years, for exam-

ple. Pay close attention to the instructions for this section, if there are any. Selecting the people for this area is not something you should take lightly for many reasons.

Earlier, you read that by making the investigator's job easier you make your investigation run smoother, you get brownie points, and your background is finished quickly. The Personal References Section is one area where you really want to make it easy. You'll want the investigator to talk to people who know you well—who can comment on your hobbies, interests, personality, and ability to interact with others. Try to choose friends who will be honest, open, and sincere. When an investigator calls a reference and figures out quickly that the person he/she is talking to barely has an idea of who you are, the red flags will come shooting up. Investigators are suspicious people by nature. Most law enforcement professionals are. The investigator will wonder why you listed someone who doesn't know you well. Are you trying to throw them off the track? Are you afraid someone who knows you too well will let out information you don't want known? This is how an investigator will look at the situation. And, at the very least, you'll get a phone call requesting another reference because the one you listed was unsatisfactory.

Most investigators expect for you to tell the personal references that you listed them and that they will be getting a phone call or a personal visit from the investigating agency. Get the RIGHT phone numbers, find out from your references what times they are most accessible, and ESPECIALLY find out if they have any objections to being contacted. You don't need a reluctant personal reference. They often do more harm than good.

Tell your references how important it is for them to be open and honest with the investigator. Let them know that if they do not understand a question, they should feel free to tell the investigator they don't understand. It's also wise to let them know that there are no right or wrong answers to most of these questions. Investigators do not want to have a conversation with someone who is terrified about saying the "wrong thing." And that's what your personal references should expect to have with an investigator—a conversation, not an interrogation. Your goal here is to let the investigator see you as a person through the eyes of those who know you best.

Looks Aren't Everything—Or Are They?

You've filled out the practice copy you made of the Personal History Statement, made all your mistakes on that copy, answered all the questions, and filled in all the appropriate blanks. Now you're ready to make the final copy.

Part of the impression you will make on those who have the hiring and firing decisions will come from how your application looks. Is your handwriting so sloppy that investigators pass your work around to see who can read it? Did you follow the instructions directing you to PRINT? Were you too lazy to attach an additional sheet of paper instead of writing up and down the sides of the page? Did you SPELL words correctly? Do your sentences make sense to the reader? (A good tip here is to read your answers out loud to yourself. If it doesn't make sense to your ear, then you need to work on what you wrote.)

Every contact you make with the hiring agency makes an impression. The written impression you make when you turn in your Personal History Statement is one that can follow you through the entire process and into the academy. In fact, it can have a bearing on whether or not you even make it into the academy because most departments have a method of scoring you on the document's appearance.

Here are some items you might find useful as you work on your application:

- a dictionary
- a grammar handbook
- a good pen (or pencil—whatever the directions tell you to use)
- a screaming case of paranoia

The paranoia will ensure that you check your work, check it again, and have someone you trust check it yet again *before* you make your final copy.

You now have the information you need to make the Personal History Statement a manageable task. This is not a document to take lightly, especially when you are now aware of the power this document has over your potential career as a state police officer. Remember, it's important that you:

- follow instructions and directions
- be honest and open about your past and present
- provide *accurate* information
- choose excellent personal references
- turn in presentable, error-free documentation
- turn in documents on time

A recruiting department can ask for nothing better than an applicant who takes this kind of care and interest in the application process. And you will get all the credit!

C·H·A·P·T·E·R
THE ORAL INTERVIEW

14

CHAPTER SUMMARY

This is the next best thing to having someone do your oral interview for you. The oral interview process is demystified in these pages with a down-to-earth look at the ordeal. Read on for tips, suggestions, and don't-do's.

Welcome to the board. Those are the words you want to hear. That means you've survived most of the process and are one step closer to your dream. State trooper. In Florida, applicants who hear that opening phrase will be stepping into a room with an oral board comprised of three members. This panel of higher-ranking professionals will take at least 20 minutes of your life to see if you have the strong communication skills necessary for such a demanding career. In Texas, trooper applicants will speak before a board of five interviewers ranging in rank from field trooper to lieutenant. You'll have 45 minutes to knock their socks off.

The oral interview board, no matter what form it takes, is unlike any oral job interview you will ever experience. The questions are pointed, personal, and uncompromising. Vague, plastic responses will usually goad a panel of veteran state police officers into rougher questioning techniques until they get the honest response called for by the circumstances. The information you are about to receive will show you how to prepare for the oral board from the moment you decide to apply to an agency until the moment the head of the board thanks you for your participation.

HIRE ME, PLEASE!

If you're like most people you've had some experience asking someone for a job. So, it's not unrealistic to expect that the trooper oral interview board will be similar to a civilian oral interview—is it? Yes and no. There are a few similarities. Both prospective civilian and law enforcement employers are looking for the most qualified person for the job—reliable, honest men and women who will work hard and be there when they are needed.

"Hire" Expectations

Civilian employers expect applicants to show up on time for their interview, dressed professionally, and showing off their best manners, as do state police employers. When you step into a trooper's oral interview board, however, you will realize that the people who are interviewing you have more than a surface interest in you and your past experiences. And the board will have more than a two-page resume in their hands when the interview begins.

Exactly who is going to be using the details of your personal and professional life to interview you? More than likely it will be a panel of two, three, four—maybe more—individuals with one purpose in mind: to get to know you well. The board members will most likely be supervisory-level troopers who have several years' experience on the force. Some departments use civilian personnel specialists to sit on their boards, but most interview boards will be made up of experienced troopers.

These board members will be using information you have provided on your application and information investigators discover during your background investigation. Investigators will provide board members with a detailed report on your past and present life history. Yes, you'll be asked questions when board members already know the answer and when they don't know the answer. You'll be asked to explain why you've made the decisions you've made in your life—both personal and professional. You'll also be asked questions that don't have right or wrong answers. In short, you can expect an intense grilling from men and women who don't have the time or patience for applicants who walk into their interview unprepared.

Tell What You Know, Know What You Tell

Before you reach the oral interview board stage of the application process you will have had to fill out a detailed personal history statement often referred to as the Applicant History Statement, the Personal History Statement, or simply the application. Terminology differs from agency to agency. Unless you are skipping around in this book, you've probably read about it by now. Call it what you want—just don't underestimate its role in the oral interview.

The Personal History Statement guides the oral board through your past and present life. You must be willing to open your life up to the board by giving them an informative, ACCURATE tour of where you've been in your life and who you are.

Since the Personal History Statement is what background investigators use to conduct investigations and what a final report to the board is built on, then it follows that you should make that document your life when you are filling it out. Members of the oral board generally are given a copy of your Personal History Statement and then a copy of the investigators' final report on you. While you are answering questions for the board, most board members will be shuffling through the pages of your life—checking what you say against what they see on paper. Naturally, you'll want to remember what information you gave them. Instead of tossing and turning the night before your interview, your time will be well spent reading and rereading your Personal History Statement so that you know what they know about you.

How much effort you put into the Personal History Statement will have a direct impact on how difficult your oral interview will be. If board members have an accurate, detailed picture of you as a whole person from the information you have supplied, your time under the microscope will be less than the applicant who turned in a vague, mistake-laden account of his/her past and present life. If the thought of the oral interview board makes your palms sweat, then pay close attention to the chapter on how to handle the Personal History Statement. You'll feel better afterward.

There's Plenty of Time, Right?

Preparation for the oral interview board begins when you make the decision to apply. From the moment you first make contact with a recruiter, everything you say and do will be potential fuel for the oral interview board. Even walking through the doors of the recruiting office to pick up an application, you have the opportunity to make a lasting impression. You are dealing with professionals who are trained to notice and *remember* people and details.

If you show up to pick up an application wearing your favorite cutoff blue jeans and trashed out, beer-stained T-shirt from those college party days, you may be in for a shock several months later when a board member asks you why you chose to make that particular fashion statement. Dress neatly and as professionally as possible each and *every* time you make contact with the department where you want to work.

Same goes for telephone contacts—if you call a department to request an application you will make an impression on the person who answers the phone. If all you want is an information packet and/or application and you do not have any specific questions to ask, do NOT take this opportunity to tell the recruiter your entire life story from the moment of conception.

Not only are you probably the 100th person to request an application that day, the recruiter has no way, or reason, to remember the details of your life at this stage of the process. Remember, though, you have to give out your name and address to this person who will be responsible for mailing your application, so the potential for connecting your name to the impression you make on the phone is high.

As silly as it may make you feel, it's a good idea to practice what you say *before* you dial the phone. In fact, it's not a bad idea to write down what you'd like to say before you call. This will give you control over the impression you make and eliminate the possibility of the first words out of your mouth being: "uh . . . hi . . . I . . . uh . . . wanna . . . uh . . . Can you mail me a . . . uh . . . one of those . . . uh . . . I wanna be a trooper but I need a . . . application! Yeah, that's it!"

Do the same for any questions you may have. Make a list and as you ask each question, listen carefully to the response without interruption. Above all, never ask a question that is designed to show off how much you know. The chances of you knowing more about law enforcement than the person who is already working in the field is slim. Your opportunity to impress the agency will come later in the appropriate setting—the oral interview board.

Self-Awareness—Don't Show Up Without It!

You wouldn't want to show up for a car race on a tricycle, any more than you would want to try putting out a fire with gasoline. Using this same logic, it's safe to say you'd never want to sit down in front of a panel of professionals who have the power to offer you a career dealing with people without a good measure of self-awareness.

Self-awareness is knowing yourself—being aware of what you do and why you do it. Many of the questions you'll hear from the board are designed to reveal how well you know yourself and how honest you can be about your talents and your shortcomings.

Big Tip!

Do NOT pay any attention to consultants or books suggesting that you downplay, or do not admit to, weaknesses. If you can remember only one piece of advice from this chapter, please let it be this! If an oral board member asks you to list the weaknesses you believe you have and you can't think of any, they will be more than happy to bring up a few instances in your life to illustrate the weaknesses you aren't able to identify.

You should be able to list your weaknesses with the same unhesitating manner with which you list your strengths. And you should be able to tell the board what you are doing to correct or compensate for your weaknesses. If you truly aren't aware of your failings, ask trusted friends and relatives for their input. Write down what you think your weaknesses are and then compare your list with what your friends and family have said. Don't forget to ask them about your strengths as well. Some applicants find talking about strengths as difficult as talking about weaknesses. You must be able to do both.

Don't You Remember? YOU Put It On Your Application!

Part of being self-aware is knowing what others know about you. Hardly any of the questions during your oral board interview should come as a surprise to you if you have taken the copy of your application that you made *before* turning it in and studied it.

Before showing up for the board you must take the time to go back over your application and carefully think about each piece of information in this document. The questions put to you by the board are generated mostly from the information you write in the Personal History Statement. As you review your copy of the Statement, think about the questions such information could generate.

For example, if one of the questions on the application directed you to list any instances where you've

been fired from a job, think about how you would answer the question, "Mr. Smith, can you tell the board why you got fired from Tread Lightly Tire Shop in 1993?" Although you may have told the investigator why you were fired during an earlier conversation, the board will want to hear it for themselves.

HELP YOURSELF!
Tame Public Speaking Fears

Being interviewed by a group of people is a lot like having one of those dreams where you show up to work in nothing but a pair of socks. You experience anxiety, sweaty palms, and a burning desire to be some place else. Public speaking classes will go a long way toward easing your fear of talking to groups.

Strongly consider taking a speech class at a nearby community college or through an adult education course. At the very least, have a friend ask you questions about yourself and have them take notes about any annoying mannerisms you may exhibit while speaking. Then practice your speaking and learn to control those mannerisms.

Practice is one of the keys to success on an oral board. If you've ever truly practiced something—batting a ball, for instance—you know that once you have the motion down you can rely on your muscles to "remember" what to do when it comes time to play the game. The same rationale holds true for practicing oral board answers.

One effective technique is to mentally place yourself in a situation and visualize how you want to act or respond when the pressure is on. Some troopers call this mental exercise "What if . . ." and they use this technique to formulate a plan of action for those times when split-second decisions rule the moment. Visualizing a successful performance ahead of time can help trigger that response once you're in the actual situation. This technique will work for you if you practice, practice, practice.

Right On Time? Tsk, Tsk!

Show the board how much you want this job. They'll check to see when you arrived for your board. An early arrival means you planned ahead for emergencies (flat tires, wrong turns, etc.), that you arrived in enough time to prepare yourself mentally for what you are about to do, and that you place a value on other people's time as well as your own.

Packaging Sells Product

You may feel like you don't have much control over what happens to you in an oral interview setting, but this is one area where you have total control. The initial impression you make on board members is up to you and this is the perfect opportunity to score points without ever opening your mouth. The way you dress sends a signal to the people who are watching you walk into the room.

Blue jeans and a "nice shirt" tells the panel you wouldn't mind having the job if someone wouldn't mind giving it to you. Business suits (for men and women) tell them you *want* this job, you take this interview seriously, and there's nothing casual about the way you are approaching it.

If you don't own businesswear, borrow it. Rent it. Buy it. Wear it! Chances are you've already invested time and money into the education necessary to get most criminal justice jobs. This is not the time to balk at spending money on appropriate clothing. Just go get the suit any way you can.

Make Mama Proud

After you've earned bonus points with your professional appearance, it's time to earn more with your manners. Most law enforcement agencies are paramilitary organizations—your first clue should be the uniforms and the rank structure. In the military it's customary to address higher-ranking men and women with courtesy.

"Yes, ma'am" or "yes, sir" or "no, ma'am" or "no, sir" is expected from military personnel. If you have military experience you will be ahead in this area.

If you are not accustomed to using these terms of courtesy, practice them! Make a conscious effort to use them. It's rarely considered rude to simply respond "yes" or "no" to a question, but you'll *always* be on shaky ground if "yeah" or "uh huh" are your customary responses.

Location is important. If you've flown from New York to Texas to apply for a job, you definitely do not want to say "yeah" or "what?" in your oral board. People in the South raise their children to say "yes, ma'am" and "no, sir" and hearing "huh?" or "yeah" is at best an irritant to southern ears. This may not be an issue in other parts of the nation, although it'd be a safe bet to assume many board members have either been in the military at some point in their lives or like the paramilitary structure of law enforcement. You won't go wrong with "yes, sir" instead of "yeah" or "Could you repeat the question?" instead of "what?"

No doubt you realize that an oral board sees many, many applicants when a department is in a hiring phase. Most oral boards typically schedule five or six applicants in one day for interviews. Some agencies schedule boards for one day during the week and some departments have oral boards set for every day of the week. The point here is that you are talking to people who are more than likely quite tired of listening. That means the "little things" take on an extra importance.

YES IT ALL MATTERS

What you've read so far may seem inconsequential. This is far from the truth. You walk a fine line when you appear before an oral board. They want you to appear self-confident and poised, but not cocky or arrogant. You're expected to be nervous, but not so nervous that you can't communicate beyond an occasional grunt or nod. You're expected to be polite, but you're not expected to fawn all over the board. Above all, you are expected to be yourself and not who you *imagine* the board might want. Which brings up another point—what exactly *is* the board looking for in an applicant?

People Talent—Gotta Have It

The men and women patrolling the highways today are expected to be highly responsive to the public they protect. Agency officials are looking for applicants who have excellent verbal skills and a strong desire to "be there" for the public. To give you an idea how most agencies feel about their mission, consider the motto for the Department of Public Safety troopers in Texas: "Service, Courtesy, and Protection." So, no, it's not a secret that the successful applicant will need superior people-handling skills. But what about skills that may be less obvious?

Oral interview boards are faced with the formidable task of hiring individuals who have the skills and talents equal to the demands of modern law enforcement. The men and women most highly sought after by agencies are those who are not only good with people, but with modern technology as well. When you open the door to your patrol car, the first thing to catch your eye might not necessarily be the radio and siren box. It may well be a computer. Computers are here to stay—in the office and on the road. If you think a keyboard is a chunk of wood you hang patrol car keys on, you are in for a surprise. You can bet your competition is in class hunched over a keyboard at this moment because they know oral boards love to hear "Why, certainly" to the question, "Have you ever used a computer?" If you haven't already, now's the time to brush up on your typing skills and sign up for a computer class.

Then there's the liability issue. Lawsuits and threats of lawsuits have law enforcement agencies scurrying to find applicants who have specific qualities and skills that will keep them out of the headlines and civil courtrooms.

Show Your Stuff

Yes, law enforcement agencies want it all. There's *always* room for men and women who can leap tall buildings and do the speeding train thing, but even if your cape isn't red, you can still compete if you can convince the board you have the following qualities:

- Maturity
- Common sense
- Good judgment
- Compassion
- Integrity
- Honesty
- Reliability
- The ability to work without constant supervision

These qualities aren't ranked in order of importance because it would be hard to say which should come first. They are all of importance in the eyes of the board and your task in the oral interview setting is to convince them you have these qualities. Since you are in an obvious question-and-answer setting, you'll do your convincing through how and what you say when you respond to questions.

YOUTH AND INEXPERIENCE—PLUS OR MINUS?

The question here is will an oral board think you have enough life experience for them to be willing to take a chance on hiring you. Local, state, and federal law enforcement agencies have never been as liability conscious as they are today. Incidents like the Rodney King trial and subsequent Los Angeles riots, not to mention the O. J. Simpson trial, have heightened the awareness of legal departments around the country.

This concern ripples straight through an agency and eventually arrives to haunt recruiters, background investigators, oral boards, and everyone who has anything to do with deciding who gets a badge. The first question you hear when trouble hits an agency is, "How did that person get a job here anyway?" As a result, applicants are scrutinized even more closely than ever before and agencies are clearly leaning toward individuals who have proven track records in employment, schooling, volunteer work, and community involvement.

Youth and inexperience are not going to disqualify you from the process. You should be aware that if you are 21 years old and have never held a job, have never been responsible for your own care, feeding, and life in general, you will have a more difficult time getting hired as a trooper than someone who is older, has job references to check, and who is able to demonstrate a history of reliability and responsibility.

Maturity is a huge concern with state agencies. They can no longer afford to hire men and women who are unable to take responsibility for their actions or the actions, in some cases, of those around them. Although maturity cannot be measured in the number of years an individual has been alive, departments will want to see as much proof as possible that you have enough maturity and potential to risk hiring you.

Get Out in the World

Make it as easy as possible for the oral board to see how well you handle responsibility. Sign up for volunteer work *now* if you don't have any experience dealing with people. If you are still living at home with parents, be able to demonstrate the ways in which you are responsible around the home. If you are on your own, but living with roommates, talking to the board about this experience and how you handle conflicts arising from living with strangers or friends will help your case.

You may want to work extra hard on your communication skills before going to the board. The more articulate you are the better you will be able to sell yourself and your potential to the board if you are young. Your need to open up and let the board see you as a worthy investment will be greater than an older applicant who has plenty of personal and business history to pour over.

Older and Wiser Pays Off

Being older certainly is not a hindrance in law enforcement. Oral boards are receptive to men and women who have life experience that can be examined, picked apart, and verified. Maturity, as has been mentioned before, is not necessarily linked with how old you are. Older applicants can be either blessed or cursed by the trail they've left in life. Many applicants have gone down in flames because they were unable to explain incidents in their past and present that point to their immaturity and inability to handle responsibility.

Applicants of any age who have listed numerous jobs and have turned in Personal History Statements too thick to run through a stapling machine should be extra-vigilant about doing homework before the oral board stage. If you fall into this category, you should carefully pour over the copy of the application your background investigator used to do your background check. Be fully aware of the problem areas and know what you will most likely be asked to explain. And decide now what you are going to say. Prepare, prepare, prepare.

Don't Leave The Meter Running

The longer your history, the longer you can expect to sit before an oral board. If a board is not required to adhere strictly to time limits, you may be required to endure a longer session than other applicants simply because there's more material to cover. The more you know about yourself and the more open you are about your life the smoother your interview will run. This advice holds true for *all* applicants.

THE NITTY-GRITTY

Questions. What kind of questions are they going to ask? Isn't that what everyone is really worried about when they are sitting in the chair labeled "NEXT" outside of the interview room? You will hear all kinds of questions—personal questions about your family life, questions about your likes and dislikes, questions about your temperament, your friends, and even a few designed to make you laugh so you'll get a little color back into your face. Don't look for many questions that can be answered with simply "yes" or "no" because you won't get that lucky. Let's look at the types of questions you are likely to hear.

Open-Ended Questions

The open-ended question is the one you are most likely to hear. An example of an open-ended question is:

Board Member: "Mr. Jones, can you tell the board about your Friday night bowling league?"

Board members like these questions because it gives them an opportunity to see how articulate you can be and it gives them a little insight into how you think. This is also a way for them to ease into more specific questions. Example:

Board Member: "Mr. Jones, can you tell the board about your Friday night bowling league?"

Jones: "Yes ma'am. I've been bowling in this league for about two years. We meet every Friday night around 6 p.m. and bowl until about 8:30 p.m. I like it because it gives me some-thing to do with friends I may not get to see otherwise because every-one is so busy. This also gives me time to spend with my wife. We're in first place right now and I like it that way."

Board Member: "Oh, congratulations. You must be a pretty competitive bowler."

Jones: "Yes ma'am, I am. I like to win and I take the game pretty seriously."

Board Member: "How do you react when your team loses, Mr. Jones?"

That one question generates enough information for the board to draw a lot of conclusions about Mr. Jones. They can see that he likes to interact with his friends, he thinks spending time with his wife is important, and that competition and winning are important to him. Mr. Jones' answer opens up an avenue for the board to explore how he reacts to disappointment, how he is able to articulate his feelings and reactions, and they'll probably get a good idea of his temperament.

Open-ended questions allow the board to fish around for information, granted, but this is not a negative situation. You should seize these opportunities to open up to the board and give them an idea of how you are as a person.

Obvious Questions

This is the kind of question boards ask when everyone in the room already knows the answer. Example:

Board Member: "Mr. Jones, you were in the military for four years?"

Jones: "Yes sir, I was in the Marines from 1982 until 1986."

Board Member: "Why did you get out?"

The obvious question is used most often as a way to give the applicant a chance to warm up and to be aware of what area the board is about to explore. It's also a way for the board to check up on the information they've been provided. Board members and background investigators can misread or misunderstand information they receive. Understanding this, board members will usually be careful to confirm details with you during the interview.

Fishing Expeditions

The fishing expedition is always a nerve-racking kind of question to answer. You aren't certain why they are asking or where the question came from and they aren't giving out clues. Example:

Board Member: "Mr. Jones, in your application you stated that you've *never* been detained by police. (Usually they will pause a few seconds and then get to the point.) You've *never* been detained?"

If your nerves aren't wracked by this kind of questioning, someone probably needs to check you for a pulse. In the example above, if the applicant has been detained by police and failed to list this on his application then he'll be wondering if the board KNOWS this happened. The odds are sky-high that the board does know the answer before asking the question. If the applicant has never been detained then paranoia is certain to set in. Did someone on his list of references lie to the background investigator? Did someone on the board misread his application? Did.... These questions race through his mind as the board scrutinizes him.

Chances are, the board is simply fishing to see what he'll say. In any event, don't let these questions cause you a dilemma because if you are honest there can be no dilemma. You simply MUST tell the truth at ALL times in an oral board. Your integrity is at stake, your reputation, and, not least of all, your chance to become a trooper is at stake. Don't try to guess at WHY the board is asking a question. Your job is to answer truthfully and openly.

Situational/Ethics Queries

Who doesn't dread these? You hear the words "What would you do if . . ." and your heart pounds wildly. Example:

Board Member: "Mr. Jones, assume you are a state police officer and you are helping another trooper transport several people he has arrested. You see your fellow trooper take a $20 bill out of a prisoner's wallet and put it in his pocket. Your buddy doesn't know you are watching. What do you do?"

Some oral boards are almost exclusively one situational question after another. Other agencies may ask one, then spend the rest of the interview asking you about your past job history. Your best defense here is to decide ahead of time what your ethics are and go with how *you* honestly feel. The only possible right answer is *your* answer. If the board doesn't like what they hear then you may be grilled intensely about your answer; however, you CANNOT assume that you've given the "wrong" answer if the board does begin questioning you hard about your answers. Boards have more than one reason for hammering away at you and it's never safe to assume why they are doing it.

Keep in mind, too, that it's not uncommon on police boards for one board member to be assigned the task of trying to get under an applicant's skin. The purpose is to see if the applicant rattles easily under pressure or loses his/her temper when baited. The person assigned this task is not hard to spot. He/she will be the one you'd love to push in front of a city bus after you've had to answer such questions as: "Why in the world would we want to hire someone like YOU?"

Expect boards to jump on every discrepancy they hear and pick apart some of your comments—all because they want to see how you handle pressure. Not all departments designate a person to perform this function, but someone is usually prepared to slip into this role at some point in the interview.

Role Play Situations

Answering tough questions is stressful enough, but doing it under role play conditions is even tougher. Many departments are using this technique more and more frequently in the oral board setting. A board member will instruct you to pretend you are a trooper and ask you to act out your verbal and/or physical responses. Example:

Board Member: "Mr. Jones, I want you to pretend that you are a state police officer and that you have just pulled over a driver. He becomes uncooperative while you are talking to him and you want him to step out of his vehicle. I want you to stand up now and tell him to get out of his vehicle."

Board members may set up a bit more elaborate role playing scenes for you. Try to enter into these situations with a willingness to participate. Most people are aware that you are not a professional actor or actress so they are not looking for Academy Award performances. Do the best you can. Role playing is used heavily in almost all academies and training situations today so expect to do a lot of role playing during your career as a law

enforcement professional. Shy, reserved people may have difficulty working up enthusiasm for this kind of interaction. Practice how you'd handle this scene and prepare yourself mentally as best you can.

They Can't Ask Me That, Can They?

"They" are the members of the oral board and they can indeed ask you just about any question that comes to mind. Applying for a job in public safety puts you in a different league than the civilian sector applicant. Yes, federal and state laws may prohibit civilian employers from seeking certain information about their applicants. But law enforcement agencies are allowed more freedom of movement within the laws for obvious reasons.

For example, you'll rarely find a space for an applicant's birth date on an application for employment in private industry. This is the result of age discrimination litigation. Law enforcement agencies, as well as other agencies dealing with public safety, need such information to perform thorough background investigations and do not have many of the same restrictions. You will be expected to provide your date of birth and identify your race and your sex before you get very far in the application process for any law enforcement agency. You are applying for a sensitive public safety job and must expect information you may consider highly personal to come to light.

In short, law enforcement agencies can ask you any question that may have a bearing on your mental stability, your ability to do the physical tasks common to state police work, your integrity, honesty, character, and reputation in the community. There's not much left to the imagination after all of this is covered. If some of the questions are probing and perhaps even offensive, it is because you are being held to a higher standard by both the courts who allow these questions to be asked and the departments who want to hire you to protect life and property.

ANSWERS—HOW MANY ARE THERE?

While you are sitting in the interview hot seat you may feel like only two kinds of answers exist—the one you wish you had given and the one you wish you could take back. There isn't a law enforcement officer in uniform today who doesn't have a war story about the one thing he wishes he hadn't brought up in his oral interview board. And this is to be expected. Nerves, pressure, and that random attack of stupid often conspire at the most inappropriate times. To help you be on guard for these moments, let's look at the mysterious "wrong" and "right" answer.

The Wrong Answer

The wrong answer to any question is the answer you think you should say because that's what you've been told the board wants to hear. Do not take well-meant advice from friends or troopers who haven't been before an oral board in the last five years and can't remember much about the one they did go through except that it made them nervous. Boards will often overlook answers they don't "like" if they feel you have good reasons for what you say and if you are being honest with them.

If the board fails you, it will not be because you gave the wrong answer. It will be because you are not the kind of person they are looking for, OR there are some things you need to work on about your life or yourself and the board feels you need some time to work on these matters before they consider you for a job in law enforcement.

The Right Answer

The answers the board wants to hear are the ones only *you* can give. They want *your* opinion, *your* reasons, *your* personal experiences, and they want to know what *you* would do under certain circumstances. No one else matters but you and how you present yourself in the oral interview. If you try to say what you think the board wants to hear you will almost certainly give them a shallow, unsatisfying response to their question.

What DO I Say?

It's not so much *what* you say as *how* you say it. The best way to answer ANY question is with directness, honesty, and brevity. Keep your answers short, but give enough information to fully answer the question. The board won't be handing out prizes for conserving words, but they also don't want to have to pull answers out of you like an old country dentist pulling teeth just so that they can get enough information.

There's a few ways you might want to avoid answering questions. Try not to play "if you ask the question *just* the right way, I'll give you the right answer" with the board. Here's an example:

Board Member: "Mr. Jones, I see you've been arrested once for public intoxication while you were in college? Is that true?

Jones: "No, sir."

Board Member: "Really? That's odd. It says here on page seven that you were arrested and spent the night in the city jail."

Jones: "Yes, well, I wasn't exactly *arrested* because the officer didn't put handcuffs on me.

Don't play word games with the board. You won't win. In this case the applicant clearly knows that the board is aware of his arrest record but he's trying to downplay the incident by trying to duck the question.

Then there's the "you can have the answer if you drag it out of me" and you also want to avoid this technique. For example:

Board Member: "Mr. Jones, tell the board why you left the job you held at Tread Lightly Tire Shop."

Jones: "I was fired."

Board Member: "Why were you fired?"

Jones: "Because the boss told me not to come back."

Board Member: "Why did the boss tell you not to come back?"

Jones: "Because I was fired."

Board Member: "What happened to cause you to be fired?"

Jones: "I was rude."

Board Member: "Rude to whom and under what circumstances?"

You get the picture. This question could have been answered fully when the Board Member asked Jones why he left the tire shop job. The board would prefer that you not rattle on and on when you answer questions, but they would also appreciate a little balance here. This applicant also runs the risk of being labeled a smart alec with this kind of answer. An oral board's patience is usually thin with an applicant who uses this answering technique.

Let's not forget the "you can have any answer but the one that goes with your question" technique. Avoid it, too. Example:

Board Member: "Well, Mr. Jones, we know about some of the things you are good at, now tell us something about yourself that you'd like to improve."

Jones: "I'm really good with people. People like me and find it easy to talk to me for some reason. I guess it's because I'm such a good listener."

If he is a good listener, Mr. Jones didn't demonstrate this quality with that answer. It's important to listen to the question and answer directly. If you duck the question then the board will assume you have something to hide or you are not being honest. If you don't understand how to answer the question, tell the person who asked it that you don't understand. They will be happy to rephrase the question or explain what they want. Be specific and above all, answer the question you are asked, not the one you wish they'd asked instead.

REALITY CHECK

By now, you should have a reasonable idea of what an oral board is looking for and how best to not only survive the experience, but come out ahead on your first board. You've had a lot of material to absorb in this chapter. Read the following scenarios illustrating the wrong way and the right way to tackle an oral interview. As you read, try to put yourself in the shoes of the oral board member who is asking the questions.

Scenario #1

Mary Smith is sitting before her first oral interview board. She is wearing a pair of black jeans, loafers without socks, and a short-sleeve cotton blouse. As the questions are being asked she is tapping her foot against the table and staring at her hands.

Board Member: "Ms. Smith, can you give the board an example of how you've handled a disagreement with a coworker in the past?"

Smith: "Nope. I get along with everybody. Everyone likes me."

Board Member: "I see. So, you've never had a disagreement or difference of opinion with anyone you've ever worked with."

Smith: "That's right."

Board Member: "Well, I see by your application that you were once written up by a supervisor for yelling at a fellow employee. Can you tell us about that situation?"

Smith: "That's different. It was his fault! He started talking to a customer I was supposed to wait on so I told him off."

Now read the second situation.

Scenario #2

Mary Smith is sitting before her first oral interview board dressed in a gray business suit. She is sitting still, with her hands folded in her lap and is looking directly at the person asking her a question.

Board Member: "Ms. Smith, can you give the board an example of how you've handled a disagreement with a coworker in the past?"

Jones: "Yes sir. I can think of an example. When I was working at 'Pools by Polly' I had an argument with a coworker over which one of us was supposed to wait on a customer. I lost my cool and yelled at him. My boss wrote me up because of how I handled the situation."

Board Member: "I see. How do you think you should have handled the situation?"

Smith: "If I had it to do again, I'd take James, my coworker, aside and talk to him about it in private. If I couldn't work something out with

him I would ask my supervisor to help out."

Board Member: "What have you done to keep this sort of thing from happening again?"

Smith: "I've learned to stop and think before I speak and I've learned that there is a time and place to work out differences when they come up. I haven't had a problem since this incident."

So, which scenario left the best taste in your mouth? In scenario #1, the applicant is obviously unwilling to accept responsibility for her actions, she isn't showing any evidence that she is mature, and she isn't honest with herself or the board members when she said everyone liked her and she's never had disagreements with coworkers.

On the other hand, in scenario #2, the applicant is able to admit her mistakes and take responsibility for her part in the incident. Although she may have wished she could present herself in a better light, she did illustrate maturity by being honest, open, and straightforward in talking about the disagreement. In scenario #2, the applicant may have had to endure a long, hard interview in order to sell herself, but she was able to articulate what she did to correct a fault.

On the other hand, you can bet she had a very short interview and a "we're not interested, but thanks" from the board in scenario #1. Let's not even talk about the way the applicant was dressed in scenario #1 or her irritating mannerisms!

These two situations may seem exaggerated, but unfortunately applicants all over the country are making these mistakes as you read.

What Do YOU Think?

Since you are all warmed up, read the following situation. Pick from Answer A, B, or C—decide which response you think is most appropriate for the question.

Alfred Wannabe's oral interview board is today at 9 a.m. at the training academy. He's parked in a chair outside of the board room by 8:40 a.m. awaiting THE CALL.

When it comes, Alfred is ushered into the room and introduced to all of the board members. He sits where he's told and waits. It begins.

Board Member: "Mr. Wannabe, what would you like for us to call you this morning?"

Wannabe: (A) "I don't know. It doesn't matter. Alfred is okay, I guess."

(B) "Alfred is fine, sir."

(C) "I go by Al."

Board Member: "Why do you want to be a state trooper?"

Wannabe: (A) "I don't know. I guess because it's fun and you get to help people. I want to be there when somebody needs something."

(B) "I'd like to be a trooper because I'm very interested in the work. I love to be around people. I like the variety of duties. And I like the challenge of trying to figure out what's really going on in a given situation."

(C) "I've always wanted to be a state trooper."

Board Member: "I see. Well, we have a few standardized questions for you and I know a few others will crop up as we go along. First, can you tell us about your personality. What are you like to be around on a social basis?"

Wannabe: (A) "Oh, I don't know. I'm okay, I guess. My friends like me."

(B) "My friends tell me I'm usually fun to be around. I'm not particularly shy. I'd say I'm outgoing. I like meeting new people, talking, and I can be a pretty good listener, too. I am even-tempered. I get mad sometimes, but if I do I get over it quickly. I have a good sense of humor and don't mind being teased as long as I get to tease back."

(C) "I'm easy to talk to, friendly, very social—I like being around lots of people—and I'm laid-back."

Board Member: "I see here that your background investigator found that you once got thrown out of a friend's house during a party because you were picking fights with the other guests. Tell us about this experience."

Wannabe: (A) "Well . . . that was just that once. I had a little too much to drink I guess. I walked home from there."

(B) "That happened about five years ago in my very early college days. I had just discovered beer and I don't think I handled myself well at all in those days. At that party I kept trying to get everyone to agree to switch the stereo to another station and was quite a jerk about it. My friend asked me to leave so I walked home. I was a jerk again the very next weekend and had to be asked to leave again. That wised me up. I realized I didn't need to be drinking like that so I did something about it."

(C)   "Yes, that did happen. I got into an argument with friends over what music we'd listen to. I had been drinking. My host asked me to leave. I did."

Board Member: "What steps have you taken to make sure this type of situation doesn't happen again?

Wannabe: (A)   "I guess I just watch how much I drink. I don't go to that guy's house anymore, either."

(B)   "I learned to eat before I went to parties where there was alcohol being served and then carried around the same drink for a while. I limited myself to two beers during an evening. I went home happy that way and so did all my friends. I still follow the same rules for myself today."

(C)   "I limit myself to two beers at a party and I don't drink much any other time. I'm responsible about the way I drink now."

All of the choices you read are responses candidates have made in oral board situations—not verbatim, but awfully close to it. If you chose Answer (A) for all your responses you will be guaranteed to grate on the last nerve of every board member. It's not hard to see why. Phrases like "I don't know" and "I guess so" and "I think so" tell the listener that the speaker isn't sure of himself. It says the speaker probably has never thought about what you asked and is giving the answer without bothering to think about it now.

Answer A does not give the board much to go on. The answers don't offer explanations, although the open-ended question gives the applicant all the necessary room to do so. The board would be left with a wishy-washy impression of this candidate at best.

If you liked Answer B, you've kept yourself awake for most of this chapter. Answer B shows the applicant has manners, but he doesn't go overboard. He is direct, but not so direct that he comes across as blunt. He has either thought about the kinds of questions that will surface in the interview or he thinks about what he wants to say before he speaks.

He comes across as confident, willing to discuss his past life, and not ashamed to admit mistakes. He also has a detailed explanation for how he's handled the drinking situation and the potential for future problems. It's at this point the applicant needs to be the most vocal. Board members are especially interested in how you handle your life in the present and what you will most likely do in the future.

If Answer C is what you chose, you probably won't blow the interview but if you pass it will be a squeaker. He's not rude, but he walks a thin line. He should elaborate more on how he feels about this career choice because this is one of his opportunities to show the board how well he can express himself. People have different reasons for wanting to go into law enforcement. Some are good and some are marginal, but for the most part this question is designed to warm you up and let the board warm up, too.

It'd be hard to come up with a truly wrong answer for this question, although people have managed to do so. ("I love to shoot guns" would not win extra points here.) The board gets a feel for how you are going to be as an interviewee with this standard question. You don't have to deliver the Gettysburg Address, but give them *something* to go on. By now, you shouldn't have to think about this response anyway. It's a freebie.

Answer C is the type of response quiet, self-assured people often tend to give. They don't use up a whole lot of words and usually answer questions with directness. The danger here is that this applicant may not say enough to convince the board that he will deal well with the public and with other troopers and supervisors.

These kinds of answers will most often force the board to switch to different kinds of questions that will force the applicant into lengthier responses. Don't make them work too hard getting the answers, though, unless you want a *really* short interview.

PULLING IT ALL TOGETHER

Chances are the postal service is looking pretty good right about now. But don't let all of this information become overwhelming. Make yourself step back and look at the big picture. You know what kind of overall impression you are most likely to make. If you don't, you should. And cut yourself a little slack. The people who interview you aren't perfect and have no real desire to hire someone who is, considering they may have to work with you some day.

Keep your sense of humor intact while you're going through this process. No, don't go into the board cracking jokes, but if you can keep your sense of humor close at hand you might actually be able to come out of interview shock long enough to react if the board jokes with you about something. It wouldn't be unusual for this to happen. Most law enforcement personnel like to tease or joke around to relieve stress. Let the board lead the way in this area, though.

Self-confidence is key. Relax, believe in yourself, and let it all come out naturally. If you feel like you are "blowing it" during the interview, show the board your self-confidence by stopping yourself. Take a deep breath and tell them that's not exactly what you'd like to say, then tell them what you'd like to say. Now THAT'S self-confidence. Be firm if a board member tries to rattle your cage. "Firm" doesn't mean inflexible—change your mind if you need to—just don't do it every other sentence. There's always the wishy-washy label to consider—and avoid.

Ready, Set, GO

You are as ready as you'll ever be if you follow these suggestions. There are no secrets to give away when it comes to oral interview boards. You can't change your past, your job history, or your educational status at this point in the process, nor can you change your personality or go back and do a more thorough job on your Personal History Statement. And you can't fake maturity if you are not a mature individual. But you can put your best foot forward, fight for your cause, and be as well-prepared as possible.

Many troopers you see on the road today failed on their first attempt to be hired by their department's oral board and then passed the board after working on shortcomings and correcting problems. Your goal, of course, is to make it through the process on the first try. If that doesn't happen and you decide to try again, you owe it to yourself to come fully prepared the next time around.

If you follow the tips you've read so far you should keep from making many mistakes that tend to eliminate otherwise well-qualified candidates. You will certainly be ahead of the applicant who has the same qualifications you have, but doesn't have a clue as to how to prepare for an oral interview board. Good luck.

SOME FINAL WORDS OF ADVICE

Dr. Rick Bradstreet is a 17-year veteran psychologist for the Austin Police Department in Austin, Texas. He holds a law degree from Stanford University and a Ph.D. in Counseling Psychology from the University of Texas in Austin. His specialty is communication skills and conflict resolution. Throughout his career with APD, Dr. Bradstreet estimates that he's sat on about 250 to 300 oral interview boards and has had plenty of opportunity to observe applicants in oral interviews. He offers the following advice to those who see a law enforcement oral board in their future.

- Make eye contact. Applicants who fail to make eye contact with interviewers can expect a negative reaction from the board. Making eye contact makes the speaker feel like what he or she is saying is being heard and is being taken seriously.
- Sit erect in your chair, but not so stiffly that you appear to be ripe for the woodsman's axe. You should not have the same posture that you would have if you were sitting at home in your living room, yet you want to appear somewhat relaxed and alert.
- Keep your hands in your lap if you have a tendency to wring your hands together when agitated. Wringing hands are generally perceived as signs of nervousness.
- Drumming fingers—try not to drum on the table. Although this behavior is most often interpreted more as a sign of someone who has excess energy and is not necessarily seen as nervous behavior, it can be distracting to those around you.
- Feel free to shift positions periodically. It's perfectly natural to move around as you speak and is expected during normal conversation. An oral board is not meant to be an interrogation so you are not expected to sit frozen in place for the duration.
- Speak up. If a board member lets you know you are mumbling then project your voice. Speaking in a voice so soft that no one can hear you does nothing to enhance the image you want to project— that of a self-confident, take-charge person who knows what you want.
- Focus on explaining how you are as a person and not responding to questions defensively. Once again, this is not an interrogation. Try to have a normal, respectful conversation with the board members and your body language will take on a more natural, confident look.
- Get out of the self-conscious mode. Your goal is to let the board see you and your experiences as unique. Do not try to mold your experiences and answers to questions according to what you "think" the board may want.

C·H·A·P·T·E·R

PSYCHOLOGICAL ASSESSMENT

CHAPTER SUMMARY

The psychological assessment, which includes an interview and testing, is an important step in the police officer selection process. The following chapter describes what to expect and how to prepare for it.

Psychologists can have a fearsome reputation. Whenever there's a terrorist or serial killer, someone sticks a microphone in a psychologist's face to ask: "Why did he do it? What's he like? When will he do it again?" In court, psychologists are asked to describe a stranger's past state of mind: "Was the defendant insane when he committed the murder two years ago?" All of this gives the impression that psychologists have special powers to predict the future and travel the past, and that they can make accurate diagnoses of people they haven't even met. The media enjoy this dramatic image, and play it up— which makes many people believe it.

But the truth is psychologists are neither fortune tellers nor mind readers. They are just skilled professionals who make educated guesses about people, recognizing that they cannot know everything about anyone. They try to produce fair evaluations based on their training and experience and all the available information.

During your assessment it may be helpful to remember that, more than anyone else, psychologists recognize that everyone has weaknesses and makes mistakes (including themselves). In fact, they're less interested in your specific mistakes than in how you handled them—for example, did you learn from them, keep repeating them, and/or blame them on other people?

The point of the psychological assessment is not to criticize or "nail" you; no one expects you to be perfect or even wonderful. Your value as a human being is not on the line here. The goal is only to discover whether your individual pattern of good and bad points matches the profile of most police officers, which says nothing about how successful you may be in other areas and careers.

PSYCHOLOGICAL TESTING

Testing is part of the assessment process. Most police departments use some form of the Minnesota Multiphasic Personality Inventory (MMPI), which has 560 simple true/false questions, together with perhaps one other, shorter test. Both are designed to produce a general psychological profile and to detect extremes in attitudes and behaviors. The results may or may not be explained to you, depending on the policies of the department; explanations are very time-consuming and thus impossible to do for everyone.

You cannot study for a psychological test. Besides, you already know the subject matter better than anyone else. You are the world's foremost expert on your own feelings, attitudes, and behaviors, and that's what the testing is about. But while you can't study, there are ways to prepare yourself for it.

One is to remember that testing is only one piece of the picture. You've already filled out a lengthy application and had a background check and probably at least one interview—if you were totally unfit for police work, you wouldn't have gotten this far! If the test results

raise any questions, your meeting with the psychologist enables you to answer them face-to-face. So try to relax as much as possible, since tension can make it difficult to concentrate (a few deep breaths will help).

It is crucial to be honest in your answers. Don't try to figure out the "right" answer or what each question is getting at. The tests are designed to make this difficult, so you'll only waste time and make yourself more nervous in the process. If you fake your answers, someone is sure to notice (you won't add up right). Besides, if you don't give a true picture of yourself, you may begin a career for which you are poorly suited. And this is not in anyone's best interest, least of all yours.

THE PSYCHOLOGICAL INTERVIEW

It's important to show up for your interview on time and neatly dressed. Respond politely to the questions, but don't volunteer too much information—this is not a social event where you can get loose and friendly. The psychologist (or psychologists—some departments use a team) may spend a few initial moments breaking the ice, but the rest of the 60–90 minutes will be focused and business-like.

It may feel strange to discuss personal things with strangers. It's almost like going to a medical doctor, where you may feel embarrassed about sharing certain information, but must do it for your own good. In the same way, being evasive or defensive in the psychological interview will not do you any good at all.

And yes, you are expected to be nervous. Who wouldn't be? This is a hurdle you have to jump on the way to your goal. At some time in their lives, most people wonder whether they're crazy or not, and you may be afraid that this psychologist will finally confirm it. Even though it's a myth, that all-powerful, all-seeing shrink image may come to mind. For these and other reasons, it's normal to be nervous. And if you are, it's a good idea to admit it, for this shows honesty and mature self-acceptance. If you are nervous and try to deny it, this suggests a lack of confidence and a tendency to lie, neither of which will gain you any points.

Remember that the psychologist who interviews you is not interested in your full history, only what's relevant to being a police officer. And don't be surprised if the questions are more personal than in other job interviews you've had. One simple reason is that this job comes with a gun—in other words, when public safety is on the line, the courts allow interviewers to get really nosy.

So you may be asked about your childhood, relationships/marriage(s), and military and high school experiences. Expect questions about which supervisors you liked and didn't like on jobs you've had; this shows how you deal with authority. If you've jumped around from job to job, but there were good reasons for it, be ready to explain them if asked.

Of course you'll be asked why you want to be a police officer. It's easy to tell a good answer from a bad answer on this one. Good answers: "I want to help people." "I want a secure job with a pension." "My relative (friend) is a cop and I think the work is interesting." Bad answers: "I want to have power over people." "I like excitement and danger." "I can't wait to put all those jerks in jail." Answers that are rehearsed or not really "you" will be obvious, so, once again, just be honest.

Last but certainly not least, don't try too hard to sell yourself. Nervousness is fine, but desperation is not. If you are right for this profession, you must be able to meet challenges with confidence—including the challenge of a brief psychological assessment.

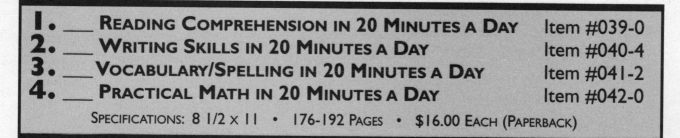